Amazin' Upset

Amazin' Upset

The Mets, the Orioles and the 1969 World Series

JOHN G. ROBERTSON *and*
CARL T. MADDEN

McFarland & Company, Inc., Publishers
Jefferson, North Carolina

ALSO BY JOHN G. ROBERTSON

When the Heavyweight Title Mattered: Five Championship Fights
That Captivated the World, 1910–1971 (McFarland, 2019)

Too Many Men on the Ice: The 1978–1979 Boston Bruins and
the Most Famous Penalty in Hockey History (McFarland, 2018)

The Babe Chases 60: That Fabulous 1927 Season, Home Run by Home Run
(McFarland, 1999; paperback 2014)

Baseball's Greatest Controversies: Rhubarbs, Hoaxes, Blown Calls,
Ruthian Myths, Managers' Miscues and Front-Office Flops
(McFarland, 1995; paperback 2014)

BY JOHN G. ROBERTSON AND ANDY SANDERS

The Games That Changed Baseball: Milestones in
Major League History (McFarland, 2016)

A's Bad as It Gets: Connie Mack's Pathetic
Athletics of 1916 (McFarland, 2014)

LIBRARY OF CONGRESS CATALOGUING-IN-PUBLICATION DATA

Names: Robertson, John G., 1964– author. | Madden, Carl T., author.
Title: Amazin' upset : the Mets, the Orioles and the 1969 World Series /
John G. Robertson and Carl T. Madden.
Other titles: Amazing upset
Description: Jefferson, North Carolina : McFarland & Company, Inc.,
Publishers, 2021 | Includes bibliographical references and index.
Identifiers: LCCN 2021022832 | ISBN 9781476684758 (paperback : acid free paper) ∞
ISBN 9781476642901 (eBook)
Subjects: LCSH: New York Mets (Baseball team)—History. | Baltimore Orioles
(Baseball team)—History. | World Series (Baseball) (1969) | BISAC:
SPORTS & RECREATION / Baseball / History
Classification: LCC GV875.N45 R63 2021 | DDC 796.357/64609—dc23
LC record available at https://lccn.loc.gov/2021022832

BRITISH LIBRARY CATALOGUING DATA ARE AVAILABLE

ISBN (print) 978-1-4766-8475-8
ISBN (ebook) 978-1-4766-4290-1

Front cover: New York Mets pitcher Tom Seaver (National Baseball
Hall of Fame Library, Cooperstown, New York)

Printed in the United States of America

McFarland & Company, Inc., Publishers
Box 611, Jefferson, North Carolina 28640
www.mcfarlandpub.com

This book is dedicated to the surviving members
of the 1969 New York Mets and Baltimore Orioles.
It is also dedicated to all the sporting world's underdogs
who have scored startling upsets in the past
and will undoubtedly do so in the future.
They are the reason the games are played.

Acknowledgments

The authors would like to gratefully acknowledge the assistance they received from the following individuals and groups:

- The Baltimore Orioles' customer service department
- The Baltimore Orioles Alumni Association
- The Society for American Baseball Research
- The good folks who lovingly maintain the fabulous Internet sites baseball-reference.com and baseball-almanac.com. They are truly invaluable to anyone who does historical research on the grand old game.
- John Horne of the National Baseball Hall of Fame Library in Cooperstown, New York, for his assistance in procuring photographs for this book.

Contents

Introduction

"In 1969 man performed two feats that staggered the imagination of the American public: One took place in mid–July, 250,000 miles from planet Earth, when man first landed on the moon. The other took place in October, here on planet Earth, on a baseball diamond, when the 100–1 underdog New York Mets became the world champions of baseball."[1]—Curt Gowdy's introduction to MLB's official film of the 1969 World Series

Nineteen-hundred-sixty-nine was indeed the year of the moon landing. It was also the famous summer of Woodstock, the infamous Chappaquiddick Incident, and the horribly bloody murders orchestrated by Charles Manson's followers. In January, Richard Nixon was inaugurated as the 37th president of the United States. It was the year Hollywood released *Midnight Cowboy*, *Easy Rider*, and *Butch Cassidy and the Sundance Kid*. In the literary world, *Portnoy's Complaint*, *Slaughterhouse-Five* and *The Godfather* were all published. *Sesame Street* debuted on PBS. *The Great White Hope* captured the Tony Award as Broadway's best play with James Earl Jones winning rave reviews in the starring role of Jack Jefferson. Zager & Evans sang about what mankind could expect in the year 2525, while Simon and Garfunkel ruefully wondered where Joe DiMaggio had gone. It was also the year of an astonishing upset in Major League Baseball—and it had been authored by a most unlikely source.

For seven inept seasons the New York Mets had routinely been the bottom-feeders of the old and proud National League of Professional Baseball Clubs. They were a generally lovable and entertaining bunch, but they had garnered little respect being something akin to an MLB comedy sideshow. They had achieved considerably more laughs than wins in their bumbling history. Their cumulative record entering the 1969 season was 394 victories, 737 losses, and five ties. That calculates to a dismal winning percentage of just .348 and an average record per season of 56–105–1. The Mets' aura of losing was about to change dramatically.

Led by the sturdy resolve of popular, second-year manager Gil Hodges and a supporting cast generally comprised of players badly underestimated by their rivals, the Mets roared to life in August and blew away their competition in the newly formed National League East Division. The West Division champs, the Atlanta Braves, were vanquished just as convincingly in the first National League Championship Series. The heavily favored, star-studded American League champions from Baltimore—winners of 109 regular season games (nine more victories than the Mets accrued)—were little more than a minor speed bump on the Mets' road to glory in capturing the 1969 World Series. It was not a bad season at all for a team that was listed by Las Vegas bookmakers as 100–1 underdogs to win the NL pennant when spring training began. In fact, they lived up to their formerly sarcastic nickname: The Amazing Mets.

Although the history of the Mets and their 1969 season will be briefly examined to give what followed its proper perspective, the primary focus of this book will be those five compelling World Series games, played over a span of six days in the middle of October, that made the Mets one of MLB's storied and historic giant-killers. After all, how many baseball fans would even remember the 1969 Mets' stunning turnaround if they had lost to the Braves in the NLCS or to the Orioles in the World Series?

Every play of all five World Series contests will be recapped, batter by batter—along with ample commentary—so the reader can replay the games and relive the growing drama as it unfolded that October, practically moment by moment. They are worth recollecting by those who are old enough to recall the Mets' championship run or by those experiencing the thrills of the 1969 World Series for the first time.

Of all the superlatives and hyperbole used to describe the New York Mets' unlikely triumph, perhaps the best comment is a humble one from a Met outfielder: Art Shamsky. He said the following in explaining why the 1969 Mets' victory still resonates today:

> History will show that a team that was a 100-to-1 longshot at the beginning of the season became the toast of the sports world seven months later. I have always said that the 1969 New York Mets probably weren't the greatest baseball team to win the World Series, but they were certainly one of the most memorable.[2]

The Bottom of the Heap

The New York Mets, 1962 to 1968

"Mr. Stengel, I don't know too much about baseball; in fact, I'm pretty dumb about it, but I do know about New Yorkers. I think we've needed an underdog team for a long time. The same people who were rooting for the [Brooklyn] Dodgers and a lot who have rooted for [you] in the past ... will be out screaming their heads off for the Mets."—*What's My Line?* panelist Dorothy Kilgallen addressing Casey Stengel on the April 15, 1962, episode

> Meet the Mets! Meet the Mets!
> Step right up and greet the Mets!
> Bring your kiddies! Bring your wife!
> Guaranteed to have the time of your life!
> —Lyrics from "Meet the Mets" (1963)

When the Brooklyn Dodgers and New York Giants—two storied clubs that had been in existence since the 19th century—callously abandoned New York City for the glittering prospects of California riches following the 1957 season, the Big Apple was without National League baseball for the first time since 1882. Dating back to 1903 there had always been three big league teams in the city. That abruptly and dramatically changed. For four seasons—from 1958 to 1961—the Yankees were Gotham's only Major League Baseball club.

In 1960 there were talks of a new baseball circuit—the Continental League— springing up in untapped markets to rival both the AL and NL. This threat, which never came to pass, had one lasting effect: It prompted MLB to expand—and reestablish a new NL team in New York City. In 1962, the New York Mets were born from a proposal presented by civic leader William Shea. In a homage to the city's NL past, the Mets chose team colors of orange and blue. Orange had been the color of the New York Giants (1883–1957) while the Brooklyn Dodgers (1890–1957) sported blue. The orange-and-blue color combination was a nice touch. "Mets" was chosen as the team nickname, also for historic reasons that were known to only the most scholarly baseball fans: The New York Metropolitans had been an American

Association club from 1880 to 1887. "Mets" also made sense for a practical reason: It was short enough to easily appear in most newspaper headlines. The Houston Colt .45s—later renamed the Astros—were the other NL expansion outfit that began play in 1962.

The Mets were officially awarded an NL franchise on October 17, 1960. They would not begin play until 1962, but it gave the club a valuable year to acquire affiliations with minor league clubs. Accordingly, for 1961, the Mets fostered working agreements with the Class AA Mobile Bears of the Southern Association, the Raleigh Capitals of the Class B Carolina League, and the Lexington Indians of the Class D Western Carolinas League. Prospects from those circuits might blossom in the future, but the Mets would largely rely upon a special expansion draft following the 1961 season to initially stock their team. A pool of unprotected players was provided by the eight existing NL clubs. Both the Mets and the Colt .45s had to pay between $50,000 and $125,000 per player to compensate each drafted player's former team. For the money spent by the two expansion teams, there was not much quality for the buck. Of New York's 22 picks, the most noteworthy were 37-year-old Gil Hodges, 33-year-old Gus Bell, and 37-year-old Félix Mantilla. The others were generally known only to the most stalwart of baseball fans. The Mets and the Colt .45s would be works in progress for the immediate future and would be at a decidedly competitive disadvantage on the field in 1962.

The bathtub-shaped Polo Grounds, the abandoned and antiquated former home of the departed Giants in upper Manhattan, was dusted off and used as the Mets' home ballpark for two seasons while a glitzy and modern facility—Shea Stadium—was being constructed in the Flushing section in the borough of Queens.

Casey Stengel ("the Old Perfesser," the veteran writers liked to call him) was lured out of a forced retirement to be the team's first field manager. Despite a résumé that included a remarkable total of 10 AL pennants in 12 years with the New York Yankees and a winning percentage of .623, Stengel had been dropped as manager by the perennial AL champions after the Yankees lost in an upset in the wild 1960 World Series to the Pittsburgh Pirates. Stengel was born in 1890, and his advancing age was the predominant factor for his dismissal. "They told me my services were no longer desired because they wanted to put in a youth program as an advance way of keeping the club going," he explained. Stengel then added one of baseball's most memorable quotes: "I'll never make the mistake of being seventy again."[1] Stengel's employment with MLB's most glamorous and successful franchise thus ended rather shabbily.

The fact that the likable Stengel possessed name recognition, was truly one of baseball's great characters, and was beloved by sports journalists everywhere were the primary reasons why he was hired to pilot the nascent Mets. At least he could be counted on for laughs, sometimes intentional, often times not. When Stengel was formally introduced as the club's first manager, he proudly announced, "It's a great honor for me to be joining the Knickerbockers."[2] With that auspicious start it was bound to be an interesting first season … or two … or three for the expansion Mets.

During the team's first spring training, Stengel noted in a TV interview that if a young, promising player joined the Mets organization he was guaranteed one thing: rapid advancement. The yuks would be sorely needed as a balm because wins would be in scarce supply in the early years. In fact, for the first seven years of their existence, the Mets never climbed above a ninth-place finish in the 10-team NL.

Sensing the public's enthusiasm for the new team, in 1961, Mets president George Weiss announced a contest to create an upbeat team song. Nineteen entries were received. The winner was adjudged to be "Meet the Mets" created by the professional songwriting duo of Ruth Roberts and Bill Katz. They were not new at this. The twosome had a history of writing tunes featuring baseball themes. Previously they had composed "I Love Mickey" (a tribute to Mickey Mantle) recorded by Teresa Brewer in 1956, and "It's a Beautiful Day for a Ballgame" which became popular at Los Angeles Dodgers games in 1960. "Meet the Mets" was recorded by Glenn Osser's orchestra, but strangely not until 1963. During that second season of Mets baseball, fans could buy 45-rpm copies at the Polo Grounds or by mail-order for $1 apiece.

The Mets' first official NL game was supposed to be played in St. Louis on Tuesday, April 10, 1962; it was postponed due to rain. The next day the Mets, at last, took the field at Busch Stadium—and lost badly to the Cardinals, 11–4. St. Louis got two runs in the bottom of the first inning. (As a harbinger of the inept baseball the Mets would produce in their first season, starting pitcher Roger Craig committed a balk that inning too. Craig went down in the history books as the first Mets pitcher to be saddled with a loss.) New York pitching would surrender 948 runs in 1962—an average of nearly six runs per game. The second most porous team in the NL only gave up 827. Of those 948 runs scored by opposing teams, 147 were unearned as the team made 210 errors—55 more than the NL average. Stengel could only marvel at his team's defensive misadventures. "I've seen new ways to lose that I never knew existed before,"[3] he exclaimed with wonder.

Regardless of the quality of baseball it would witness, so grateful was New York City to once again have an NL franchise as an attraction that the Mets were feted with a grand tickertape parade the day before their first home game. It was ominously scheduled for April 13—Friday the Thirteenth. The route concluded on the steps of City Hall where speeches followed. Richie Ashburn recalled William Shea addressing the assembled fans not with enthusiasm but with a heartfelt plea for patience "until we can get some real ballplayers in here."[4] Spurred by that ringing vote of non-confidence, the following day the Mets trudged to the Polo Grounds and narrowly lost their home opener to the Pittsburgh Pirates, 4–3. In the crowd was a 17-year-old high school student named Ed Kranepool. Before the 1962 season ended, he would be playing for the team he was paying to see that day.

The Polo Grounds had a rich history well before it became the New York Mets' first home in 1962. The last version of the Polo Grounds served as the home of the New York Giants from 1891 through 1957. This photo is from the 1923 season (Library of Congress).

On Opening Day the following year, Kranepool would be batting third for the Mets and playing right field. Rapid advancement indeed.

The payroll for the entire 1962 Mets roster was only about $600,000. One sportswriter later cackled, "They got what they didn't pay for."[5]

Yet, the "Amazing Mets" (a tongue-in-cheek term coined by Stengel himself and promptly adopted by New York's baseball writers) swiftly garnered a huge following. Old, disenfranchised fans of the Dodgers and Giants—as well as legions of other New Yorkers—embraced the new, pitiful team. The lowly Mets needed encouragement, the ticket-buyers figured. They figured correctly. Accordingly, the Mets' faithful followers trooped religiously to an area of urban decay in New York City to watch something that was at least billed as National League baseball. Stengel, who was routinely known to mangle names, occasionally called it "the Polar Grounds," perhaps by accident, perhaps not. Some zealous Met supporters began carrying inspirational and optimistic banners to the old ballyard to support their cellar-dwelling Mets, a novelty in professional sports at the time. Soon the old ballpark was festooned with banners and placards for every home game. Writer Roger Angel sensed why the Mets easily gathered new fans. "The Mets were human. There is more Met in all of us than Yankee," he explained. "The [Mets franchise] was probably antimatter to the Yankees."[6]

It was certainly a fun atmosphere at the Polo Grounds—but just as certainly it was not a winning one. After nine starts the Mets were a godawful and demoralizing 0–9. (Amusingly, the Mets were 9½ games out of first place at that time.) They lost their first eight home games before rewarding the club's loyal supporters with an 8–6 victory over Philadelphia on April 28 to finally get a win on their ledger. A brief period of respectability followed. After sweeping a Sunday home doubleheader versus Milwaukee on May 20, the Mets were in eighth place in the NL standings with a lofty 12–19 record. Alas, New York then fell into a dreadful slump, losing 17 straight games. In July, another long losing skein—11 games—befell them. It was more of the same in August when the Mets lost 13 consecutive games. The longest Met winning streak of the season was a measly three games, occurring in the first week of August. Against the Houston Colt .45s, the other 1962 expansion team, New York won just three of 16 games. The Colts would win 24 more games than the Mets did in 1962.

Nevertheless, the poor results did not seem to faze the unflappable Mets fans in the slightest. Despite accruing a horrible record of 40–120, the 1962 Mets were a tremendous hit at the box office where they won just 22 of 80 games at home. In an era when seasonal attendance of one million was considered terrific, the Mets nearly attained that mark. They drew 922,530 fans to the unappealing Polo Grounds to watch a handful of ballplayers long in the tooth (e.g., Gil Hodges and Richie Ashburn) and a coterie of delightful, bungling misfits acting as a supporting cast. That number was good enough for seventh best in the NL—sixth if one goes by average attendance. (The '62 Mets lost one home date due to a rainout that was never made up.) The Mets easily outdrew the Chicago Cubs, Milwaukee Braves, and Philadelphia Phillies and were close to matching the home attendance of the St. Louis Cardinals, Cincinnati Reds and Houston Colts. Only once in their final five seasons at the Polo Grounds had the dearly departed New York Giants drawn as well as the 1962 Mets.

While New York's star-studded AL team won another World Series in 1962 and drew more than 1.4 million fans to Yankee Stadium, it was the city's lackluster NL reps who became the darlings and clear favorites of the New York City media. Journalists enjoyed the novelty of covering the comical misadventures and uphill battles of the ultimate underdogs. Moreover, wrote Stengel biographer Bill Bishop, "[The Mets] were considered the fun team, a sharp contrast to the corporate image projected by their American League competitors, the Yankees."[7]

With the Mets getting plenty of ink in the New York City dailies, the players became famous for their unintentionally funny behavior and comments. Clarence (Choo-Choo) Coleman, a catcher from South Carolina, was asked by a writer about his wife. "What's her name and what's she like?" was the scribe's simple question. "Her name is Mrs. Coleman ... and she likes me!"[8] was Choo-Choo's memorable reply.

Harry Chiti was one of seven catchers to appear in at least one game for the 1962 Mets. A minor leaguer, Chiti was acquired from the Cleveland Indians organization for a "player to be named later." The player sent to Cleveland turned out to be the inept Chiti himself after he batted just .191 in 15 games. It was the first instance in MLB history where a player had been traded for himself. (One wag suggested that the Mets had gotten the short end of the Chiti-for-Chiti swap.) Chiti was never seen again on an MLB diamond.

On September 30, the last day of the season, another forgettable Met backstop, Joe Pignatano, simultaneously ended a New York rally and his major league career by lining into a triple play versus the Cubs at Wrigley Field. With Met runners Sammy Drake and Richie Ashburn on second and first base respectively, Pignatano hit a pitch that was caught by Chicago's second baseman Ken Hubbs. Here is how Edward Prell of the *Chicago Tribune* saw it:

> The runners were on the way when it appeared as if Pignatano's pop fly would be out of Ken's reach. After he speared it, Hubbs had time to set himself for the throw to [Ernie] Banks at first. Neither was there any urgency for Ernie to hurry his throw to [shortstop] André Rodgers because Drake never had a chance to get back to second base.[9]

Stengel was reputed to have muttered, "We've got to learn to stay out of triple plays."[10] (There were two triple plays in all of MLB during the 1962 season. Against all odds, both involved the Mets. On May 30, the Mets turned a triple play against Los Angeles at the Polo Grounds. The Dodgers still won the game, 6–5.) It was a wholly appropriate way to conclude the disastrous 1962 campaign for New York's NL newcomers. Pignatano would later become a very valuable coach under Gil Hodges and would serve on the Mets' staff for 14 years.

June 17, 1962, was a particularly memorable day at the Polo Grounds for first baseman and bumbling fan favorite Marv Throneberry of Tennessee. Accurately described as "the best symbol of the team's spectacular ineptitude,"[11] Throneberry had a triple versus the Chicago Cubs nullified on an appeal play because he had not touched second base on his trip around the base path. Manager Stengel angrily rushed onto the field—as fast as his 72-year-old legs could carry him—to squawk about the call. He was stopped before he even began. "Don't bother arguing, Casey," said veteran NL umpire Dusty Boggess, who probably thought he had seen everything that could possibly happen in a professional baseball game. "He missed first base too." It was indisputable. Years later Richie Ashburn recalled, "We could all tell from the dugout that Marv didn't really come close to touching first base." After a slight pause to weigh the evidence, Stengel reputedly replied, "Well, I know he touched third base because he's standing on it!"[12] By the end of the 1962 season, the good-natured Throneberry, facetiously dubbed "Marvelous Marv" by the New York press, reputedly boasted a fan club numbering more than 5,000 members. Throneberry (whose initials were MET!) was released in May 1963, but his fame endured. For about five years beginning in the mid–1970s, he appeared in a series of comical, self-deprecating television commercials for Miller Lite beer and garnered a new generation of fans. "I don't know why they asked me to do this commercial,"[13] was Throneberry's common refrain. In one ad he ruefully said, "If I do for Lite Beer what I did for baseball, I'm afraid their sales might go down."[14] (Throneberry died of cancer in 1994. His son reported that Marv was still receiving and answering fan mail to the very end. As late as December 2018, in a poll of Met fans, Throneberry was ranked 122nd out of 1,067 Mets in all-time popularity.)

Perhaps the most amusing story told about the woeful '62 Mets is the one involving a not-so-skillful shortstop from Venezuela named Elio Chacón and center fielder Richie Ashburn, an aging, onetime star, formerly of the Philadelphia Phillies. Ashburn, at age 35, was playing out the string with New York and wanted to end his career in one piece. Ashburn had several near-collisions with the 160-pound Chacón on fly balls that were hit to center field. Chacón spoke no English, so he did not understand when Ashburn was trying to call him off so he could make the play instead of his backpedaling shortstop. It was suggested that Ashburn learn a smattering of Spanish to solve the problem. With a bit of tutoring, Ashburn learned the phrase "¡Yo la tengo!"—meaning "I have it!" Soon thereafter, on a short fly ball to center field, Chacón drifted into the outfield grass, but he dutifully backed off when he heard Ashburn shout "¡Yo la tengo!" Alas, Ashburn was flattened by charging left fielder Frank Thomas who did not understand Spanish— and weighed 200 pounds. After both outfielders got to their feet, Thomas reputedly asked Ashburn, "What the hell is a yellow tango?"[15]

Despite having a reasonably productive season for the woeful Mets in which he batted .306, Ashburn retired at the end of the 1962 campaign. In his amusing book about that dreadful team, author Jimmy Breslin noted, "[Ashburn] sat on the bench for a while with another team once and it bothered him badly. He said that if he ever had to be a benchwarmer for the New York Mets he'd commit suicide."[16]

For a time, the 1962 Mets remarkably had two players named Robert L. Miller on the roster. Both were pitchers, adding to the confusion. (Stengel was never especially strong with remembering players' names, even in his younger days. He solved the ambiguity problem, sort of, by referring to one of the Millers as "Bob Nelson." However, Stengel further muddled things by referring to Mets broadcaster Lindsey Nelson as "Miller.") Neither Robert L. Miller contributed very much to the overall welfare of those original Mets. The left-hander compiled a 2–2 won-lost record. His right-handed counterpart was a thoroughly miserable 1–12.

At least righty Miller was in good company: The 1962 Mets were the first MLB team since the 1936 Philadelphia Phillies to have two pitchers who lost at least 20 games apiece: Roger Craig (24) and Al Jackson (20). Craig Anderson, who compiled a 3–17 record for New York, finished the season by losing 16 consecutive games. The Mets' pitching staff allowed 71 wild pitches to set a modern NL record, and surrendered 192 home runs to set an MLB record.

In 1963, again under Casey Stengel's watch, the Mets improved, but they still finished in the NL cellar with a dismal 51–111 record. Nevertheless, the crowds at the old ballpark continued to grow throughout the long, hopeless summer. The

Mets ranked fourth in NL home attendance with a seven-figure total: 1,080,108 customers passed through the Polo Grounds turnstiles. Another familiar face from yesteryear was welcomed back to New York for reasons of nostalgia: Duke Snider, the former Duke of Flatbush, batted .243 in 129 games. He attained both his 400th career home run and his 2,000th hit while toiling for the lowly Mets. He would be sold to the San Francisco Giants prior to the 1964 season where his MLB career concluded in obscurity. Snider's former teammate, Gil Hodges, retired as an active player early in May when he had the chance to manage the Washington Senators, the American League doormats. The Senators sent Jimmy Piersall to the Mets in exchange for Hodges. No one could have foreseen at the time that one day Hodges would return to the Mets as their manager and achieve wonderful and quite miraculous things.

Seventy-four-year-old Casey Stengel remained at the helm when the Mets moved into their fancy new and modern Shea Stadium home in Queens in 1964. Of course, the novelty of the club's new ballpark sparked an even greater jump in attendance to 1,732,597. Only the Los Angeles Dodgers drew more fans in the NL. However, for the first time, Stengel began receiving serious criticism from the New York media. On his radio program, ABC's Howard Cosell began to frequently question Stengel's ability to manage an MLB team at his age. Worse, Stengel was accused of occasionally falling asleep on the bench during games. The most notable game for the 1964 Mets occurred in the first game of a Father's Day doubleheader at Shea Stadium. In defeating the home team 6–0, Jim Bunning of the Philadelphia Phillies threw the first perfect game in the NL since John Montgomery Ward of the Providence Grays set down all 27 Buffalo Bisons he faced on June 17, 1880. (That feat occurred so far in the distant past that Ward, by rule, was pitching underhand!) New York again finished in the NL basement, this time with a slightly improved 53–109 record.

Within a short time, the futility of New York's NL team transcended baseball and became part of general American culture. Allusions to their inept play crept into other forms of entertainment. A George Carlin comedy routine on a 1965 episode of *The Merv Griffin Show* featured the following quip: "He's a veteran of two wars, the Depression, and a Mets doubleheader."[17] That same year the plot of an episode of the sitcom *Bewitched* focused on a man named Adam Newlarkin who is victimized by a malicious magical spell. It contained the line "He's on the list … right between the New York Mets and Richard Nixon."[18]

The 1965 season was a critical one for the Mets franchise. Stengel was still the manager, having signed a new contract, but his fragility now became an issue. During spring training, the Mets played an exhibition game at West Point. Stengel slipped on a patch of wet pavement at the military academy and broke his wrist. The regular season began with Stengel's arm in a sling, but he did not miss any games. On July 24 the Mets lost 5–1 at home to the Philadelphia Phillies. Prior to the official NL contest, the Mets played their fourth annual Old-Timers Game and specifically saluted Stengel as his 75th birthday, on July 30, was nearing. At a post-game function at Toots Shor's famous restaurant, Stengel had another mishap. This time he slipped in the establishment's men's room and broke his hip. The following day he underwent surgery to have the broken hip replaced with an artificial one.

Edna Stengel, Casey's beloved wife of 41 years, urged her husband to retire from baseball. Casey agreed; he and Edna relocated to California by the end of 1965. The Mets kept Stengel on the payroll, listing him as the club's head of west coast scouting. Stengel's #37 jersey was retired by the team in 1965. Wes Westrum, who had been a superb defensive catcher

A young Casey Stengel is shown here circa 1915 in a Brooklyn uniform. When Stengel was hired as the Mets' first manager, he became the only man to have worn the uniform of four New York MLB teams: the Yankees, Giants, Dodgers and Mets (Library of Congress).

for the New York Giants for 11 seasons and was a coach on the Mets' staff, replaced Stengel as manager for the final 67 games of the 1965 season. The team staggered to the finish, in last place again, with a 50–112 record. They were 47 games out of first place and 15 games behind ninth-place Houston. Still the home attendance increased. It rose to 1,768,389 in 1965.

The 1965 Mets had acquired the aging Warren Spahn, easily one of the top 10 pitchers in MLB history. However, the 44-year-old future Hall-of-Famer was merely a shell of his former daunting self. He started 19 games for New York and went 4–12. As an indication of Spahn's advancing years, his MLB career was launched with the 1942 Boston Braves. That team had been managed by Casey Stengel—the first MLB club he ever piloted. When Spahn was released in midseason, he humorously and somewhat bitterly told the press, "I'm the only guy to play for Casey before and after he was a genius."[19] Spahn was a living linchpin of 58 years of baseball history. One of Spahn's teammates on the 1942 Braves was Paul Waner. Waner's MLB career had begun in 1926. During the 1965 season, Waner died on

August 29. On the reverse side of the coin, one of Spahn's teammates on the 1965 Mets was youthful rookie pitcher Tug McGraw whose lengthy MLB career ended in 1984.

The drab Wes Westrum returned as the Mets' manager in 1966 and guided the club out of the NL basement for the first time ever. Their 66–95 record elevated them to ninth spot, 7½ games ahead of the Chicago Cubs. Westrum was not nearly as quotable as his predecessor had been—in fact he was often described as downright dull—but he did come up with a Stengel-like malapropism. After a particularly tight game, Westrum told the press it had been "a cliff-dweller." Remarkably, the steadfast Met fans, with precious little to cheer about in 1966, continued tradition and established another new home attendance record of 1,932,693. Amazing!

In 1967, Met fans first glimpsed right-handed pitcher Tom Seaver of Fresno, California. Although Seaver was 6'1" and weighed 195 pounds, he was not perceived to be especially physically intimidating, but he had pinpoint control. Sometimes he was disparagingly labeled as "chubby." He starred at the University of Southern California and spent just one year in the Mets' minor league system. Not quite 23, Seaver pitched 18 complete games for the Mets in 1967. He struck out 170 batters, posted a 2.76 ERA, had a 16–13 won-lost record, and tossed 18 complete games. He was named NL Rookie of the Year. The strikingly handsome Seaver, not surprisingly, became the most popular Met and the face of the still-struggling franchise.

Even with Seaver's fine season, the Mets still finished 1967 at the bottom of the NL heap with a 61–101 record. Frustrated at not having been guaranteed a contract for 1968, Wes Westrum resigned as the Mets' manager with 11 games left on the schedule. He was quickly hired by the San Francisco Giants as a base coach. Francis James (Salty) Parker guided the Mets to a 4–7 record the rest of the way. Attendance at Shea Stadium declined by nearly 400,000 in 1967—the first time it had ever dropped. Mets historian Peter Golenbock noted, "Fans, no longer the rebels they once were, and no longer interested in lovable losers, stayed home in droves. Without Stengel, these Mets were no longer lovable. Under the colorless Westrum, they were just another bad ball club."[20] Despite having a wonderfully catchy nickname for a baseball manager, Salty Parker was just hired as an interim pilot. Somebody new would have to take command of the team in 1968. The Mets definitely had someone specific in mind.

Since leaving the Mets organization in 1963, Gil Hodges had capably managed a subpar Washington Senators team to a level of respectability while personally gaining credentials and experience as a major league bench boss. In 1967, the Senators' sixth-place finish in the AL was considered just slightly short of miraculous. The Senators did not want to lose Hodges' services, but the Mets wanted desperately to acquire him to manage the club in 1968. Eventually the substantial sum of $100,000 and right-handed pitcher Bill Denehy were sent by New York to Washington in exchange for the Senators making Hodges available. Fans in Washington were generally perturbed at losing Hodges for a pile of cash and a journeyman hurler. So were the city's baseball journalists. One disenchanted *Washington Post* sports scribe described the deal as something akin to "wife-stealing."[21] On November 27, 1967, Gil Hodges officially became the fourth manager in New York Mets history. Jim Lemon replaced Hodges as the Senators' manager in 1968. Lemon lasted just one season in D.C. as the Senators lost 96 games and plummeted back to last place in the AL.

Although Hodges did not technically assume the managerial reins of the Mets for more than another month, his imminent hiring had been announced during a press conference held at the 1967 World Series. The timing was no accident. Bing Devine, the Mets' general manager, wanted Hodges to study the AL champion Boston Red Sox. "I merely wanted Gil to get a good look at a team that went from ninth place to a World Series in one year,"[22] Devine recalled. The underdog Red Sox had beaten 100–1 odds in 1967 to win the AL pennant.

For Hodges, the Mets were a great fit. Gil's wife, Joan, a Brooklyn girl, still lived primarily in New York City and only commuted occasionally to Washington during the baseball season to see her husband. "Gil and I had never discussed the possibility that he would manage the Mets," Joan recalled for one biographer of her husband. "He was very happy with the progress of the Senators and liked being in Washington. The Mets were still considered the clowns of baseball, so he was a little nervous about that. There was a lot of work ahead of him."[23]

But the idea of a return to New York was a great allurement for the 43-year-old Hodges. He still maintained financial interests in some Brooklyn bowling alleys from his years with the Dodgers. Hodges was enormously popular throughout the city too. Although he grew up in Indiana, Hodges was one of the few Brooklyn players who resided year-round in the borough, a gesture the fans truly appreciated. At the height of Hodges' popularity, Dodger owner Walter O'Malley once said, "If I had sold or traded Hodges, the Brooklyn fans would hang me, burn me, and tear me to pieces."[24]

As a member of the great Brooklyn Dodgers clubs of the late 1940s and 1950s, Hodges was an outstanding defensive first baseman—a right-handed one—who possessed capable offensive skills too. (He hit 370 career homers—361 of them for the Dodgers. As of 2020, Hodges is still sitting in second spot in Dodger history, trailing only Duke Snider's 389 home runs.) Patrons of Ebbets Field absolutely loved Hodges. "Those [Brooklyn] fans knew their baseball," recalled teammate Clem Labine decades later. "Gil was the only player I can remember whom the fans never—and I mean never—booed."[25] A 1966 Topps baseball card glowingly said that Hodges "epitomizes the courage, sportsmanship and integrity of America's favorite pastime."[26] Although he was physically imposing—he looked the part of a stereotypical ex–Marine—Hodges was perceived by the public as a modest, pious, quiet, gentlemanly everyman.

While a member of the U.S. Marine Corps during the Second World War, Hodges had been awarded the Bronze Star for heroism under fire during the brutal and bloody fighting on Okinawa, but he would never discuss his specific battlefield experiences with anyone—not even his family members. (Until informed otherwise, his son, Gil Jr., believed for years that his father had only a mundane desk job in the service.) Future Dodger teammate Don Hoak, who served in the navy in the final year of the war, did catch wind of some unverified tales, though. "We kept hearing stories about this big guy from Indiana who killed Japs with his bare hands."[27] After getting to know Hodges after the war, Hoak concluded that Hodges must have been that superhuman Marine he had heard about.

"I think it's very nice to be back in the National League," Hodges told a reporter from *Sports Illustrated* during the middle of May 1968. "I'm very encouraged that, in my opinion, the Mets have some very fine young ballplayers. It's a question of giving them the experience they need."[28] Hodges specifically cited his young pitchers—Tom Seaver, Jerry Koosman and Nolan Ryan—as being reasons for growing optimism. Hodges also mentioned a promising young outfielder from Baltimore, Ron Swoboda, who had recently been featured on the May 6, 1968, cover of *SI* under the caption "Movin' Mets."

The New York Mets retired Gil Hodges' number 14 in 1973, a year after he had suffered a fatal heart attack. Hodges' name is still absent from the Hall of Fame despite being one of the best first baseman of the 1950s and his skillful management of the 1969 Miracle Mets (National Baseball Hall of Fame and Museum, Cooperstown, NY).

Hodges' return to New York was more than just a feel-good story for Mets fans. The team had also improved markedly from 1967. Hodges led the Mets to a respectable 73–89 record in 1968, easily the team's best seasonal result in their seven years in the NL. The Mets were just four games under .500 when the All-Star break arrived, uncharted territory for them at the midway point of any prior season. It was MLB's final season of pre-divisional play. Still, the Mets finished in ninth place, only one game in front of last-place Houston, but also only four games out of sixth place. New York was starting to get solid pitching—the foundation of a championship club—but too often the offense let them down. For example, a promising right-handed pitcher named Jim McAndrew lost five times in 1968 in games where his Met teammates did not score a single run for him.

Very late in the season, while the Mets were in Atlanta for a series with the Braves, Hodges suffered a mild heart attack on September 24 and was hospitalized. Hodges was outwardly a calm figure on the New York bench, and was generally good-humored in dealing with the press, but he hid the stress of being a big-league manager well. A smoking habit that Hodges had picked up during the war was also a likely factor in his heart attack. (While a member of the Brooklyn Dodgers, Hodges appeared in print ads for Chesterfield cigarettes.) A doctor ordered him to quit the cigarettes and lose 24 pounds before returning to pilot the Mets in 1969.

With four more expansion teams entering the big-league fold in 1969, the composition of MLB would be forever changed. Would the traditional powerhouse clubs retain their grip on the sport, or would the new era usher in an age of new champions in baseball? The 1969 New York Mets would provide a surprising answer.

Baseball fans, like no others, enjoy searching for omens. Those who looked deeply enough found one obscure augury that favored the Mets' chances in 1969. Starting with the 1965 season, the MLB team whose farm club won the Florida Instructional League title went on to win the pennant at the major league level the following year. The Mets' affiliate won the championship of the 13-team FIL in 1968.

2

The 1969 Mets' Miracle Pennant

"We're a young team. We're just coming. We all played together last year and we're together again this year. When you play together a few years, you get to know each other, and things improve. Yes, sir, there's a different feeling on the team this year. There's more togetherness. There's more pride. We're a close-knit team."[1]—Mets catcher Jerry Grote, assessing his team during spring training 1969

"The Mets are getting so good I hear they are thinking of moving to California."[2]—an anonymous "cynic," quoted during the 1969 NLCS

In 1969 MLB celebrated the 100th anniversary of the professional game. It was a noteworthy season throughout the majors. A new era was unfolding.

The Montreal Expos and San Diego Padres joined the NL in 1969. The Seattle Pilots and Kansas City Royals were added to the AL, increasing the number of MLB clubs by 20 percent from 20 to 24. Baseball's leadership deemed that the longstanding simplicity of one set of standings per league would no longer do; thus the division system was foisted on the public. It was something entirely new to baseball, although the other three major team sports in North America had all adopted some form of it. The two major leagues would henceforth be split into East and West divisions, creating four "pennant races" instead of the traditional two. Interdivisional play would exist, but interleague play during the regular season was still decades away from becoming a reality. To qualify for the World Series, a team would now have to finish atop its respective six-team division and then defeat the champions of the other division in a best-of-five playoff (officially called the League Championship Series). Traditionalists were not especially thrilled about it. They cringed at the idea that it was now quite possible that the best team from each league would not play in the World Series.

The New York Mets were slotted into the NL East along with Chicago, Montreal, Philadelphia, Pittsburgh and St. Louis. The NL West teams were Atlanta, Cincinnati, Houston, Los Angeles, San Diego and San Francisco. The 162-game schedule was retained, which meant it was an unbalanced one. Over the course of the 1969 regular season, each team would meet their other divisional rivals 18 times and play the six teams from the other division 12 times.

Given a clean bill of health, Gil Hodges was back on the Mets' bench in 1969. "If I thought I was going to be bothered in any way, I just would not have come back," he told a reporter. "After all, your first concern is your life and your family. Since [my doctors] tell me I can do everything, I'm back. I'm happier doing this than anything else. We all have problems in regular life. I just won't let [the pressure of managing the Mets] get to me."[3]

Despite the promising upturn in the team's fortunes in 1968, no one seriously expected too much from the New York Mets in 1969. Baseball writer Joseph Durso was typical of most prognosticators. He picked the Mets to finish fourth in the NL East, ahead of only the Pirates and the expansion Expos. (Cynics said at least it was no longer possible for the Mets to finish in ninth or tenth position as sixth place would now put them squarely in the divisional cellar.) Gil Hodges raised a few skeptical eyebrows when he predicted his Mets would win the lofty and thoroughly respectable total of 85 games in 1969.

In its 1969 baseball preview issue, *Sports Illustrated* did not think much of Hodges' troops' chances to win their division, citing a dearth of quality substitutes as the primary reason. "New York's Mets lack many things, among them reserves. The best thing that can be said of the bench is that it is made of wood; the worst thing, that it is made of deadwood."[4] *SI* picked the defending NL champs from St. Louis to take top honors in the new NL East. In fact, the periodical figured it would be no contest. "Had the St. Louis Cardinals made no moves at all to strengthen themselves for the 1969 season, they would still be lopsided favorites to win in the East,"[5] wrote one of *SI's* prognosticators.

In 2019 Art Shamsky recalled a speech that Hodges gave to the Mets during spring training regarding what had often happened to them in the 1968 season. "He basically said, 'You know, you guys are better than you think. You lost a lot of one-run games. If you can find some way to win those close games, anything can happen.' Basically, he was right."[6]

Opening Day had never once produced a win for the Mets in their seven previous seasons dating back to 1962. On Tuesday, April 8, 1969, at Shea Stadium, that futility streak continued. Their eighth loss in their eighth season opener was especially embarrassing for the Mets as it was an 11–10 setback to the Montreal Expos in the first MLB game ever played by a team located beyond American borders. (At one point in the 1969 season, the Expos would lose 20 consecutive games, just three defeats shy of the modern NL record.) "They're coming up with awesome remedies for heart disease," wrote Ted Blackman in the next day's *Montreal Gazette*, "but yesterday's game was not designed to keep Gil Hodges healthy."[7] The Mets were certainly gracious and accommodating in more ways than one: The home team invited Montreal's mayor, Jean Drapeau, to throw out the ceremonial first pitch to Jerry Grote! (They also recruited Canadian operatic contralto Maureen Forrester to sing "O Canada.")

Second baseman Ken Boswell made two errors in the top of first inning (and three overall) to aid the Expos in scoring two runs. The Mets, trailing 11–6 with two out in the ninth inning, made a game of it by scoring four times and having two runners on base with Rod Gaspar coming to bat. With drama running high, Gaspar was struck out by Carroll Sembera to secure Montreal's first NL victory. In recalling the ugly Opening Day loss, New York starter Tom Seaver noted that he was so bad that Expo relief pitcher Dan McGinn homered off him. (The ball bounced off the top of the right-field fence; it was the only home run McGinn smacked in his five-year MLB career.) Yet somehow Seaver also sensed a strange feeling of optimism in the Met clubhouse despite the embarrassing loss. "The defeat really didn't depress us. We knew that no team could be as bad as we looked in the opener. My reaction was typical of the locker room: 'My God, wasn't that ridiculous!'"[8] Seaver would have numerous outings in 1969 that were much better than Opening Day at Shea Stadium.

The Mets did beat the upstart Expos in the remaining two games of that first series of the 1969 season. In the second inning of the game on Thursday, April 10, Tommie Agee hit the longest home run in the history of Shea Stadium. It was served up by Larry Jaster. The ball landed 505 feet from home plate in the left field upper deck. The game was not televised, so there is no video record of it—only the lasting impression it made on the small gathering of 8,608 spectators and the awestruck players who witnessed it. On-deck batter Rod Gaspar declared, "I've never seen a ball hit like that! Just incredible!"[9] A commemorative plaque was eventually installed on the seat where the ball touched down. As an encore, Agee hit a second homer that day in New York's 4–2 win.

Despite taking two of three games from Montreal, the Mets fell into a slump shortly thereafter. They had a poor 3–7 record after 10 games and a thoroughly unimpressive 9–14 mark after 23 contests. To all observers, it looked like another long, fruitless season at Shea Stadium was at hand.

On June 15—the trading deadline—the Mets acquired a player from the Montreal Expos who would play a large role in their eventual success: first baseman Donn Clendenon. He got to New York in 1969 in a roundabout way. He had been a member of the Pittsburgh Pirates since 1961. However, the Pirates left Clendenon unprotected in the expansion draft. The Montreal Expos claimed him. The Expos intended to trade him and Jesús Alou to the Houston Astros for Rusty Staub.

Things became complicated, however, when Clendenon refused to report to the Astros. His gripe concerned Harry Walker, Houston's new manager. Clendenon, a black man, had played under him in Pittsburgh and considered the Mississippi-born Walker to be a racist. Clendenon threatened to retire rather than report to the Astros. (By the end of the 1969 season, Clendenon and Walker were on friendly terms—so much so that Walker was offering batting tips to his former player before and during the World Series.) Eventually Commissioner Bowie Kuhn helped settle the issues by insisting the Expos send other compensation to the Astros to complete the deal for Staub. It was mid–April by the time Clendenon played his first game for Montreal. Two months later, after playing in only 38 games for the Expos and batting just .240, he was traded to the Mets for Kevin Collins, Steve Renko, and a pair of minor league players. Clendenon and longtime Met Ed Kranepool would share the duties at first base for New York for the remainder of the 1969 season.

The Mets won 11 consecutive games at one point in the season, but still trailed the Chicago Cubs by 5½ games in the NL East. Many baseball historians like to cite July 8 as the key date when the 1969 New York Mets truly became something special. That day the New York City newspapers carried a disparaging quote uttered by Chicago third baseman Ron Santo in which he claimed that none of the Mets' youthful infielders was good enough to play for the Cubs' AAA affiliate in Tacoma. (The 29-year-old Santo was likely the least respected Cub among the Mets. His shtick of merrily jumping and clicking his heels after each Chicago win was thought to be beneath the dignity of an MLB player—at least according to Gil Hodges.) That night at Shea Stadium, with the Cubs as the visitors, the Mets dramatically rallied to score two runs in the bottom of the ninth inning to tie the game, 3–3. Fan favorite Ed Kranepool drove in the winning run in the home half of the 12th inning. Earlier in the game, Kranepool had opened the scoring with a solo home run.

The following evening, Wednesday, July 9, Tom Seaver came within two outs of pitching a perfect game versus the Cubs. Seaver's bid failed when Jim Qualls, an obscure rookie outfielder, lined a clean single into left-center field. Qualls was a lifetime .223 hitter who played in just 63 MLB games over three seasons. Seaver recalled the moment the dream died:

> I decided to throw Qualls a sinker, but the ball didn't sink. It came in fast, too high, and almost waist-high over the heart of the plate. Qualls swung and hit the ball to left-center field. Cleon Jones broke over from left field. Tommie Agee raced over from center … and neither of them could reach the ball. It fell in: a clean single. Never in any aspect of my life, in baseball or outside, had I experienced such a disappointment.[10]

In the franchise's history, no Met had thrown a no-hitter before Seaver's close shave—and none would until Johan Santana did it on June 1, 2012, versus St. Louis. Seaver would write about that game, "When I warmed up before my imperfect game against the Cubs, my shoulder was tight, restricting me. For about ten minutes I just couldn't seem to get loose. Then I retired the first 25 batters who faced me."[11] Deprived of perfection, Seaver and the Mets still defeated Chicago 4–0 that evening. After a nine-game Mets homestand, the Cubs' lead in the NL East was whittled down to just four games.

A harbinger of wonderful things to come in October came in mid–July when light-hitting Al Weis, the Mets' occasional second baseman, hit home runs on consecutive days (July 15 and 16) at Chicago's Wrigley Field. New York won both games. Cubs manager Leo Durocher was perplexed and tormented by Weis' uncharacteristic display of power. "Weis…. Weis…. Why Weis?"[12] he was heard mumbling after the second loss.

The 1969 MLB All-Star Game was played in Washington on the afternoon of Wednesday, July 23, because of a rainout the previous night. Three Mets were chosen for the NL roster. Only one was a starter: outfielder Cleon Jones, who hit two singles in four at-bats. Jerry Koosman gave up a hit and struck out one AL batter in 1⅔ innings of relief pitching. Tom Seaver did not get into the game.

One date that has entered New York Mets lore is Wednesday, July 30, 1969. It is noteworthy for a single incident that may have turned the Mets' season completely around. The Houston Astros were playing a doubleheader at Shea Stadium on a drizzly night. The footing in the outfield was not especially great that evening. In the first game, the visitors erupted for 11 runs in the top of the ninth inning—including two grand slam homers—to turn a close game into a 16–3 Houston romp. In the third inning of the second game, the Astros nearly duplicated the feat, scoring 10 runs to assume a huge lead. With Houston having scored seven runs already, the second-to-last Houston hit of the inning, by Johnny Edwards, dropped into left field where it should have only been a single. However, Cleon Jones made only a half-hearted effort to chase it down swiftly on the wet and muddy outfield. Jones then compounded the sin by making a poor throw to the infield. Houston's Doug Rader scored all the way from first base on the hit as Edwards coasted into second base with a double. At the time, Jones was nursing a hamstring injury, but he was also vying for the NL batting lead. (He had finished in sixth spot in 1968.) Manager Gil Hodges was steamed by what he saw. He asked for time and then slowly but purposefully entered the field to have an up-close chat with his left fielder.

According to Jones, the conversation was brief and very one-sided. This is what Jones recalls Hodges saying to him: "If you're not running good [sic], why don't you just come out of the ball game?"[13] Hodges did not wait for a reply; instead he turned around and headed towards the Met dugout. "I knew he had something more than my leg in mind, and I followed him in,"[14] Jones noted. In effect, Hodges had yanked him from the game—and Jones perceptively knew it. Ron Swoboda took Jones' spot in left field. The next batter, Houston pitcher Larry Dierker, hit a two-run homer. (Dierker's next home run would occur in the 1976 season.) Houston eventually won the game, 11–5. Cleon Jones finished 1969 with a .340 batting average—a new club record—but it only put him third in the NL batting race behind winner Pete Rose (.348) and runner-up Roberto Clemente (.345).

When Hodges pulled his best hitter for not hustling sufficiently in the outfield in a one-sided game, his action gave a clear message to the team, the home fans, and the entire NL: The Mets were no longer going to accept being the league's laughingstocks. Following the disastrous doubleheader, the Mets were in second place in the NL East, five games behind the Chicago Cubs, with a record of 55–43. They won 45 of their remaining 64 games from that point onward. Years later, Joan Hodges recalled that her husband had not deliberately intended to make the Cleon

Jones incident a grandiose show of his authority and his expectations for his players. It just happened in the heat of the moment. She recalled Gil explaining to her after the game, "I never realized [what I was doing] until I passed the mound—and [then] I couldn't turn back."[15]

The Houston Astros—the Mets' NL expansion brothers from 1962 who were threatening to win the West Division—came to New York and swept three games at Shea Stadium from August 11 to 13. Those setbacks dropped the Mets to third spot in the NL East, trailing both the front-running Chicago Cubs by 10 games and the St. Louis Cardinals. Following two days off, the Mets regrouped and swept doubleheaders on consecutive days from the lowly San Diego Padres to start their remarkable charge toward the top of the division. On August 21, a nifty 6–0 two-hitter pitched by Jim McAndrew over San Francisco gave the New Yorkers their sixth straight victory and put them within 6½ games of faltering Chicago.

Once the Mets got going on their unstoppable winning track, nothing could derail them. Even when things went wrong, they still somehow ended up right. Their August 30 game at San Francisco's Candlestick Park provides an excellent example. The Mets and Giants were locked in a 2–2 tie in the bottom of the ninth inning. San Francisco's Bob Burda was at first base with one out. Willie McCovey, who would win the NL MVP Award for 1969, was at bat with Tug McGraw pitching for New York. Rookie Rod Gaspar was the Mets' left fielder, but he was positioned in left-center because McCovey was renowned as a left-handed pull hitter. McCovey connected and drove the ball, against his nature, down the left-field line. It was fair by about a foot and landed near the warning track. Years later this was how Gaspar recalled the play unfolding:

> The field was wet. There was no way I could catch the ball. My only thought was Burda was the winning run and I had to throw him out at home plate. As I approached the ball it was stuck in the ground. I grabbed it bare-handed, pivoted off my left foot, and threw blindly toward home plate. Thankfully it was a strike to catcher Jerry Grote.[16]

Burda, who was not especially fleet of foot—he had just two stolen bases in his seven-year MLB career—was gunned out at home. However, Grote lost track of how many outs there were! Believing the inning was over, Grote rolled the ball toward the pitcher's mound that McGraw had vacated to back up Gaspar's throw. McCovey, who was standing on second base after his hit, broke for third base. Fortunately for New York, Mets first baseman Donn Clendenon alertly saw Grote's mistake. He raced to the mound, picked up the ball and threw McCovey out. It was a highly unusual 7–2–3–5 double play to end the ninth inning and preserve the tie. The Mets won the game 3–2 in 10 innings when Clendenon hit a solo home run off Gaylord Perry. Amazing!

Tuesday, September 9 was the night of what was certainly the most famous oddball incident at Shea Stadium to occur during the 1969 regular season. During a Cubs-Mets game, a black cat somehow ended up on the playing field. It walked around Chicago's Ron Santo who was standing on the on-deck circle. Then it strangely peered directly at the Cubs in their dugout before scampering down the warning track toward left field. The symbolism was clear: The Chicago Cubs were a hexed baseball team.

Ed Kranepool remembered there were quite a few stray felines who made their homes in the vast crevices of Shea Stadium, feasting on plentiful rats and discarded food morsels for sustenance. Thus, cats were not exactly scarce at the Mets' home ballpark. Still, none had previously ever roamed onto the field during a game, much less a black one apparently focused on the division-leading visitors. "It was just so weird that it came up right in front of [the Cubs'] dugout, around the on-deck circle, and just stared at Leo [Durocher]," marveled Kranepool many years later. "It really was like some voodoo thing."[17]

Art Shamsky wrote in 2019, "It was like this cat was mechanical and had been programmed to just walk around and stay in the Cubs' area. If it would've come over to the Mets' side [of the infield], I think it would've freaked all of us out. We were all very superstitious."[18]

Donn Clendenon always suspected that one of Shea Stadium's groundskeepers, Pete Flynn, had something to do with letting the cat loose on the playing field. If that were truly the case, Flynn, who died in 2017, forever kept quiet about any involvement he may have had in orchestrating such a memorable stunt.

Of course, the Mets won that night, 7–1, in what the Associated Press described as "a carnival atmosphere."[19]

On Wednesday, September 10, the Mets reached a historic milestone. Combining a twi-night doubleheader sweep over Montreal at Shea Stadium with a Chicago loss to the Phillies in Philadelphia, New York's formerly woebegone Mets were residing in first place for the first time in their dreary eight-year history. "Look Who's No. 1…" read the Shea Stadium scoreboard as it displayed the updated NL East standings. The Cubs had been in first place for 155 days, since winning on Opening Day on April 8. According to an Associated Press story, "After the jubilant Mets romped off the field, Mrs. Joan Payson, the club's principal owner, left her box seat alongside the Mets' dugout for a triumphant stroll behind home plate. The crowd gave her a standing ovation."[20] That action was unusual for the 66-year-old Payson; she typically tried to avoid being in the spotlight. At least that was what she insisted when she gave interviews.

The Mets had won 22 of 28 games since August 13 when they trailed the Cubs by a daunting 9½ games. On the other side of the coin, Chicago had only won 11 of 27 games in that same period. The loss to Philadelphia was the fading Cubs' seventh consecutive setback. New York would not relinquish their grip on first place. A common theory espoused by baseball historians for the changing fortunes of the two contenders for the NL East title was that Leo Durocher overused his regular starting eight Chicago players throughout 1969 while Gil Hodges' platoon system provided valuable rest for his Mets over the course of the long season.

Two days after attaining first place, on Friday, September 12, the Mets won an extraordinary twi-night doubleheader in Pittsburgh before 19,000 fans at Forbes Field. Remarkably, both games ended in 1–0 shutouts—and in each contest the game's only run was driven in by a Met pitcher: Jerry Koosman in the opener and Don Cardwell in the nightcap. It was Koosman's first RBI of the 1969 season; Cardwell had not recorded an RBI since May. Back in March, Pittsburgh had been one of the experts' favorites to win the NL East title, but the sweep put the Pirates 10 games in arrears of the Mets and the Cubs 2½ games behind. It also extended the New York winning streak to nine games. It truly seemed that the hand of destiny was guiding the Mets.

Another omen that the baseball gods were clearly favoring the Mets came on Monday, September 15, at St. Louis. That night, Steve Carlton of the Cardinals struck out 19 Mets to set a modern MLB record for whiffs in a game. Nevertheless, New York still won, 4–3, thanks to a pair of two-run homers by Ron Swoboda. Both home runs came on two-strike counts. It was the first time Swoboda recorded multiple home runs in a game since his rookie season in 1965. In a SABR piece, author Richard Cuicchi wrote that the game "was characteristic of [the Mets'] late-season surge to glory."[21]

En route to the division title, the Mets survived one last hiccup, losing the first three of a five-game home series versus Pittsburgh over two days on September 19 and 20. (The third loss was a 4–0 no-hitter tossed by Bob Moose.) Nevertheless, New York rallied to win the next two contests—and seven more games in a row to finish the season quite strongly. Jack Lang of *The Sporting News* wrote with a sense of wonder,

> In the space of one week, the Mets were victims of an historic, record-breaking 19-strikeout performance by Steve Carlton, the victims of a doubleheader defeat by the limbo-bound Pirates, and victims of a no-run, hot-hit game by 21-year-old Bob Moose. Through all this embarrassment, the Mets did not lose ground, they actually gained on the Cubs.[22]

On September 23, the Mets clinched at least a tie for the NL East by beating St. Louis, 3–2, in a comeback effort in 11 innings at Shea Stadium. Most Cub fans had thrown in the towel on the 1969 season. Before a pitifully small turnout of 2,217 at Wrigley Field the next afternoon, the Chicago Cubs beat the Montreal Expos 6–3 to temporarily stay alive in the divisional race. But that night, a nifty, four-hit, 6–0 shutout over the Cardinals authored by Gary Gentry clinched the East Division title for the Mets. New York scored five runs off Steve Carlton in the home half of the first inning to siphon much of the drama out of the occasion. A 6–4–3 double play concluded the game. Such was the historic significance of the event that Met broadcaster Lindsey Nelson felt compelled to give the precise time that Mets had won the NL East: 9:07 p.m.

Joe Torre was the Cardinal who hit into the game-ending twin-killing. Before the 1969 season, when Torre was with Atlanta but embroiled in a contract dispute, the Mets had tried to acquire him in a trade. However, they balked at the price the Braves demanded: young pitchers Nolan Ryan and Gary Gentry. (Atlanta eventually traded Torre to St. Louis for Orlando Cepeda, who had won the 1967 NL MVP Award.)

For the first of three times in 1969, crazed fans at Shea Stadium brazenly ignored police and ballpark security personnel to invade the field. They gleefully tore large portions of the sod from the diamond. Meanwhile, the giddy Met players celebrated in the clubhouse by pouring bottle after bottle of champagne over each other and anyone else who happened to pass by. Gil Hodges, now the toast of New York City, was quietly pleased by what he and his squad had accomplished. Surveying his unbridled, merrymaking Mets, Hodges told a reporter, "I'm a little bit older than they are. Take off 25 years and I'd be running wild too."[23]

Amid the tumult, a grateful Tommie Agee sought out Hodges in his office to personally thank his manager for not giving up on him. Agee had endured a terrible 1968 season in which he batted just .217 and hit only five home runs, but Agee rebounded well in 1969. He swatted 26 homers and batted .271. "The man had faith in me. I'll never forget that."[24] Agee would be named the NL Comeback Player of the Year for 1969 by *The Sporting News*.

"This is the best," declared Ed Charles above the clamor. "We're going all the way."[25]

The next step would be the first National League Championship Series where they would confront Hank Aaron and his Atlanta Braves, winners of the NL West. They too had played excellent baseball in September.

During the very memorable 1969 regular season, the New York Mets drew 2,175,373 fans to Shea Stadium. No other MLB team in either league came within 300,000 of the Mets' attendance total. The superb Baltimore Orioles did not draw 50 percent of what the Mets had.

On October 1, in their second-to-last outing of the season, the New York Mets, who habitually accrued campaigns of triple-digit losses, won their 100th game of 1969 by edging the Chicago Cubs 6–5 at Wrigley Field in 12 innings. They were indeed the Amazing Mets—without any sarcasm attached to the adjective. In all the years since 1969, the Mets have only achieved a triple-digit win total in two other seasons: 1986 and 1988.

The Vaunted 1969 Baltimore Orioles

"If we were allowed to bet, I'd have put every nickel on this ball club. It was the best team I'd ever, ever seen."[1]—Catcher Clay Dalrymple, acquired by the Baltimore Orioles before the 1969 season

"The Orioles should win this [AL East] division. Last year the Orioles found themselves too far behind [Detroit] at the All-Star break. If Baltimore starts well, watch out."[2]—*Sports Illustrated* 1969 Baseball preview edition

The modern Baltimore Orioles were once the Milwaukee Brewers. It sounds strange, but it is true. When the Western League was transformed by Ban Johnson in 1901 and became the American League, one franchise was located in Milwaukee and was locally known as the Brewers. Johnson, the AL's president, preferred to have a team in the more populous St. Louis, so after a potential owner came forward in 1902, the Brewers were abruptly shifted to St. Louis and became the Browns. There they remained for the next 52 baseball seasons.

For a while, the Browns were a better gate attraction in St. Louis than the more established St. Louis Cardinals, their intra-city NL competition. More often than not, however, the Browns played generally bad baseball in St. Louis' Sportsman's Park for half a century. Crowds were small—especially after the Cardinals became the more fashionable team to support in St. Louis. Three times during the 1930s the Browns drew fewer than 94,000 paying customers all season—an average of little more than 1,000 people per game. Wisecracks about the poorly supported club abounded. It was said that no spectator would dare heckle anyone on the home team because the Browns players outnumbered the fans. Another joke had a fan telephoning the Browns' box office to inquire about the starting time of that day's game. "What time can you be here?" was the reply.

The St. Louis Browns captured just one AL pennant—in 1944—when major league rosters were badly depleted by the manpower demands of the Second World War. The greatest Brown player was undoubtedly George Sisler, a .340 lifetime hitter who once accrued a mind-boggling 257 hits in a season and twice won the AL batting championship in the early 1920s. Tellingly, though, the most famous St.

Louis Brown was probably tiny Eddie Gaedel. He was the midget who made a bizarre pinch-hitting appearance (and drew a four-pitch walk) as a publicity stunt in 1951. By the early 1950s, the franchise was hemorrhaging money and few tears were shed in Missouri—or elsewhere—when the Browns bid St. Louis adieu, were shifted to Baltimore, and became the Orioles beginning in 1954.

For the rest of the 1950s, the Orioles retained the longstanding but demoralizing tradition of the Browns by finishing well out of contention in the AL pennant chase. A fifth-place finish in 1957 being their best effort. The 1960s would see a dramatic shift in the franchise's fortunes. Only twice in the decade did the Orioles finish below .500. Starting with a terrific second-place finish in 1960 (just eight games out of first place), the Orioles soon established themselves as legitimate pennant contenders. They were also starting to get some fine players. Shortstop Roy Hansen was named AL Rookie of the Year in 1960. Third baseman Brooks Robinson—who was attracting scouts while playing American Legion baseball in Arkansas—was the AL's Most Valuable Player in 1964.

In 1966 everything came together for the Orioles. Led by no-nonsense manager Hank Bauer, Baltimore captured the franchise's first pennant since coming from St. Louis. Baltimore won 97 games and finished nine games ahead of second-place Minnesota. Frank Robinson, acquired from the Cincinnati Reds, won the AL Triple Crown and was the obvious MVP winner. "We had an awesome, nasty lineup," first baseman John (Boog) Powell recalled. "We pounded on people. We rolled. And we had a ton of fun."[3] The Orioles drew more than 1.2 million fans to Memorial Stadium, a mark that would not be equaled until 1979. In the World Series, the Orioles humiliated the Los Angeles Dodgers in an impressive four-game sweep. The Dodgers had been favored because of their two superstar pitchers, Don Drysdale and Sandy Koufax. But Frank and Brooks Robinson both homered off Drysdale in the first inning of Game #1 to dispel any fears. Ironically, it was the Orioles pitchers who shined in the 1966 World Series. Los Angeles only managed to score two runs in 36 innings—both of which came early in Game #1. Hank Bauer was named the MLB Manager of the Year by *The Sporting News*.

The following season, 1967, the Orioles surprisingly stumbled to a sixth-place finish with a mediocre 76–85 record. Injuries to pitchers and other star players were largely to blame, but Bauer was criticized in the media and by Orioles owner Harry Dalton for being too hands-off when it came to his handling of the team's veterans and too hard on the younger players. By the All-Star break in 1968, with the Orioles languishing in third place, Bauer was fired only 21 months after winning the World Series. A new face—Earl Weaver—was named the Baltimore manager. Writer George Will noted, "Earl Weaver was what a manager ought to look like: short, angry, florid, impatient, intemperate—like a great many managers."[4]

A cherubic face betrayed Weaver's fiery temperament. He had never played a game in the major leagues, but he had proven himself to be a capable and cagy field pilot in the Orioles' minor league system. He was also a favorite of Harry Dalton.

"In short, I believe Earl Weaver is a winner,"[5] Dalton told the media when introducing Weaver as the team's new manager. From Weaver's first day at the helm until the end of the 1982 season, no MLB team won more games than the Baltimore Orioles did. In writing Weaver's biography for the Society for American Baseball's website, Warren Corbett noted, "Weaver ... became the revered Earl of Baltimore, while fighting with umpires, his own players, and English grammar."[6] Under Weaver, the Orioles won 48 of their last 82 games in 1968, made a run at the AL pennant, but ended up finishing second to a talented Detroit Tigers team.

The Orioles' brain trust thought Weaver had done a fine job in his half season with the club in 1968. Accordingly, on September 27, the team rewarded him with a 30 percent raise for 1969—increasing his salary from $25,000 to $32,500. "I think Earl accomplished a lot in a short time," said Harry Dalton, Baltimore's director of player personnel. "Under his direction, our club created the only semblance of a pennant race in either major league this year. Considering the great year Detroit has had, it took some doing to cut 6½ games of their lead in the first seven weeks he managed."[7]

Despite having no major league playing career largely because of his diminutive height (5'7"), Weaver did have one advantage: He was typically familiar with the ballplayers he was managing, having already managed many of them in the Baltimore farm system. Weaver did not tolerate any arrogance on his team. This sentiment was reflected on a sign he had posted in the Baltimore clubhouse: "It's what you learn after you know it all that counts."

Weaver also encouraged his Orioles to be generous to fans with their time as a way of gelling as a team. (Previously, Frank Robinson had been especially reluctant to sign baseballs or engage with the ticket-buyers.) Some Orioles, however, did not need any prodding to interact with the customers. Weaver's star third baseman was already famous for his excessive friendliness with awestruck admirers of all ages. "When fans ask Brooks Robinson for his autograph," Oriole broadcaster Chuck Thompson fondly remembered, "he complied while finding out how many kids you have, what your dad does, where you live, how old you are, and if you have a dog. By the time the press got [to the clubhouse after the game], Brooks was in the parking lot signing autographs."[8] Interestingly, although Robinson batted right and threw right, he held a pen with his left hand.

Apart from Baltimore dropping their 1969 home opener to Boston in 12 innings (on the same day the Mets dropped theirs to Montreal), everything went swimmingly for the Orioles during the 1969 regular season. Frank Robinson played very nearly as well as he had in his Triple Crown year. Brooks Robinson had fully recovered from a 1967 concussion and once again guarded third base as no one had ever done before. Paul Blair was back at 100 percent from a broken ankle he had suffered playing winter ball in Puerto Rico in December 1967. (Blair was the only center fielder in MLB to record more than 400 putouts in 1969.)

After enduring two years of arm injuries, promising 23-year-old Jim Palmer pitched superbly. Mike Cuellar, acquired from the Houston Astros in a trade for Curt Blefary, was thought to be washed up. He was far from it. Cuellar had a dream season in 1969, winning 23 games and throwing five shutouts in his new surroundings. (He would share the 1969 AL Cy Young Award with Detroit's Denny McLain. He was the first Oriole to win the league's top pitching trophy.) A 26-year-old left-hander from Montana, Dave McNally, rolled off 15 consecutive wins en route to a terrific 20–7 record. One of those wins was a 5–0 one-hitter in Minnesota on May 15 in which César Tovar of the Twins got the home team's only hit—a single—with one out in the ninth inning. McNally also had 12 no-decisions within that streak. Baltimore won three of those games in which McNally failed to go five innings; the shortness of those outings deprived McNally from getting credit for any of those victories.

Excellent pitching was always a hallmark of the championship Oriole clubs. Paul Blair once said, "With Cuellar, McNally, and Palmer, you could almost ring up 60 wins for us when the season started because each of them was going to win 20."[9] Dave Leonhard, who compiled a 7–4 record for the 1969 Orioles, gave Weaver credit for knowing which buttons to push to get the most out of each Baltimore pitcher. He said Weaver knew "how and when to turn it on and off. He knew some guys would respond to screaming and others needed a pat on the back. That was what made him a success as a manager."[10]

At the beginning of the 1969 season, *Sports Illustrated* rated the AL East to be the toughest of

Earl Weaver's 1,354 wins for Baltimore rank him first among the 42 Oriole managers in the club's history—as do his 919 losses. Stymied by the Mets in 1969, Weaver would steer his club to a World Series victory over Cincinnati the following season. The Orioles retired his number 4 in 1982. Weaver was inducted into the Hall of Fame in 1996 (National Baseball Hall of Fame and Museum, Cooperstown, NY).

baseball's four divisions in its MLB preview edition. (One leading factor was that it did not contain any of the new expansion teams.) Weaver—a man who loved and understood numbers—did not think so. He calculated that his club was clearly the team to beat in the AL. He told his players that if they could win seven more games than they lost each month, they would win the newly formed AL East. Weaver was correct. In 1969, the first year of divisional play in MLB, Baltimore made a mockery of the mini pennant race. Midway through August, the Orioles' record was 86–35. On September 25 they were 60 games over .500. The Orioles attained first place nine games into the season and never relinquished it. Baltimore easily romped to the first-ever AL East title with 109 wins. At one point in September, the Orioles were 22 games ahead of their closest pursuers. They finished 19 games in front of second-place Detroit—the 1968 World Series winners—clinching the division on September 13 with a 2–1 home win over Cleveland. Five of Baltimore's 53 losses came at the very end of the season—in games #157 through #161—long after the AL East title had been settled.

The Orioles had such an easy time of it throughout most of the 1969 AL season that reliable Brooks Robinson felt it was okay to take a well-earned midseason rest. On Tuesday, August 19 he did not play versus the California Angels in Anaheim, sparking cries of "What's wrong with Brooks?" among Oriole fans. It was certainly a conspicuous absence—and it generated headlines across America's sports pages. Robinson had played in every game for the Orioles in 1968 and in all 120 of Baltimore's previous 1969 contests in accruing a consecutive-games-played streak of 282. The record books showed Robinson had also not been absent from any game in 1961, 1963, or in his AL MVP season of 1964.

Robinson explained to alarmed baseball journalists that he was not injured and that his sitting out was completely a voluntary move, with his manager's approval. "It's become apparent since the All-Star Game that we are going to win our division," he stated, "and I think it would be a good time for me to take a couple of days off. I told Earl [Weaver] last week that I was going to [take some time] off at Anaheim. I'm a little arm-weary—my swing, that is—but I'll be right back in there on Thursday night."[11] Without their regular third baseman in their lineup (Don Buford was moved to the hot corner), the Orioles still won Tuesday's game, 10–0, as Mike Cuellar tossed a seven-hit shutout over the Angels. Baltimore lost the following night, 3–2, however.

Robinson, who was having a slightly off year offensively, said Weaver had asked him if he wanted to sit out an occasional game when the Orioles had an 11-game lead in the AL East. "That lead is now 17," noted the great third baseman, "so I figure a couple [days off] now and a couple more when we clinch it will help me and will help the club because I'll be a fresher player [for the postseason games]."[12]

It was reported on September 1 that Weaver had happily signed a new contract for 1970 that provided him with a $10,000 increase over his 1969 salary: a significant 33 percent bump from $30,000 to $40,000. "He richly deserves the substantial salary raise he will receive next year," said Harry Dalton, the Orioles' director of player personnel, "and I hope there will be many more to follow."[13] At the time of the announcement, the Orioles were in a bit of a rut, having lost eight of 12 games, but they still had a substantial lead—12½ games—over their closest divisional rivals, the Detroit Tigers.

The Orioles were a scary team for any opponent to face in 1969. Five of Baltimore's most potent regulars combined to hit 128 home runs. Frank Robinson and Boog Powell each knocked in at least 100 runs while batting over .300. Leadoff hitter Don Buford used an amalgam of speed and power to be among the AL leaders in doubles for most of the year. (He finished tied for sixth place with 31.) Defensively, the Orioles were unmatched in the AL. They made just 95 errors all season. William Leggett of *Sports Illustrated* admiringly declared, "The left side of the [Baltimore] infield, with Brooks Robinson at third base and Mark Belanger at shortstop, is one of the best that baseball has ever seen."[14] Furthermore, the Orioles boasted

the finest pitching staff in the AL. They had 50 complete games and 19 shutouts. Although 11 different Baltimore pitchers recorded wins in 1969, the threesome of Mike Cuellar, Dave McNally and Jim Palmer combined for 59 of them. The Orioles' team ERA of 2.83 was the AL's best.

At the 1969 All-Star Game, five Orioles were on the AL roster, including starters Boog Powell and Frank Robinson. Dave McNally, Paul Blair, and Brooks Robinson were also present. Dave Johnson was supposed to take part too, but he did not make the trip to Washington due to a nagging back injury that sometimes prevented him from sitting comfortably. McNally was the best of the Birds: he pitched two shutout innings in relief. The NL won the game handily, 9–3.

Hall-of-Famer Brooks Robinson's impressive résumé includes 16 consecutive Gold Glove Awards, 18 All-Star appearances, and 1970 World Series MVP. The slick-fielding third baseman was aptly nicknamed "The Human Vacuum Cleaner" and is widely considered by baseball historians to be the greatest third baseman of all time (National Baseball Hall of Fame and Museum, Cooperstown, NY).

SI's William Leggett was certainly no supporter of the new, unfamiliar MLB postseason format for 1969, and thought it unfairly minimized sustained excellence over the long baseball season. He spoke for legions of the sport's purists when he wrote,

> There are quite a few people, many of them not living in Baltimore, who believe that the Orioles enter the playoffs somewhat disadvantaged. Why, some ask, must a team be exposed to being beaten in a short series after having won more games than any other during the 162-game regular season and thus be deprived of playing in baseball's biggest showcase, the World Series?[15]

Indeed, on the eve of the ALCS Frank Robinson seemed annoyed by the extra tier of postseason games which meant that Baltimore might become the only team in AL history to win the most games during the regular season and not attain a spot in the World Series. He told an Associated Press reporter that the Orioles "shouldn't have to prove again" that they are the best baseball club in the AL. "We've already proved that over 162 games," he grumbled. "Now we have to prove it again in a five-game series."[16] Baltimore had beaten Minnesota eight times in the teams' 12 games during the regular season.

"That 8–4 [record] shows we're the superior club over a season," Brooks Robinson insisted, "but it doesn't mean a whole lot now, not in a five-game series. The best club doesn't necessarily win a short series like that. It depends on who has the hot hand."[17]

Despite Baltimore's fine 1969 season, and whatever views the two Robinsons personally held about the matter, it made no difference. The ALCS was now part of MLB's new era. Accordingly, Earl Weaver's vaunted Orioles still had to get by the dangerous West Division champion Minnesota Twins to claim the AL pennant and World Series berth that most fair-minded baseball followers believed they wholly deserved.

Some observers figured the Orioles had gotten the short end of the stick in the ALCS scheduling, as Minnesota would have three home games if the series went the maximum five games. William Leggett of *Sports Illustrated* was one of them. In a preview piece about the two LSC, he wrote,

> "Haven't new Commissioner Bowie Kuhn and his staff bungled the playoff setup by not giving to the winningest team the home-field advantage? Baltimore plays the first two games in Memorial Stadium, then the remaining [three] games in Minnesota. Not even the National Basketball Association, seldom cited for its great foresight, ever let that happen during its playoffs."[18]

The Orioles also were quite respectful and wary of the Twins' strong lineup. It was Minnesota who had ended Dave McNally's personal 17-game undefeated streak that dated back to 1968. When Minnesota and Oakland were battling for the AL West title, 30 Oriole players and coaches were polled to find out which of the two combatants they would rather meet in the ALCS. Only three respondents selected the Twins while 20 said Oakland. The other seven pollees declared themselves to be undecided.

From a strategic standpoint, first-year Twins manager Billy Martin said he planned to continue doing the things that had won the Twins the AL West title—especially emphasizing aggressive baserunning. He promised to "run against the Orioles quite a bit. Sometimes in crucial games, teams change and become more conservative. We're going to play our game and run. That could lead to errors and mental mistakes [by Baltimore]."[19]

Martin also respectfully added the following coda: "We're impressed with Baltimore's 109 wins." Then he noted, "But that's history."[20]

4

National League Championship Series
New York Sweeps Atlanta

"The 1969 baseball season was a new and exciting experience for me, for almost all of the New York Mets. We seemed to have hurtled straight from our first pennant race into our first [NLCS]."[1]—Tom Seaver

"With momentum going for both teams, the New York Mets and Atlanta Braves will start their ace pitches Saturday in the opening game of the best-of-five series for the National League championship and a spot in the 1969 World Series."[2]—Ed Shearer, Associated Press

When the American and National Leagues each split into two divisions for the 1969 season, MLB hyped the radical change from its past as a means of creating more excitement for its fans—four championship races instead of two—and an extra level of postseason drama. *Sports Illustrated* called it "a new deal for an old sport."[3] In 1969, however, MLB produced just one nail-biting divisional race and two League Championship Series that were over in the minimum amount of games.

Only the NL West provided anything close to a photo finish, with the Atlanta Braves crossing the finish line three games in front of the San Francisco Giants. (Five of the six clubs in the NL West were vying for first place at some point in the season. Only the expansion San Diego Padres, losers of 110 games, were non-factors in the divisional race.) Atlanta had been a fifth-place club in 1968, finishing with an 81–81 record. The champions of the NL East, the New York Mets, pulled away from the rest of the pack in the last month of the regular season to finish eight full games ahead of the Chicago Cubs. The AL had no drama at all with Baltimore laughing their way to a monstrous 19-game edge on their closest rivals (Detroit) in the East. The high-scoring Minnesota Twins also galloped home in the AL West without experiencing too much difficulty. At the end, they held a comfy nine-game margin over the Oakland Athletics. The new LCS meant that for the first time in the 20th century there were official playoffs in MLB that were not used to break first-place ties at the end of the regular season.

Intra-league playoffs were not entirely unknown in MLB history, but one had to go way back to the 1890s to find them. For a short time in that decade, the NL held a postseason Temple Cup series between its first- and second-place finishers. The tangible prize was an $800 silver trophy donated by and named after William Chase Temple. He was a coal and lumber magnate who owned a share of the Pittsburgh Pirates. Known today by only the most scholarly of baseball fans, the Temple Cup series was a best-of-seven affair that was played annually from 1894 to 1897 with the winning team getting 65 percent of the gate receipts; the losing squad got 35 percent. (W.C. Temple was the epitome of a true altruist; his mediocre Pirates never came close to qualifying for any of the four postseason series.)

Few people took the Temple Cup competition seriously, though; it was generally viewed as superfluous fluff. In most fans' minds, the team that won the pennant by compiling the best record over the long season was the true NL championship club. (For evidence, one only needs to look at the cover of a rare copy of an 1895 Temple Cup scorecard from Baltimore. It proclaims the Orioles as NL champions of 1894 and 1895 even though they lost both those seasons' Temple Cup series.) Those 19th century Baltimore Orioles—whose star-filled lineup featured the likes of Wee Willie Keeler, John McGraw and Hughie Jennings—appeared in all four Temple Cup series, winning three of them. Apathy also engulfed many players when the games' gate receipts proved to be highly disappointing. No one cared too much when the Temple Cup series was discontinued after 1897. The trophy was returned to Temple. It was forgotten for more than 40 years until the folks at the Hall of Fame went looking for it. It was found in the home of one of William Chase Temple's descendants, who, according to some sources, had no idea what it was. The Hall of Fame paid $750 for it in 1939. It resides in a display case in Cooperstown today and usually draws only cursory attention from most museum visitors.

Beginning in 1969, the two LCS were going to be clearly more important than the Temple Cup series ever was. From this point forward, their respective winners would each earn a coveted World Series berth.

As would be the case through 1984, both LCS were best-of-five affairs. Both series began on Saturday, October 4, and were to be contested over five consecutive days, if need be, with no day set aside for travel. It was predetermined that the NLCS would start in the NL West champions' ballpark. Thus, the series would open in Atlanta for the first two games and then move to New York for Game #3 (and #4 and #5, if necessary). The ALCS had the reverse occurring, starting in Baltimore and moving to Minnesota for its conclusion. *Sports Illustrated* called the newfangled intra-league playoffs "a necessary prelude to that most honorable and ancient tradition: the World Series" as MLB's postseason had now been elongated into a "two-week-long tournament."[4]

A *Sports Illustrated* scribe figured the Mets were entering the NLCS playing with the house's money. "[They are] the one club with very little to lose," wrote William Leggett. "Their season has already been a tremendous success because few of their followers thought the team had progressed to the point, after seven years of existence, where it could beat out powerful contenders. In preseason odds, St. Louis was 2 to 5 to take the title in the East, Chicago was 3 to 1, and the Mets 25 to 1."[5] In keeping with their collective underdog persona, the Mets had again failed to win the respect of Las Vegas oddsmakers. The Braves were installed as 11–10 betting favorites to win the NLCS. Perhaps it was because Atlanta had won 10 consecutive games before dropping their meaningless regular-season finale on October 2 versus Cincinnati.

Despite a midseason slump that almost caused Atlanta to fall out of the NL West race, Braves manager Chalmer Luman (Lum) Harris entered the NLCS with confidence. "We're a better team now than when the Mets last met us [August 10]," he insisted. "We're much the same as we were early in the season when we got off to a good start. There's no comparison between this team now and a month ago."[6] Nevertheless, Sam Lacy of the *Baltimore Afro-American* wrote, "The resurgence in the wigwam notwithstanding, the pick here for the NL representation in the World Series beginning next Saturday is the New York Mets."[7]

Game #1 of the NLCS began at 4 p.m. in Atlanta Stadium. October baseball was a novelty in the southern city in 1969. (The Braves had shifted to Georgia from Wisconsin in 1966; the franchise had not won anything since the once-fashionable Milwaukee Braves had last captured the NL pennant in 1958.) Slightly more than 50,000 people were on hand for the Atlanta Braves' postseason debut. Both clubs' best pitchers were on the mound for the opener, but the matchup seemed to favor New York, at least if recent history had any bearing on it. Tom Seaver had beaten the Braves three times in 1969, while Phil Niekro had lost three games to the Mets. Overall, the Mets had beaten Atlanta in eight of their 12 regular-season clashes.

The huge crowd saw the Mets draw first blood in the top of the second inning off Braves starter Phil Niekro. Catcher Jerry Grote rapped an RBI single with two runners on base. Shortly thereafter, second baseman Ken Boswell scored from third base on a passed ball that eluded Atlanta catcher Bob Didier. New York surged into an early 2–0 lead.

The Braves sliced the visitors' lead in half in the bottom of the second inning on Clete Boyer's sacrifice fly off Tom Seaver with runners on both second and third base.

Three consecutive doubles in the third inning gave the Braves a 3–2 advantage—their first lead of the game—in the bottom of the third inning. The home team did not hold onto that lead for very long, though. The Mets immediately regained the advantage in the top of the fourth on Bud Harrelson's timely two-run triple. (Harrelson had accrued just 17 extra-base hits all season.) Strong offensive showings by unlikely contributors would be a hallmark of the Mets' October.

Atlanta fought back. The Braves Tony González tied the seesaw game at 4–4 in the home half of fifth inning with the first home run ever struck in NLCS play. Hank Aaron gave the Braves a 5–4 lead with a home run of his own in the bottom of the seventh. Aaron was a holdover from the 1957 and 1958 Milwaukee Braves who had played in consecutive World Series versus the New York Yankees. (In a pre–NLCS newspaper story, Hodges had told reporters that his pitchers would, whenever possible, do their best to pitch around the slugging Aaron, who had finished second in the NL home run race with 44, just one behind Willie McCovey of the Giants.)

The Braves were just six outs from winning Game #1 of the NLCS when things suddenly unraveled for them. In the top of the eighth inning, Wayne Garrett led off with a double. He was promptly driven home by Cleon Jones' single, tying the score 5–5. The Mets' rally continued. Art Shamsky hit a single, advancing Jones to second base. Al Weis pinch-ran for Shamsky. With Boswell attempting to bunt, Jones broke for third. Boswell missed the pitch. Jones should have been an easy put out, but Braves catcher Bob Didier threw high to third base. Jones was safe and was generously credited with a stolen base on the broken play.

With nobody out and runners at third and first, Boswell's at-bat continued. He smacked a ground ball back to Atlanta pitcher Phil Niekro. Niekro took a moment to hold Jones at third base, but then threw to second base to force out Weis. There was no time to turn a double play however; Boswell reached first base on the fielder's choice. With one out the Mets had runners at the corners.

New York first baseman Ed Kranepool hit a ground ball to his Atlanta counterpart, Orlando Cepeda. Jones broke for home. Cepeda opted to try to nail Jones at the plate, but he made an inaccurate throw. Jones was safe; New York now led 6–5. Boswell moved to second base on the play while Kranepool got to first base on the fielder's choice. Up next was Jerry Grote. He grounded out, but Boswell and Kranepool moved to third and second bases respectively. There were now two out. Bud Harrelson, batting in the number-eight spot, was walked intentionally to load the bases and bring Tom Seaver to the plate.

Gil Hodges removed Seaver from the game and inserted pinch-hitter J.C. Martin into the number-nine spot. It proved to be a great strategic move. Martin slashed a base hit to right-center field. Two runs scored easily. Harrelson made it three when outfielder Tony González misplayed the ball. Martin had moved to second base on the play—and tried for more—but he was thrown out at third base by González. The damage had been done, however. In another amazing rally, New York had scored five runs in the top of the eighth inning to assume a 9–5 lead. Niekro had surrendered all nine of New York's runs in Game #1, but just four of them were earned.

Ron Taylor came in from the New York bullpen and pitched two shutout innings. Two Braves reached base in the ninth inning, but Taylor retired the side to preserve the visitors' 9–5 victory. It was not a masterpiece. Mets broadcaster Lindsey Nelson described it as "a somewhat loosely played but exciting baseball game." Tom Seaver looked vulnerable in getting the win. (In fact, one New York writer asked Seaver if he was embarrassed to have won by a 9–5 score.)

Nevertheless, the Mets had won the first game in NLCS history and seized the important momentum.

In Game #2 the following day, before another Atlanta crowd in excess of 50,000 baseball lovers, the Mets leapt out to a 9–1 advantage going into the bottom of the fifth to quickly discourage the home team's fans. Not everyone present was cheering for the hometown Braves. A few banner-carriers praising the Mets got into scuffles with supporters of the home team. One large sign, which strangely proclaimed, "The Mets Got Schmaltz," was quickly reduced to tatters by unaccommodating Braves fans. (One witty Pittsburgh sportswriter wondered who that Schmaltz fellow was as he could not find such a name on the New York roster.) Some Braves fans brought banners of their own. One, alluding to 17th-century American history, read, "New York isn't worth $24."

Atlanta's starter was Ron Reed, a 6'6" right-hander who had been a multi-sport athlete at Notre Dame. The 26-year-old had played two seasons in the NBA with the Detroit Pistons before pursuing a professional baseball career. He did not survive two innings before getting yanked from the mound. Milton Richman of United Press International commented, "The Mets tore into Reed like they had never heard of his 18 wins this season and thought he was still just a pro basketball player." Tommie Agee swatted a two-run homer as part of the onslaught. Seventeen-game-winner Jerry Koosman was handed a healthy 8–0 lead to work with after the top of the fourth inning. "Amazingly, he couldn't last even with that,"[8] Richman reported.

A spirited Atlanta rally knocked the New York starter out of the box with five runs before Koosman could qualify for a win, the most damaging blow being a three-run blast by Hank Aaron. "Seaver and Koosman have looked far from their usual sharpness,"[9] declared Ralph Kiner on the Mets' radio broadcast, stating the obvious.

Ron Taylor, who would one day become a licensed physician in Canada, was summoned from the Mets' bullpen to staunch the bleeding. He did what he was asked to do, pitching 1⅓ innings of shutout ball. New York expanded their lead to a very comfortable 11–5 by scoring twice in the top of the seventh inning.

The last two Met runs came courtesy of a Cleon Jones homer with Tommie Agee on base. Prior to the home run, Agee, on his own, decided to try to steal home. Agee had been studying the delivery of Atlanta pitcher Cecil Upshaw and figured he could pull off the daring baserunning feat. This gutsy—and highly dangerous—maneuver totally surprised Jones. Jones saw Agee approaching the plate only after he had swung and made contact. The ball sailed just past Agee's head before veering foul. Correspondent Richman described Agee's individualistic attempt to steal home "one of the weirdest plays of the season."[10] Roy McHugh of the *Pittsburgh Press* wrote, "Afterward the only question was whether the ball or Jones' bat missed Agee's head by a narrower margin."[11] Agee, after seeing his life flash before his eyes, reputedly told Jones, "Now you'd better get a hit."[12] Jones' two-run blast over the left-field fence followed shortly thereafter.

Tug McGraw pitched the final three innings for New York to earn a save. In the ninth inning, Atlanta got two runners on base with nobody out, but McGraw coolly struck out Hank Aaron on three pitches and got the next Brave, Rico Carty, to hit into a game-ending 4–6–3 double play. There would not be another postseason baseball game in Atlanta until 1982.

Roy McHugh was utterly unimpressed with the quality of play in Game #2—especially by the hometown Braves. "Yesterday's game, like Saturday's, was an artistic monstrosity," wrote the Pittsburgh scribe. "The Braves, at times, looked like the Chicago Black Sox playing the Cincinnati Reds in 1919. They were butchering ground balls, forgetting to cover bases, interfering with Met runners, trapping Mets off base and letting them escape. Hank Aaron, trying to nail a runner at the plate, threw the ball over the catcher's head. Orlando Cepeda dropped a throw at first base."[13]

McHugh singled out Atlanta's Rico Carty as being especially useless. McHugh declared, "Carty, the Braves' left fielder, has dislocated his shoulder three times this year and can't throw. For left fielders, throwing is fairly important. It seemed that every time the ball went to left field, there were Mets running the bases and Carty was almost reduced to carrying the ball into the infield like a messenger boy."[14]

Game #2 had taken three hours and 10 minutes to play—an eternity by 1969 standards. Again, it had not been pretty, but it was a win for New York. The Mets' 11–6 victory, in which they belted three home runs and got 13 total hits—three by Tommie Agee—off six Atlanta pitchers, brought them a game away from a World Series berth. The people who had wagered money on the Mets to win the NL pennant at 100–1 odds back in the spring—if there really were any—were salivating.

An unsightly scuffle followed Game #2, but neither team was involved. Instead, fists flew in the Mets' clubhouse between two groups of reporters: television crews and the print media. The veteran scribes were told by MLB they could interview players without their questions being filmed and shown television newscasts; the TV folks were supposed to conduct their own separate interviews afterwards. Not everyone got the memo—and tempers flared. Dick Young of the New York Daily News, whacked by a large television light, was apparently the only notable casualty of the brief melee.

Game #3 was slated for Shea Stadium the following afternoon. Gil Hodges certainly did not want a Game #4 or Game #5. "My aim," he told reporters after the game, "is to wrap this up as soon as possible."[15] Atlanta manager Lum Harris was decidedly pessimistic. He told the media his club had one foot in the grave heading to New York for the rest of the NLCS.

"Our boys, I think, are underrated as a hitting club,"[16] Hodges commented when asked about the Mets' 11-run outburst.

Jerry Koosman, who was deprived of the win because he failed to last the required five innings, was undeterred by his no-decision. "The main thing is winning ball games," he said. "The way we are hitting I have all the confidence we'll get another win."[17] Koosman blamed the cool, breezy weather—and the long intervals between bottoms of innings when he had to pitch—for his subpar outing.

Before an excited Shea Stadium crowd, Game #3 began at 1 p.m. Gary Gentry was on the mound for New York. He fell behind in the very first inning as Hank Aaron hit a two-run homer. (It was the last postseason game Aaron ever played. Impressively, the home run was Aaron's third of the NLCS.) When the first two Brave batters reached base in the top of the third inning, manager Gil Hodges replaced Gentry with Nolan Ryan. Described by the Associated Press as "the fire-balling 22-year-old right-hander who commuted between the Mets and a Texas army camp all summer,"[18] Ryan bailed out Gentry with two quick strikeouts—and Atlanta failed to score.

Atlanta pitcher Pat Jarvis, a right-hander, held off the Mets for two innings, but Tommie Agee slugged a solo homer in the third inning and Ken Boswell hit a two-run blast in the bottom of the fourth inning. The Mets were ahead 3–2. It was the suddenly potent Boswell's second home run of the NLCS. Prior to this series, Boswell had not homered since July.

In the top of the fifth inning Ryan faltered just a bit. He issued a two-out walk to Rico Carty. Orlando Cepeda followed with a two-run homer to give Atlanta a 4–3 lead. The Mets responded in kind in the home half of the fifth inning. Ryan himself singled. Two batters later Wayne Garrett homered. (Garrett, who once played in Atlanta's farm system, had hit one home run all year—precisely five months earlier on May 6—and unimpressively batted just .218 in 1969.) The Mets had swiftly regained the lead, 5–4, but they had not finished their scoring in the fifth inning. Cleon Jones hit a double, prompting Atlanta manager Lum Harris to replace Pat Jarvis with left-hander George Stone. Ken Boswell singled off Stone to drive home Jones. New York's lead expanded to 6–4.

In the bottom of the sixth inning, the Mets tacked on a seventh run. Jerry Grote led off with a double. Bud Harrelson bunted Grote to third base. Cecil Upshaw, a right-hander, replaced Stone on the mound. Two batters later Tommie Agee singled home Grote, extending New York's lead to 7–4.

Atlanta mounted a serious threat in the top of the eighth inning. Rico Carty and pinch-hitter Mike Lum both got base hits off Ryan. With two men out and two men on, pinch-hitter Felipé Alou made good contact, but he lined out sharply to the Mets' shortstop. The Braves' threat dissolved in Bud Harrelson's glove.

Ryan came to bat in the bottom of the eighth inning and received a standing ovation. He singled but was stranded on base.

In the top of the ninth inning, the Braves went down quietly. The Mets' boisterous rooters were not so silent, though. An alarming chant of "We want blood!" echoed from some sections of Shea Stadium. One wag in the press box commented that not that long ago, in the dark days of Met ineptness, "fans who rooted for a base on balls ... would have been glad to get a single white corpuscle."[19]

Two routine ground balls and a fly out ended the game. Nolan Ryan had pitched seven innings in relief, faced 26 Braves, and had given up just three hits and two bases on balls. (Ryan aided his own cause offensively, rapping out two of New York's 14 hits.) Tony González was the final Atlanta batter of the Series. He hit a ground ball to Wayne Garrett at third base. Garrett threw to first baseman Ed Kranepool for the final out. It was fitting. Kranepool was the last of the hopeless and comical 1962 Mets remaining on the team's roster. Shea Stadium exploded into bedlam. In seemed unbelievable, but the New York Mets—"once the laughingstocks of baseball,"[20] according to one wire service story, and dubbed "former ragtag clowns"[21] in another—were the NL pennant winners of 1969 and would play in the World Series six days hence.

Utter mayhem followed on the field. A wave of human locusts invaded. At least one base and home plate were stolen. "Big chunks of infield and outfield were stripped down to bare earth," noted one reporter. Another stated, "Thousands of Flushing fans spilled onto the field. When they got finished souvenir-hunting [it] looked like a battleground. If the playing field at Shea Stadium can be put back together in a week, the unbelievable Mets will be World Series hosts."[22] Luckily the 1969 World Series was scheduled to start in the AL representative's ballpark.

Jack Hugerich, the sports editor of the *Schenectady Gazette*, commented,

> When Tony González grounded out to Wayne Garrett and the Mets' third baseman completed the final out, it was the signal for the fans to take over. The players escaped to the safety of their clubhouse, but the field was left at the mercy of their young fans. To the Mets' faithful, this was sacred land. They wanted a part of it, and they took it.[23]

A scribe from the Associated Press noted, "Even a World Series victory will have a hard time topping this celebration. Some thought it was wilder than the night they clinched the East Division title on Sept. 24."[24]

Beginning the following day, John McCarthy, the head groundskeeper at Shea Stadium, had a crew of 25 men working furiously to patch the holes in the infield and outfield. McCarthy saw the glass as half full. "It wasn't as bad as last time," he shrugged. "They got home plate and second base, but they didn't get the pitching slab."[25]

An Associated press reporter took his life into his hands by attempting to interview some of the field invaders. One declared the Mets' NLCS win to be "the greatest day in the history of the world."[26] Another insisted, "Don't worry about the World Series. This team is so psyched up it could beat the 1927 Yankees."[27]

The Mets had swept the Braves, but it had not gone exactly according to the script. The team's strength was supposed to be its pitching, but the Met hurlers allowed 15 runs to the Braves in three games—not an especially good statistic. The Mets' offense, however, described by one writer as "Punch and Judy hitters,"[28] came alive in the NLCS with 27 runs and 37 hits. New York compiled a team batting average of .327 in the Series. During the regular season the Mets batted just .242. Amazing!

In the rowdy Mets' clubhouse after the game, Gil Hodges was asked how this NL pennant compared to those he had won so often as a player with the Dodgers. "None compares to this," he proudly told Lindsey Nelson. As for what was the key in turning the Mets into champions, Hodges credited an abundance of old-fashioned confidence in his charges. "They just have so much that they cannot lose," he said. Then Hodges quickly added, "And they will not lose."[29]

One Met saw the great significance in how his team would now be perceived given they were the 1969 NL pennant winners. "I'll walk down the street in New York now and people will say, 'There's Art Shamsky of the Mets.' People used to laugh. They won't anymore."[30] Had there been such a thing as the NLCS MVP Award in 1969, Shamsky would have been the likely recipient.

Ken Boswell told the media the Mets had been overlooked all season. He noted, "Up to this series we hadn't even been on the TV *Game of the Week*."[31]

Jerry Koosman was reminded by a writer that neither he nor Seaver had looked especially sharp in the Mets' wins over Atlanta. He was unconcerned. "I see no reason," Koosman confidently asserted "why we should have the same trouble [in the World Series]. We'll probably both go out and throw shutouts."[32]

New York outfielder Cleon Jones exuded unlimited confidence. "Nobody can stop us," he proclaimed. "Atlanta, Baltimore ... nobody!"[33]

Also celebrating the sweep in the Mets' clubhouse was Donn Clendenon, who played first base for New York when Gil Hodges' platoon system allowed for it. Because he was a right-handed hitter and the Braves had used three right-handed starters in the NLCS, Clendenon saw no action whatsoever in the three games versus Atlanta. However, he expected to see considerable playing time in the World Series if the lefty-heavy Orioles won the ALCS.

Wayne Garrett, the Mets' surprise hitting star of Game #3, was featured on the front page of the October 7 issue of the *Sarasota Herald-Tribune* for good reason. With New York's NLCS victory, Garrett was going to be the first Sarasotan to appear in a World Series. "We all knew we were going to win [the pennant]," the 21-year-old infielder told John Brockmann, the sports editor of his local daily newspaper. He said with a smile, "We've known since April."[34]

In the clubhouse of the defeated Braves, Hank Aaron praised the winners from New York, saying he knew they were for real long before the NLCS. "I've always believed 'em," he stated, "ever since they've had those two guys named Seaver and Koosman." Aaron thought the victors' offense was underappreciated. "[The NLCS] was built up as [their] pitching against [our] power," he noted, "but it was just slugging—mostly by the Mets."[35] Braves manager Lum Harris was impressed by Nolan Ryan's relief work. "That's the first time I've seen Ryan pitch this year," he said. "I wish the heck I hadn't seen him today."[36]

Other observers found the Mets were full of surprises during their NLCS victory. "The long-ball hitting of Boswell and Garrett was almost as unexpected as Nolan Ryan's fine hurling. Boswell only hit three home runs all season, yet [he] belted two in the playoffs, while Garrett blasted only one home run in the regular season."[37]

Lowell Reidenbaugh of *The Sporting News* assigned the blame for the Braves' loss squarely on the team's pitchers. He wrote, "In two of the three games the Braves held leads. But the pitching that carried them to ten consecutive victories and 17 wins in 20 decisions during their drive to the NL West title betrayed them in the clutch."[38]

With the Orioles on the verge of sweeping the Minnesota Twins in the ALCS, the champagne-soaked New York City mayor John V. Lindsay was asked by Lindsey Nelson if he had anything to say to Baltimore's mayor (Thomas D'Alesandro III). Lindsay the mayor told Lindsey the broadcaster the Orioles would be welcomed with hospitality to his city for the World Series, but they would certainly leave town as second best.

Team owner Joan Payson was more succinct. When she was asked about the prospect of her team facing the mighty Baltimore Orioles, she simply said, "Bring 'em on!"[39]

In 1969, Payson was the only female to be a principal owner of an MLB club; she had held at least partial ownership of the Mets since 1962. Payson was genuinely touched when Ed Kranepool presented her with the ball from the game's final play. "The first thing I'm going to do when I get to Baltimore is get [all the players] to sign it," she told a reporter. "They're like my own children."[40]

An unnamed United Press International correspondent summarized the state of Mets baseball as the club approached the 1969 World Series. "The New York Mets have lost their mystique," he wrote. "They are now full-fledged champions and are beginning to bear a vague resemblance to the old New York Yankees." The scribe concluded his analysis by noting, "Everything fell right for the Mets in the [NLCS], just like everything went superbly for them in the regular season. Everything comes so easy now for the Mets. Do the Baltimore Orioles dare challenge them for the world championship?"[41]

5

American League Championship Series

Baltimore Sweeps Minnesota

"The Orioles, deep in pitching and strong up the middle, are throwbacks to classic Yankee teams. But the Twins' Harmon Killebrew, finishing an awesome year, has his own heroic thoughts."[1]—William Leggett, *Sports Illustrated*

While Baltimore was an expected AL success story in 1969, the Minnesota Twins were a bit of a pleasant surprise. They had finished in seventh place in the 10-team AL in 1968 with a 79–83 record. The following year, the fiery Billy Martin replaced the unpopular Cal Ermer as Minnesota's manager. The Twins responded well to Martin's truculent style of leadership and became the best of the AL West in the new divisional setup. Since the Twins and Orioles were the top two AL teams in runs scored in 1969, plenty of scoring was expected in the best-of-five series.

Minnesota had played .770 baseball in the last month of the regular season while Baltimore had cooled down considerably after clinching the AL East title. Sam Lacy of the *Baltimore Afro-American* managed to express both caution and confidence about the favored Orioles when he wrote in the October 4 issue of his newspaper, "The Birds could have a rude awakening. It just may be—as so often happens—the club has relaxed too much, and when the time comes to get back in the groove, the urge will be missing. I'm gambling against this and picking the Orioles to wrap up the flag in three games, four at the most."[2]

The ALCS opened at Baltimore's Memorial Stadium on Saturday, October 4 with the unsettling reality that more than 15,000 seats had gone unsold. Right-hander Jim Perry, a 33-year-old 20-game winner, was the starter for Minnesota in Game #1. Frank Robinson smashed a solo home run in the bottom of the fourth inning off Perry to break the 0–0 tie. However, Minnesota fought back in the top of the fifth inning to tie the game. Tony Oliva hit a leadoff double off Baltimore's lefty screwball hurler Mike Cuellar and advanced to third base when Frank Robinson, misplayed the ball in right field. He was charged with an error. Bob Allison drove Oliva home with a line-drive sacrifice fly to Oriole left fielder Don Buford. Game #1 was tied 1–1 at its midway point.

The usually light-hitting Baltimore shortstop, Mark Belanger, batting eighth, contributed a rare home run in the bottom of the fifth inning to put the home team back into the lead, 2–1. After the game, Twins manager Billy Martin, with the benefit of 20/20 hindsight, rued not issuing an intentional base on balls. "If we walk Belanger, it doesn't hurt us with two out and the pitcher up."[3]

The home runs continued in the top of the seventh inning. With Harmon Killebrew on first base courtesy of a walk, Tony Oliva, who had socked 24 homers in the regular season, rocked a hanging Cuellar curveball for a two-run jolt with one out to put the visitors back on top, 3–2. An upset was in the making in Game #1.

Minnesota maintained their advantage to the bottom of the ninth inning. In the top of the ninth, the Twins missed a valuable opportunity—which proved to be costly—to pad their slim one-run lead. Baltimore relief pitcher Pete Richert walked two Twins (one was intentional) but he managed to squirm out of further trouble without the score changing.

With prospects looking grim for the home team, Baltimore first baseman Boog Powell led off the home half of the ninth with a towering, majestic, 400-foot home run that sailed over the right-field fence. Powell's blow leveled the score at 3–3 and shifted the game's momentum back to the Orioles.

When the next Baltimore batter, Brooks Robinson, got to second base courtesy of a single and an error by left fielder Ted Uhlaender, Ron Perranoski was summoned from the Twins' bullpen by Billy Martin. Perranoski, a left-hander who had recorded 31 saves in 1969, retired the Orioles without any further scoring—but it was quite a chore. Second baseman Rod Carew surprisingly misplayed a pop-up from the bat of pinch-hitter Curt Motton. Dave Johnson was the next Baltimore batter. He popped up to catcher George Mitterwald for the first out. Mark Belanger hit into a 6–4 force play, but he was safe at first base. With two men out and runners on the corners, Perranoski smartly foiled some Baltimore baserunning chicanery: He retired Robinson when he attempted to swipe home on a double steal. It was a play the Orioles had used once before in 1969 against Oakland, but Perranoski read it. He ignored Mark Belanger trying to steal second base and threw to the plate instead. Robinson was easily put out at third base in a rundown. Extra innings would be needed to settle the first ALCS game ever played.

Baltimore stranded two baserunners in the home half of the 11th inning, so the game moved into the 12th still deadlocked 3–3. Minnesota loaded the bases in the top of the inning with one out but failed to score when Leo Cárdenas failed to lay down a squeeze bunt.

Perranoski was still on the mound for Minnesota when Baltimore came to bat. Mark Belanger led off with an infield single to third base. Andy Etchebarren bunted Belanger to second base. Don Buford grounded out, but Belanger moved up another 90 feet on the base paths. With two out and Belanger standing on third base, Baltimore's Paul Blair was next up. He was struggling, enmeshed in an awful 4-for-44 batting slump. The first pitch was a ball. Blair made a full cut at Perranoski's second offering—and missed. Acting solely on his own judgment, Blair laid down a perfect bunt toward third base that came to rest approximately 30 feet from home plate. Caught completely by surprise, neither catcher John Roseboro (who had entered the game that inning) nor third baseman Harmon Killebrew were able to make a play on the ball. Belanger, who got a good jump on the play, dashed home without a throw. "Any time Blair or Don Buford is at the plate, I'm alert for that play,"[4] Belanger told reporters afterward.

As for the man who laid down the superb bunt, Blair explained, "I decided to do it [while waiting on] the on-deck circle. I figured I would try to drive [Belanger] in first by swinging away. I haven't been hitting much and I went to the plate thinking about a bunt. I wanted to take one swing, though, with Mark on third. I figured Perranoski would throw me an off-speed pitch at that point, and that is the best kind to bunt. I think it was a screwball."[5] The defeated Billy Martin conceded to a scribe that Blair's bunt had been executed to perfection and there was no way to defend against it.

Blair's deft batting touch and gutsy strategy had given the Orioles the hard-fought first game of the ALCS by a 4–3 count. The power-hitting Orioles had gone against form and deftly manufactured a run in the bottom of the 12th inning without a ball leaving the infield. Baltimore reliever, Dick Hall, who had skillfully quashed the Twins' threat in the top of the 12th inning, was credited with the win.

Game #2 was played before another less-than-capacity crowd at Memorial Stadium. That was a shame because the 41,704 spectators who did pass through the turnstiles witnessed another nail-biter that went into extra innings. Pitching thoroughly dominated the game. Zeroes filled the line score. Baltimore's Dave McNally was superb. The left-hander went the full 11 innings and only gave up three hits to Minnesota—and all three of them were singles. McNally walked five Twins, but he also struck out 11 batters. No Twin got a hit off him after the fourth inning.

His mound opponent, Dave Boswell—no relation to Ken Boswell of the Mets—lasted almost as long McNally did. Going into the bottom of the 11th inning, Boswell had given up seven Oriole hits. On numerous occasions, Baltimore mounted promising threats that fizzled away. They left nine runners on base through the first 10 innings. Each time, however, Boswell managed to extricate himself from any trouble. Baltimore's leadoff man reached base in each of the first four innings. In the home half of the second, the Orioles loaded the bases with none out but still failed to score a run.

However, the long game would have huge implications on the hard-throwing Boswell's baseball career. When he struck out Frank Robinson to end bottom of the 10th inning, Boswell felt an excruciating pain run through his right arm. Years later he recalled, "I threw [Robinson] a slider—and it was a rocket. He didn't even swing at it." The strikeout came at a huge price, though. "By the time I got back to the first-base line going back to the dugout," Boswell said, "my arm felt like it was going into my jaw. Then I went out [the next inning] and still tried to pitch."[6]

Boog Powell continued his heroics from Game #1. He led off the bottom of the 11th inning for Baltimore. He was walked by the ailing Boswell on four pitches. Brooks Robinson's sacrifice bunt moved Powell to second base. Dave Johnson was walked intentionally to set up a possible double play. Mark Belanger popped out in foul territory for the second out of the inning. (Harmon Killebrew made a fine play on the ball, reaching into the stands near third base to make the catch.) Minnesota manager Billy Martin then pulled Boswell from the game. "I felt like I had thrown 500 pitches out there,"[7] Boswell would later state. After the game, Boswell showed reporters the raw fingertips of his blistered pitching hand.

Ron Perranoski, a southpaw who was the tough-luck loser from Game #1, was called upon to by Martin to face Elrod Hendricks, the next Oriole scheduled to bat. Boswell defended his manager's strategy. "Perranoski is the best relief pitcher in the American League," he said. "He might be the best in both [major] leagues."[8]

However, Earl Weaver sent in a right-handed pinch-hitter, Curt Motton. Motton promptly drilled a single into right field past the outstretched arm of second baseman Rod Carew. (According to what Carew told reporters, the ball nicked his glove.) "If I had been on the edge of the grass, I would have had it. That's the way the game goes,"[9] Carew later lamented.

Powell, likely the slowest man on the Orioles' roster, chugged home all the way from second base. "Powell, no gazelle at 240 pounds," wrote an Associated Press reporter, "sprinted for the plate and just made it ahead of Tony Oliva's throw."[10]

The ball got by Twins catcher George Mitterwald, who lunged at it, trying but failing to make an acrobatic tag play on Powell who made a slight leap toward home. He lamented, "I just ticked the ball. If I catch the ball, even if he knocks me down, he's out."[11] The man who hit the ball concurred. "I watched the play," said Motton. "I thought if the catcher held onto the ball, he'd have Boog [for the third out]."[12]

On-deck batter Dave McNally was not entirely certain that Powell had touched the plate and urged him to go back and make sure. Powell assured him, "I got it."[13] McNally, not entirely satisfied, replied, "Then go back and get it again!"[14] A UPI photograph that appeared in many newspapers the following day showed Powell just barely stepping on the rear point of home plate with his right foot as he eluded the sprawling Mitterwald.

Powell later commented, "Any more of these cliff-hangers and I'm going to have myself a heart attack."[15]

"I didn't think there would even by a play [at the plate]," Baltimore manager Earl Weaver told reporters afterward, "[Oliva] made a heck of a play scooping up the ball on the short hop. He made a strong throw; he gunned it."[16]

It was a thrilling 1–0 victory for Baltimore, their second walkoff triumph in as many days. The Orioles confidently headed to Minnesota for Game #3 holding a daunting 2–0 lead in the ALCS. The Orioles were cautiously confident of a sweep, but publicly they said the right things to the media. "We still have to win one more ballgame,"[17] Dave McNally stated diplomatically. According to Bill Christine of the *Pittsburgh Press*, sports fans in Baltimore were breathing more easily after the two tight Oriole wins. He wrote,

> The local fear that the Orioles might ape the Colts and the Bullets, by blowing the egg money once the egg money got into the thousands, is all but dispelled today. Baltimoreans are confident now that there'll be no crying in their crab cakes over the end of the baseball season. Baltimore is confident. Winning two games in the fashion the Orioles did here would do that to any city.[18]

John G. Griffin of United Press International diagnosed what was ailing Minnesota. "The Twins sorely need some hitting punch," he wrote. "They were held to four hits in their 4–3, 12-inning loss on Saturday and held hitless by McNally in the last seven innings of Sunday's loss." Bill Christine concurred, noting that the Twins had tallied a mere three runs in the first two ALCS games, "one of which resulted from an error."[19]

Losing manager Billy Martin said he had played the percentages in how he instructed Perranoski to pitch to Motton, but it simply did not work out. "[Motton] is a high-ball hitter," Martin said. "It was a good pitch; it was down."[20] According to Martin, Minnesota's scouting reports on the Orioles had determined the best way to pitch to Motton was low and away.

Motton said afterward that he had been mentally preparing himself for a chance to bat when the pressure was great. "I kept walking around. I went into the clubhouse a couple of times," he noted. "I was thinking I'd get my chance. I was thinking about Ron Perranoski and Joe Grzenda and the way they pitch."[21]

When asked about his team's chances to win the next three games to take the ALCS, Martin admitted his troops plainly had their backs against the wall, but he expected they would come out fighting in Game #3 at home the following day. "I've never run scared in my life," Martin stated. "Even though we leave town two games behind, I'm not going to run scared now."[22]

Twins starting pitcher Dave Boswell did not mention his injured arm. He only admitted he was unhappy about being pulled in the 11th inning—blisters or no blisters. "I never want to come out of a game," he noted. "I still had good stuff. You can push yourself and push yourself. I wasn't about to give up. But you have to go with percentages; I accept the percentages. I'm out there to help the team win. I don't want to second-guess Billy [Martin]," Boswell continued. "I don't want to be in his shoes. We've been winning ball games all year like this."[23] Boswell's arm never recovered. (He was 3–7 the following season with a 6.42 ERA. Boswell was out of baseball by 1973.)

Game #3 of the ALCS, was played at Minnesota's Metropolitan Stadium, where the Twins had lost just 10 of 48 games since June. However, it turned out to be a series-clinching laugher for the Orioles. Commissioner Bowie Kuhn was in attendance to witness what Ralph Ray of *The Sporting News* called "Baltimore's sacking of the Twin Cities." A disappointing crowd of just 32,735 spectators was present to see their Twins absorb a beating. Ray further commented, "If Twins fans felt the series was all but over before the action came their way, they were proved correct."

Paul Blair, more known for his defense than his offense, had a fabulous day at the plate, contributing five hits—two doubles and a homer—while driving in five runs. It was the first five-hit game in his MLB career. (As of 2020, no other player has had five hits in an ALCS game.) Left fielder Don Buford, who had failed to hit safely in the first two games versus the Twins, broke out of his slump decisively and connected for four hits in Baltimore's 11–2 romp. Altogether, the Orioles drilled 18 hits off six Minnesota hurlers.

Things started well for Minnesota, however. With Jim Palmer on the mound for Baltimore, Rich Reese of the Twins struck for an RBI single in the bottom of the first inning after Tony Oliva doubled and Harmon Killebrew had been intentionally passed. The Minnesota lead was short-lived. Elrod Hendricks hit a two-run double in the top of the second inning after Brooks Robinson had doubled and Dave Johnson was safe on an error. Later that inning Don Buford singled home Hendricks. That base hit knocked Twins starter Bob Miller out of the game. (Miller was one of the two Robert L. Millers who had been on the pitiful 1962 Mets roster!) Dick Woodson replaced Miller.

In the top of the fifth inning the Orioles extended their lead to 5–1 on a two-run double by Paul Blair. Mark Belanger had led off with a triple and Don Buford had walked. Both men scored on Blair's two-bagger. Minnesota got one of those runs back when Harmon Killebrew hit a double with two men out and scored on Rich Reese's single. (It was a rarity for Killebrew to see anything good to swing at in the 1969 ALCS. Baltimore manager Earl Weaver had chosen to simply pitch around the formidable Killebrew—who had slugged a whopping 49 homers in 1969—unless he was in no position to do any substantial damage. He had been issued five walks in the first two games, and another one in Game #3.) Killebrew's run was the last one the Twins would score in their 1969 season.

Baltimore got it back in a hurry. In the top of the sixth inning, Frank Robinson's RBI single off right-hander Al Worthington—the fourth Twins pitcher of the game—knocked home Don Buford. Baltimore was now up 6–2. Paul Blair put the game out of reach with a two-run homer in the top of the eighth inning. It came off right-hander Dean Chance.

In the top of the ninth inning, Baltimore tacked on three more runs for good measure. Dave Johnson led off with a base hit. Elrod Hendricks drove in Johnson with a double off Ron Perranoski—who was making his third relief appearance in three days. (Elrod Hendricks' hit was misplayed by Tony Oliva—his second error of the game—allowing the Baltimore catcher to circle the bases.) The score was now 10–2 for the visitors. Mark Belanger singled. The sizzling hot Paul Blair lashed a double to right field, scoring Belanger, to give Baltimore their 11th and final run of the game. It was more than enough.

Two of the first three Minnesota batters managed to get hits off Jim Palmer in the home half of the ninth. Both men—John Roseboro and Graig Nettles—were stranded when Rod Carew grounded out to Dave Johnson to end the game. Although he allowed 10 hits, Palmer pitched a complete game. As in 1966, the Baltimore Orioles would be representing the AL in the World Series. It was an odd year; that meant the AL champs would host Game #1 of the Fall Classic. It would start on October 11. The three-game Oriole sweep meant that the franchise had never lost a postseason game since the St. Louis Browns had uprooted and moved to Baltimore in 1954. In seven games they were a perfect 7–0.

The Minnesota Twins—the team that had led the AL in runs in 1969—managed to just score five runs in the three ALCS games. It was an especially disappointing series for two of their biggest stars. Rod Carew, the man who had hit .332 to win the 1969 AL batting title, finished the ALCS with just one hit in 14 at-bats. He was hitless in five at-bats against Jim Palmer in Game #3. Tony Oliva's shoddy fielding in the third game—he made two egregious errors in the outfield—obscured the fact that he had had a terrific ALCS at the plate, batting .385. Oliva had at least one hit in all three contests, including a home run in Game #1 at Baltimore.

It was later revealed that the Cuban-born Oliva had hurt his arm trying to throw out Boog Powell at home plate on the final play of Game #2 and, because of his injury, probably should have sat out Game #3. He was deeply disappointed that the home crowd was booing him because of his errors. "They forget what kind of player I've been before," he lamented in broken English. "I

No pitcher won as many games during the 1970s (186) as Jim Palmer did. A three-time Cy Young Award winner and Hall-of-Famer, Palmer has the distinction of never allowing a grand slam homer in any Major League contest. His lone World Series appearance in 1969 was a disappointment, however (National Baseball Hall of Fame and Museum, Cooperstown, NY).

no understand why they boo. I no can throw. The doctors tell me I no should play today. I can ruin my career. But I have to play today. I can ruin my career, but I have to play. This is the big game. It's all or nothing."[24]

The Sporting News declared in its coverage of the ALCS,

> It is worth noting that in their dark hour, the Twins and their manager went down like champs. Martin, in particular, was available and gracious to all writers after each and every defeat, including the third-game holocaust. Martin is popular in the Twin Cities and there was some apprehension there that [the] Twins' prexy Calvin Griffith might dump him.[25]

Indeed, Billy Martin was a prominent casualty of the first ALCS. In a move that was hugely unpopular with Minnesota fans, Martin was fired by Twins owner Calvin Griffith a day before the World Series was set to begin. After being on the Minnesota coaching staff for four years, the colorful Martin was promoted to the team's manager in 1969. Griffith told the press that Martin had not been especially communicative with him all season. Griffith had a point: After the ALCS ended, Griffith asked his manager why he had chosen Bob Miller—a mediocre pitcher with a 5–5 record—to start Game #3. Martin arrogantly replied, "Because I'm the manager, that's why!"[26]

Indeed, the feisty Martin was terminated shortly thereafter. (Popular with the fans, Martin's dismissal prompted a wave of season-ticket cancellations and a call for a general boycott of Twins games in 1970.) Martin spent 1971 working for a Minneapolis radio station. He would resurface in MLB in 1972 as the new manager of the Detroit Tigers.

Inside the visitors' clubhouse, the Orioles felt both relief and euphoria having cleared a hurdle that no other AL had to do in the past to get to the Fall Classic. "Amazing!" said manager Earl Weaver, borrowing the Mets' favorite adjective. "Before this year," Weaver stated, "if you came in first after 162 games you were in the World Series. This time you had to keep winning, winning, winning. To win three in a row [in the ALCS] was amazing to me. It shows what a great ball club this is."[27]

The New York Mets had won the NLCS a few hours before the Orioles won the ALCS. Some of the Mets' postgame comments were already being heard and disseminated by their next opponents. In the joyous Baltimore clubhouse, Frank Robinson announced, "Ron [*sic*] Gaspar has just said on television that the Mets will sweep the Birds in four games. Bring on the Mets! Bring on Ron Gaspar … whoever the hell *he* is."[28]

Teammate Paul Bair, who was within earshot, felt compelled to correct Robinson's name gaffe. "It's not Ron … it's Rod, stupid!"[29] Blair pointed out.

"Okay then," retorted Robinson with a bit of comedy. "Bring on Rod Stupid."[30]

Paul Blair, who was once a prospect in the Mets' farm system, was quite determined to beat the organization that had given up on him. He said, "I'd like to beat anybody [in the World Series], but especially the Mets for not thinking I was good enough to play for them."[31]

"On paper, we have a sounder club," Clay Dalrymple, Baltimore's third-string catcher, claimed. "We figure to have more power, a better defense, and we're thick in pitching."[32]

First baseman Boog Powell told a reporter, "I don't know if [the Mets] are for real, but we're going to find out."[33]

Brooks Robinson was asked if the Orioles would sweep the Mets. He replied, "It might be tough to win four straight [games] against pitchers like Tom Seaver and Jerry Koosman, but I think we will win the Series."[34]

Veteran Baltimore relief pitcher Dick Hall, who would become a chartered accountant soon after retiring from baseball, was far more cautious in his statistical appraisal of his Orioles' supposed superiority and what it meant. Hall sensibly noted, "Even with an obvious advantage, the best team doesn't always win [a best-of-seven series] because of the nature of the game and the nature of chance."[35]

With a bit of concern, Earl Weaver stated, "The Mets are a complete mystery. They hit about .241 during the regular season and then turned around [in the NLCS] and beat one of the best hitting teams at its own game. But I have very much confidence in my pitchers."[36]

Showing that he had already been thinking ahead, Weaver outlined his club's pitching assignments for the first three World Series games. "I plan to use Mike Cuellar, followed by Dave McNally and Jim Palmer,"[37] he said.

Weaver was also grateful for the long break before Game #1 versus the Mets. "Those two extra-inning games took a lot out of our guys," he declared. "Some of them have to have tight legs after that."[38]

6

Excitement in New York,
Lethargy in Baltimore

"Vegas makes the Orioles 8–5 [favorites] to win the World Series. Vegas had the Mets at 100–1 to win the pennant. Vegas had the Colts 17 points over the Jets. Vegas is in trouble at any game you don't play on green felt or you can't set the lever."[1]—Jim Murray, *Los Angeles Times*

The day after both LCS wrapped up, World Series tickets in New York City (for the third, fourth, and fifth games) were already tough to find. Oriole players who tried to get any beyond their allotment of five found there were none available. Jim Palmer was not especially bothered. The Baltimore pitcher thought that the $15 cost for a prime seat at Shea Stadium was exorbitant. Furthermore, he said, "At those prices, I don't even want my wife to go. It would be better for her to stay home and watch the games on television."[2]

There were no such problems at the Memorial Stadium box office, however. Baltimore's third-string catcher Clay Dalrymple said on October 8 that the only advantage the Mets had over his Orioles was the large crowds they typically played in front of at Shea Stadium. It was a barely veiled criticism of the underwhelming attendance at Baltimore home games in 1969. Despite clearly having the best team in the AL, the Orioles were a poor fifth in a 12-team league in turnstile count. They barely drew over a million fans, nearly 800,000 fewer than the number who came to Fenway Park to watch a Boston Red Sox team that had finished in third place in the AL East, 22 games in arrears of the mighty Orioles.

The four idle days that both the Mets and Orioles had between the end of their LCS and the start of the World Series was unprecedented. Before divisional play was instituted, the World Series would typically start with just one or two days separating it from the last day of the regular season. (Each of the six World Series from 1963 through 1968 began on a Wednesday.) MLB and NBC had agreed that the World Series would start on the Saturday following the completion of LCS play regardless of how quickly they might finish. That way four of the seven games would be scheduled on weekends. With the Orioles and Mets both clinching their respective pennants on Monday, each team got a long break. Accordingly, both managers could plan their pitching matchups without worrying about whether their pitchers were tired.

As Will Grimsley of the Associated Press took a taxi ride through Baltimore on Friday, October 10, the 55-year-old, longtime baseball scribe could scarcely believe what he was seeing—specifically, what he was not seeing: It was the utter absence of anything to do with the hometown Orioles or the World Series itself. Where was the World Series atmosphere in the home of the terrific AL champions? Grimsley, who had been covering baseball on a national level since 1947, had never seen such lack of enthusiasm in any host city before the start of MLB's annual showcase event. It struck him as bizarre, almost surreal. Grimsley was incredulous. "No one would have believed baseball's grandest show was only 24 hours away,"[3] he sadly wrote.

"Buntings were missing from the light poles," Grimsley continued. "Men with briefcases and secretaries in miniskirts went about their business as usual. The wild excitement and hoopla that normally attended such events were noticeably missing. Hadn't Baltimore heard about the Mets? Hadn't modern communications sent the story of the Shea Stadium miracle down the coastline?"[4]

Grimsley's cabbie, a gruff fellow named Allan Diskin, offered an explanation. "Nobody here buys the Mets' miracle stuff. Or cares much. This is a football town—a Colts town." Another typical Baltimorean, Morris Taylor, whom Grimsley described as "a big, mustachioed truck driver," said the World Series was no longer a novelty in his city. "We had the Series here in 1966. It's not new anymore. I guess we're just spoiled."[5] (The Orioles drew about 1.2 million fans to their home games in 1966, only the third-best total in the AL that season.)

Then Grimsley reported the most startling statistic of all: There were about 2,000 unsold seats still available at the 54,000-seat Memorial Stadium for Game #1 the next afternoon. By all indications, a World Series game was going to be played before less than a sellout crowd for the first time since the dark days of the Second World War when people had more important things than professional baseball in the forefronts of their minds. About 300 dedicated Oriole fans had camped out in front of Memorial Stadium on a rainy Tuesday night in order to be near the front of the queue when the box office opened on Wednesday morning, but it was hardly necessary. Scalpers, usually a ubiquitous World Series fixture, were nowhere to be seen. (Two years later when Game #1 of the 1971 World Series drew a full house at Memorial Stadium, Baltimore announcer Chuck Thompson sheepishly informed the NBC-TV audience that, despite the excellent product on the field, sellouts were rarities at Oriole home games.)

"If the Mets' Cinderella climb from ninth place to the NL pennant was enough to make raving maniacs of thousands of New York fans and inspire Mayor Lindsay to poetry, it seems to elicit only boredom in this city's close-to-one-million populace,"[6] Grimsley sadly opined.

Even at the hotels that were designated as official World Series lodging places,

Baltimore's Memorial Stadium hosted three consecutive Fall Classics from 1969 to 1971. Despite having an excellent team, the Orioles often struggled with home attendance, barely surpassing the million mark in each of those championship seasons (Library of Congress).

Grimsley noted that baseball people were badly outnumbered by conventioneers who had interests in other things quite different than the national pastime. At one such inn he noticed that barber shop quartet enthusiasts, by far, comprised the dominant group of guests.

The lack of support for such an excellent team bothered baseball writers from well beyond Maryland. Bill Christine of the *Pittsburgh Press* had written in his October 4 column,

> Baltimore's baseball-goers should have plenty of cash left in their summer entertainment budget envelopes. Although the Orioles won 109 games—the third highest total in the history of baseball [*sic*]—it wasn't until their final [regular season] home game that the club finally creeped over the million mark in attendance. The Orioles managed it by only 811 patrons. [Authors' note: Officially, Baltimore's home attendance in 1969 was 1,062,069.]

In that same column, Christine wondered if a special giveaway promotion, similar to Bat Day, might have enticed more Baltimoreans to buy tickets for the two important ALCS games that were played at Memorial Stadium.

On Friday, October 10, a city-sponsored, midday rally for the team and the people of Baltimore to jointly celebrate their AL pennant and to get the fans enthused for the opening game of the World Series was hardly inspiring. "The Orioles sat in open-top convertibles and tossed small, Styrofoam baseballs into a sparse crowd who applauded politely," Grimsley reported. "There were no banners, no loud cheers. A hawker sold seven pennants on the busiest corner."[7]

Grimsley encountered a traveling Mets fan who happened to stumble into the low-key pep rally by accident. He too was shocked by the blasé attitude of the locals about the upcoming World Series. "What is this? A wake?" he asked. "Today these bums ride. Tomorrow they walk."[8]

The Orioles themselves, listed as 8–5 favorites by Las Vegas bookmakers to win the championship—and 7–5 favorites to take the opening game—oozed confidence on the eve of the 1969 World Series. Baltimore manager Earl Weaver said, "If somebody upstairs is guiding [the Mets] as we're told, then all I can say is he is guiding us better. We won 109 [games] to their 100."[9]

"Baltimore has been warned that the Mets are eerie and unreal," Grimsley wrote. "[They are] a team that seems to have made a deal with the occult, as in Douglas Wallop's *The Year the Yankees Lost the Pennant*, from which the stage play *Damn Yankees* was taken."[10]

The Orioles' popular first baseman, John (Boog) Powell, whom Grimsley admiringly called a "blond Hercules," had a ready response for the notion that fate was somehow piloting the 1969 NL champs. "That's a lot of baloney," Powell scoffed. "The Mets are a good team. They have to be a good team to win 100 games and the pennant. But we're a better team, and if we play our game, we'll beat them."[11]

Similarly, Baltimore right fielder Frank Robinson was unimpressed by other New York sports teams recently upsetting favored Baltimore clubs, and how that troubling trend might carry over to the World Series. Reporters seemed to be dwelling on it, and Robinson found the whole concept annoying. "They're telling us the Mets are going to win because the Jets beat the Colts in the Super Bowl and the Knickerbockers beat the Bullets in the basketball playoffs, and that all things come in threes," noted Robinson. "There's also the saying 'the third time is a charm.'"

Robinson continued, "We respect the Mets, sure. But they don't worry us. We know we can beat them."[12]

Baltimore center fielder Paul Blair was outwardly contemptuous of the NL champions. "They're no mystery to us," he said, downplaying the notion of any sort of divine guidance the Mets were said to possess in 1969. "They get a man around to second [base] and somebody punches him home. If the pitching's good, they win. We do everything they do, only better."[13]

On Thursday, the Orioles had what was described as a "spirited workout" by Gordon Beard of the Associate Press. Earl Weaver was in a playful mood and in top form with witty quotes. When Beard asked how the Baltimore manager was

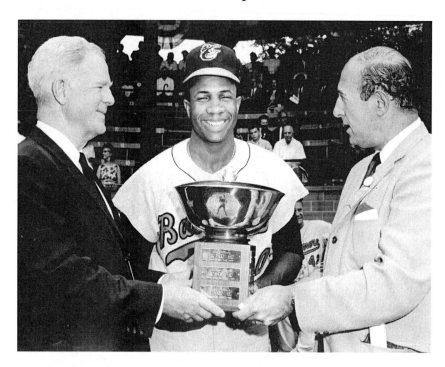

Frank Robinson, a 14-time All-Star who hit 30 home runs 11 times and batted .300 nine times, is the only player to win the Most Valuable Player Award in both the American and National Leagues. Pictured here is Robinson receiving the distinguished AL honor for 1966. (National Baseball Hall of Fame and Museum, Cooperstown, NY)

preparing for the World Series, Weaver replied, "I'm going to stick around and practice taking the lineup card to the plate. Then I might practice running to first, second and third base—in case there's an argument."[14]

There was some discussion that the rule requiring a pitcher to be removed from the game upon being visited at the mound twice in an inning might be waived for the World Series. (It was.) Beard facetiously asked Weaver how many times a manager can visit second base. Weaver had a ready answer for that too: "Until the umpire says don't come back anymore."[15]

The Mets awaited Saturday's Game #1 in Baltimore in their hotel. They were well aware they were supposed to be cannon fodder for the mighty AL champs. They disagreed with the experts. They had come too far to lose. "The Orioles are a fine club, but I think we can win it," said a respectful Ken Boswell, who shared second base duties with Al Weis in 1969. "We're not cocky but we have a quiet confidence." Boswell continued, "[The Orioles] are a real good team [*sic*]. They have big guns at every position. But that doesn't scare me or any of us. We're all looking forward to playing them."[16]

Mets manager Gil Hodges, who had been a perennial World Series partici-
pant with the Brooklyn and Los Angeles Dodgers, said, "If anything, some of our
guys are awed about being in the Series, but not one player is overawed about playing the Orioles. This is a very determined ball club. I think they'll play their type of
baseball rather than worrying about who they are playing against."[17]

A sense of surety pervaded among Baltimore supporters who did line up to
buy World Series tickets on Friday for the first two games. Josh Watson of the *Baltimore Afro-American* interviewed a few of them. "I don't give the Mets a chance,"
declared Melvin Brown. "The thing they have going for them now is momentum,
but I am sticking with the Orioles."[18] A fan from Washington named Eddie Reid
thought the upstart Mets would soon get a reality check. "The Mets have Cleon
Jones," he said, "but I want to see what he is made of when he faces Cuellar, McNally
and Palmer."[19] Reid figured Baltimore would win the Series in five games.

The newspaper itself, was, of course, foreseeing a triumph for Baltimore's
"super team"—in six games. An editorial on the day of Game #1 stated, "Our heart
belongs to the Orioles—to Frank, to Boog, to Curt, to Dave—to all that company
of beautiful people who outplayed and outclassed everything the American League
had in both divisions for the honor and glory of our town."[20]

The Associated Press summed up the situation nicely: "While the Mets are
undoubtedly the sentimental favorites because of their sudden rise after so many
years of ineptitude, the Orioles have been installed as the favorites in their first
World Series since 1966." Tom Seaver would later write, "We moved into the World
Series with 41 victories in our last 51 games—better than .800 baseball—and still
people refused to take us seriously."[21]

Shortly after the two World Series participants were finalized, NBC, in con-
junction with the Commissioner's Office, announced the lineup of television and
radio broadcasters for the upcoming 1969 Fall Classic. To no one's surprise, Curt
Gowdy and Tony Kubek from NBC's regular *Game of the Week* coverage would
be there for TV, of course. So would the reliable Jim Simpson, who would host
the pregame show with retired baseball superstars Sandy Koufax and Mickey Mantle. Simpson would do radio work too. Augmenting the crew would be Baltimore
broadcaster Bill O'Donnell and two announcers from the Mets: Lindsey Nelson
and Ralph Kiner. With a surplus of broadcasters available, Kubek would spend
most of the World Series conducting brief interviews with notable attendees.

The Mets left on Thursday for Baltimore, flying from an unusual departure
area. The team's charter flight took off from the Marine Air Terminal at LaGuardia
Airport. The Mets obtained special permission to do so to avoid a likely chaotic
scene if the team attempted to depart from the airport's main terminal. A small
mob of about 200 screaming baseball fans found them anyway. A Dixieland band
just happened to be on hand to play "Take Me Out to the Ballgame" and other
tunes. New York City mayor John V. Lindsay—a passionate supporter—was min-
gling among the well-wishers. He had a surprise for everyone: Lindsay had been

inspired to compose an optimistic poem for the occasion titled "Ode to the New York Mets" and read it aloud:

> The outlook isn't pretty for the Orioles today.
> They may have won the pennant, but the Mets are on the way.
> And when Gil Hodges' supermen get through with Baltimore,
> They'll be champions of the world—they win it all in four!
> The experts say they cannot win, but they'll just eat their words.
> When Jones and Koos and Agee pluck the feathers off the birds.
> When Gentry shuts out Robinson and Ryan does the same,
> The world will know the Mets have come to dominate the game.
> With Harrelson and Kranepool, with Gaspar and Weis,
> With Grote, Shamsky, Boswell, we've got the game on ice.
> And when we've got a manager like Gilbert Raymond Hodges,
> We've got a team that makes up for the Giants and the Dodgers.
> So good luck down in Baltimore; New Yorkers place your bets.
> We know we've got a winner with our amazin' Mets![22]

The crowd approved; the 47-year-old Lindsay was heartily cheered by one and all for his creative effort.

The Mets certainly were the choice of the average American, according to a poll of 1,200 adults conducted by Sinlinger and Co. The nationwide-survey data indicated that 52.3 percent of people asked about the upcoming World Series said they hoped New York would win. A mere 7.4 percent of those questioned said they would be rooting for Baltimore. The other 40.3 percent of respondents indicated they either did not have a preference or did not care at all.

The Mets also had backers around the world, as an Associated Press story from October 11 indicated. Twenty-three-year-old Allen Orpin of Ascot, England had flown to New York City just to watch the first two World Series games on television! Orpin had lived in New York for six years and had developed a love for baseball in general and for one MLB club specifically.

"While I lived here, I got hooked on the Mets," he explained. "I figured this World Series wasn't likely to happen again for another century, so it was worth a weekend. I miss the Mets."

Orpin explained that he had caught a flight from London to New York City on Thursday night after getting permission to be absent from work on Friday. He had also booked a return passage, scheduled to depart New York shortly after Game #2 on Sunday ought to end, so he could be back at work in England on Monday morning. Orpin added this stipulation: "But I'm staying through the second game even if it goes 48 innings." Orpin gladly offered his prediction on the World Series. "The Mets are going to win," he said confidently. "I don't see how Baltimore can stop them. The Baltimore players must be shaking in their boots. The Mets will win four games to one, no doubt about it."[23]

Game #1 of the 1969 World Series was slated for 1 p.m. the next day. New Yorkers (and Met fans everywhere) were counting the minutes. Baltimoreans ... not so much.

7

World Series Game #1

Cuellar in Control

"I think you can sum up this '69 World Series by saying if you pick [the winner] on paper, it's the Orioles. They have the best statistics in hitting, in power, lowest staff earned-run average, they've made the fewest errors. But the Mets didn't win the National League [pennant] on paper. On paper they didn't look as good as the Cardinals and the Cubs. They won it on the field."[1]—NBC's Curt Gowdy assessing the two teams prior to Game #1 of the 1969 World Series

"What astonishes most baseball men who have seen him is Seaver's unbelievable poise. For a young man of 24, he pitches with the head of a veteran."[2]—Jack Lang, *The Sporting News*

Date: Saturday, October 11, 1969
Site: Memorial Stadium, Baltimore, Maryland

The 66th World Series of the modern era began on a beautiful, balmy Maryland afternoon. Although the morning of Saturday, October 11 was cool and overcast, the temperature in Baltimore steadily improved as game time approached. It was hovering near 75 degrees when play began. It was spectacular autumn weather for the crowd of 48,400 who were predominantly clad in suits and dresses. Even a sizable number of youngsters lucky enough to be in Memorial Stadium for Game #1 seemed to be decked out in their Sunday best.

One large, professionally made sign positioned outside Memorial Stadium captured the feeling of the hometown rooters with a clever pun: "The Mets are for the Birds." On NBC radio, Ralph Kiner—who called Met games during the regular season—described the 1969 Fall classic a "David versus Goliath series" after reading both teams' lineups. He also opined that the Orioles were "one of the strongest representatives the American League has sent [to the World Series] in a long time."[3]

Strangely to outsiders, the game was not a sellout despite being played on a weekend afternoon in lovely conditions. Even odder, there were more than 2,000 no-shows for Game #1, an embarrassing statistic that was not mentioned during the NBC telecast. It was the first time a World Series game had not sold out since the all-St. Louis, Cardinals-Browns Fall Classic back in 1944 when the Second World War was raging. A United Press International story said, "The ticket windows were still open when the game started, but there weren't any fans left trying to buy tickets."[4] Perhaps Baltimore's baseball fans had been lulled into believing the 1969 World Series would be the one-sided rout that the media was generally predicting.

Rumors abounded that U.S. president Richard Nixon, an avid sports fan— or perhaps vice-president Spiro Agnew—might make the 40-mile trip from Washington to throw out the ceremonial first pitch. It was not the case; the honor was instead done by the Commissioner of Baseball, Bowie Kuhn. (First Lady Pat Nixon was present, however. She shared Kuhn's box with daughters Tricia and Julie and her son-in-law David Eisenhower. At one point in the game, the First Lady was photographed ducking for cover when a foul ball drifted into the stands close to her seat.) The lanky, six-foot-five Kuhn, the fifth commissioner since the post had been established by MLB in 1920, made two firm, right-handed throws from his box seat. One went to Mets catcher Jerry Grote; the other was tossed to Elrod Hendricks, who would catch for the Orioles on this autumn afternoon.

In the NBC broadcast booth, 50-year-old Curt Gowdy praised "the articulate and dynamic"[5] Kuhn for his outstanding leadership during his first year on the job as MLB's top man. Kuhn was supposed to be merely an interim commissioner when he succeeded William Dole Eckert on February 4, 1969, but he had recently signed to a seven-year contract by the contented club owners. The 42-year-old Kuhn was a tailor-made and utterly logical replacement for the unpopular Eckert. Unlike his predecessor—who reputedly had not even attended a professional game in the decade before he was hired—Kuhn was keenly aware of the inner workings of Major League Baseball. He had ably served as the legal counsel for MLB's owners for nearly two decades. Starting with 1969, for 16 seasons Kuhn would prominently hold his post as Commissioner of Baseball through some of the sport's most tumultuous times. In the October 18 issue of *The Sporting News*, Kuhn received praise from a fan in Kansas City who wrote to tell the periodical, "I think the lords of baseball achieved a master stroke when they named Bowie Kuhn commissioner. In this, baseball's centennial year, Kuhn has taken many steps to revive interest in a sport whose obituary had been written across the nation."[6]

By their outward appearances, both teams looked relaxed—almost jovial— during the pregame introductions as they trotted out to the baselines in front of their respective dugouts. The smiling Orioles, with their surnames on the back of their uniforms, appeared especially confident and totally at ease. Some even waved at friends and family in the stands. "The Orioles are a beautifully balanced baseball team," Curt Gowdy noted. "They are almost a team without a weakness."[7] Fifty years later, in a 2019 interview, Ron Swoboda, a Met who was born and raised in

Baltimore, recalled being anything but calm before the World Series opener. "I had worked out with the Orioles and wore their uniform as a kid before I signed with the New York Mets," Swoboda said. "I had been in Memorial Stadium, but when I ran onto the field in Game #1 of the World Series, I felt like all that history just crowded my brain. It was a little daunting. I ran out there as nervous as heck."[8]

The Baltimore crowd was surprisingly polite to the upstart New Yorkers. Perhaps they felt sorry for them based on what the experts were predicting about the Series. No one loudly booed the visitors during the Mets' introductions. In fact, many large cheers greeted the New York players, presumably from traveling Met fans. Gil Hodges was given an especially warm welcome. There was, however, one glitch in the pregame festivities: Orioles public-address announcer Bob Bolling mispronounced Jerry Grote's surname, thinking it rhymed with "boat." Apprised of his error, the very professional Bolling got the New York catcher's name right from that point forward ("grow-tee").

When Bolling announced Tom Seaver as the as the ninth batter and starting pitcher for the visitors, New York's 25-game winner received a loud general roar of approval. Seaver's photo appeared on the cover of that day's issue of *The Sporting News* alongside the caption "Prince Valiant." Of course, the hometown Orioles got a rousing welcome when they were introduced, especially manager Earl Weaver and third baseman Brooks Robinson. The popular and thoroughly reliable infielder had, to no one's surprise, recently been voted by Oriole fans as the greatest player in the 16-year history of the team since it had relocated from St. Louis. Longtime Orioles announcer Chuck Thompson always insisted that Robinson was the most popular athlete in Baltimore history, surpassing even quarterback Johnny Unitas of the Colts.

"The Star-Spangled Banner" was performed by Joseph Eubanks, a professor from Morgan State College's music department. He sang the national anthem in a deep, rich voice. Eubanks was accompanied by the full Baltimore Symphony Orchestra to add an extra level of elegance to the festive occasion.

The six-man umpiring crew—in their standard suits and neckties—assigned to work the 1969 World Series was a combination of veterans and newcomers to MLB's showcase event. Lou DiMuro of the AL and Lee Weyer of the NL were both excitedly appearing in their first World Series. DiMuro, age 38, patrolled the right field foul line in Game #1. Weyer, the youngest member of the crew at just 33 years old, was stationed on the left field line. The other four arbiters were markedly older. Crew chief Hank Soar, a 55-year-old AL ump, was behind the plate. The 1969 WS was his fifth; his first had been the 1953 Yankees-Dodgers clash. In that Series, Mets manager Gil Hodges and Yogi Berra, now Hodges' first-base coach, had been adversaries. Frank Secory of the NL, the oldest member of the crew at age 57, was assigned first base. This was his fourth Fall Classic, as it was for second-base umpire Larry Napp, age 53. Also 53 years old was Henry (Shag) Crawford—whose son Jerry would eventually umpire in five World Series. He was an NL ump stationed at third base. It was his third World Series appearance. Each of the six men in blue had earned his coveted World Series assignment based on merit.

The Mets' lineup for Game #1 featured an entirely right-handed batting order to face Baltimore's excellent southpaw Mike Cuellar. Cuellar, age 33, had led all left-handed AL pitchers in wins in 1969 with 23. (Detroit's Denny McLain, a righty, had been the overall league leader with 24 victories.) It promised to be a strong pitching matchup to open the Series. Both Cuellar and his teammate Jim Palmer had recorded victories over every AL team during the 1969 regular season. Tom Seaver had been just as dominant with his NL opponents. He had beaten each of the other 11 teams in the senior circuit at least once.

With his cap tilted slightly to the right—as was his sartorial style—Cuellar threw the first pitch of the World Series that counted to New York's leadoff batter Tommie Agee. It clipped the outside corner. Umpire Hank Soar lifted his right arm to indicate it was a strike. The Baltimore crowd cheered. Cuellar, who was in his second year with the Orioles, had an excellent repertoire of pitches, including two versions of a terrific screwball. He got ahead of Agee 0–2 but then threw three consecutive balls to make the hometown fans quickly uneasy. After a foul ball, Agee grounded to the sure-handed Brooks Robinson at third base. Robinson made the play look routine and threw out Agee at first base by a considerable margin. The partisan crowd cheered the first putout. Bud Harrelson was the next Met batter. He grounded out to Robinson as well on an easy hop. Cleon Jones, a product of the Met farm system, got the first hit of the World Series. He smacked a 1–2 pitch beyond shortstop Mark Belanger's range toward second base. It bounced into center field. Jones was stranded on first base when New York first baseman Donn Clendenon struck out swinging on a 2–2 pitch.

The bottom of the first inning started spectacularly for the home team. With a slight breeze blowing from first to third base, up to the plate strode Baltimore's Don Buford. Both he and Met starter Tom Seaver had attended the University of Southern California. Buford, powerfully built at just 5'7", showed no mercy for his fellow Trojan alumnus as he belted a surprise home run. Buford connected solidly with Seaver's second offering, sending the ball hurtling towards to right field fence about 15 feet inside the foul pole. Ron Swoboda came forward at first, but then followed the ball back toward the warning track. Swoboda, who was not known for being a defensive specialist, looked unsure of himself.

The right field wall in Memorial Stadium in 1969 was a seven-foot-tall temporary canvas structure. As such, it could not be climbed easily. As the ball continued to carry, Swoboda raised his glove above his head and leapt. He missed snaring Buford's drive by mere inches. Swoboda's leap was not especially high nor was it perfectly timed; certainly, it could have been better by MLB standards. The partisan Baltimore crowd gave a surprised roar when they saw the ball drop beyond the barrier for a leadoff home run. To their absolute delight, the home team was ahead 1–0 after just one batter. The squat Buford, a .291 hitter with 64 RBI in 1969, had hit just 11 home runs during the regular season.

"What a way to lead off a World Series!"[9] declared Curt Gowdy. But should Swoboda have caught it? Did the Met right fielder mistime his jump or miscalculate the ball's trajectory? Perhaps both? Baltimore announcer Bill O'Donnell, who was sharing the NBC television broadcast booth with Curt Gowdy for the Orioles' home games in the World Series, seemed to think so, and subtly articulated his opinion. (Former Mets manager Casey Stengel once said disparagingly of Swoboda, as only Stengel could, "He will be great, super, even wonderful. Now if he can only learn to catch a fly ball."[10]) Indeed, Swoboda was sometimes called "Rocky" by his teammates for his shaky defensive skills.

Cuban-born Mike Cuellar posted 23 wins for the Orioles in 1969 against 11 losses. In a World Series full of disappointments for the Orioles, Cuellar's 1.13 ERA over 16 innings, including the win in Game #1, was a rare bright spot for the team (National Baseball Hall of Fame and Museum, Cooperstown, NY).

Neither Gowdy nor O'Donnell dwelled on the play after a slow-motion replay showed how close Swoboda was to making a home-run-saving catch. Instead, O'Donnell commented that it was a rarity for Seaver to allow a home run. (That was a bit of a stretch; Seaver had surrendered 24 homers in 35 starts during the regular season.) Neither Jim Simpson nor Ralph Kiner openly passed judgment on Swoboda in the NBC radio booth. A pair of photos, one showing Swoboda leaping and the other showing him sitting glumly at the base of the fence without the ball, would run in many Sunday newspapers' sports sections around the continent. A large black-and-white shot of Swoboda leaping fruitlessly for the ball appeared in the October 20 issue of *Sports Illustrated*.

Fifty years later Swoboda admitted in an interview, "Every mistake you could make [on that play], I made. Yes, it's a ball I should have caught."[11] Swoboda also recalled sitting in the Mets' dugout between innings angrily muttering about not preventing Buford's home run. Teammate Ed Kranepool, with some profanity sprinkled in for effect, bluntly told him to forget about it and focus on getting the next one. "We caught everything after that," Swoboda proudly remembered. "Everything."[12] Before the 1969 World Series was over, Swoboda would redeem himself with his glove in a most timely and spectacular manner.

The 24-year-old Seaver quickly regained his usual fine control. Paul Blair went down swinging as did Frank Robinson. (Robinson possessed a quirky batting statistic that proved he was consistently productive at the plate: He had compiled a .303 lifetime batting average in the NL and, to date, a .303 lifetime average in the AL!) One Seaver pitch to Robinson was fouled sharply to third-base coach Billy Hunter. He made a skillful bare-handed play and got a rousing cheer from the already happy crowd. With two men out, Baltimore fan favorite John (Boog) Powell lashed a belt-high pitch into right field for a single to keep the inning alive. The fifth Oriole to bat in the first inning, Brooks Robinson, had a subpar offensive year in 1969, batting just .234 in 598 at-bats. The crowd got excited when he hit the ball hard to center field, but Tommie Agee easily snagged it to end any further Baltimore threat. Still, after one inning, the heavy World Series favorites from the AL were already following the script having established a quick 1–0 lead over the NL underdogs from New York.

Cuellar looked solid in the top of the second inning. Ron Swoboda, who had played one game in Memorial Stadium for Patterson Park High School, went down swinging. So did third baseman Ed Charles. It became a three-up-three-down inning when catcher Jerry Grote grounded out to smooth-fielding Oriole shortstop Mark Belanger. Belanger handled the big hop without difficulty. The hometown Birds looked like a confident bunch.

Baltimore also went down swiftly in the bottom of the second inning. Catcher Elrod (Ellie) Hendricks led off for Baltimore. He had hit 12 home runs in 1969. There was no home run in this at-bat, though. Hendricks popped up near the pitcher's mound. Third baseman Ed Charles moved forward and to his left to make the routine catch in front of Seaver. Next up was Oriole second baseman Dave Johnson. The right-handed-hitting Johnson positioned himself in front of Met catcher Jerry Grote. (The two had something in common besides baseball: They had both attended Trinity University in San Antonio, Texas.) On Seaver's first offering, the tobacco-chewing Johnson lofted a routine fly ball to Tommie Agee in center field for the second out. Mark Belanger, choking up on the bat, grounded out to Ed Charles.

Cuellar lost his control briefly at the start of the top of the third inning. Second baseman Al Weis was the first man to come to the plate for New York. Showing a good eye for the strike zone, Weis drew a base on balls on six pitches after falling behind in the count. (Curt Gowdy noted that Weis and Frank Robinson had been involved in a nasty collision when Weis was with the Chicago White Sox in which both men suffered serious injuries.) With Tom Seaver at bat, trying to lay down a bunt, Weis was very nearly picked off by Cuellar's excellent and deceptive move to first base. The crowd disagreed somewhat with umpire Art Secory's safe call, but it was clearly a correct decision. Seaver was a decent hitter for a pitcher. He batted .121 and had six RBI in 1969. Tom Terrific (as adoring Met fans called him) fouled off two bunts and took a full cut at a third pitch. He missed it completely and became Cuellar's fourth strikeout victim of the game. Leadoff hitter Tommie Agee, who had walloped 26 home runs in 1969, quickly hit a swift ground ball directly at shortstop Mark Belanger. Belanger turned an easy 6–4–3 double play to end the inning.

Baltimore failed to take advantage of a New York gift in the bottom of the third inning. Mike Cuellar got a big hand when he, Baltimore's number-nine hitter, stepped into the batter's box. He struck out on five pitches, however. After Cuellar struck out, Don Buford hit a routine ground ball to second baseman Al Weis. Weis moved to his left and seemed to have the ball in his glove, but he botched the play badly when he tried to transfer the ball to his throwing hand. The chagrined Weis had to retrieve the ball from shallow right field. Buford was safely standing on first base courtesy of the first error of the 1969 World Series. (A trio of three newspaper men collectively ruled on scoring plays: Dick Young of the *New York Daily News*; Joseph Durso of the *New York Times*; and Lou Hatter of the *Baltimore Morning Sun*.) Buford, who was known to take a big lead off first base, drew a lot of attention from Seaver. On one pitch Buford noticeably wiggled his hips in an attempt to distract the Met pitcher. It proved to be a harmless miscue, though, when Paul Blair flied out to left field and Frank Robinson grounded out to third baseman Ed Charles on a play where Buford broke for second base. One-third of the way through Game #1, Baltimore still led New York by a 1–0 score.

The top of the fourth produced a small threat but another zero in the line score for New York. The first two Mets went down quickly and quietly. Bud Harrelson, a .248 hitter in 1969, grounded out to Brooks Robinson and Cleon Jones lofted an easy fly ball to Paul Blair in shallow center field. Donn Clendenon provided the visitors with a glimpse of hope by slugging a double into left-center field. The Mets' second hit of the game was wasted, however, when Ron Swoboda lofted another high, lazy fly ball to Blair in center field to end the inning. Cuellar was making things looks easy.

Before the bottom of the fourth inning began, Tony Kubek interviewed Ted Williams for NBC television. The former Red Sox superstar had just finished his first year as manager of the Washington Senators. Williams declared the Orioles were certainly the cream of the AL because of their well-balanced lineup and terrific pitching staff. Kubek congratulated Williams on the Senators' surprisingly strong 86–76 record in 1969. Kubek also politely told Williams he could expect to garner many votes for the MLB Manager of the Year—an annual award presented by *The Sporting News*. That prize would be won by Gil Hodges.

The bottom of the fourth inning proved to be the game's most decisive frame.

Seaver began the inning with the same dominance he had shown since Buford opened the game with a leadoff home run for Baltimore. Boog Powell hit a check-swing grounder to shortstop Bud Harrelson and was retired easily at first base. Brooks Robinson followed Powell's out by popping up to Al Weis at second base. "Since that homer by Buford, Seaver has been tough on the Orioles,"[13] declared Curt Gowdy.

Gowdy spoke too soon. With two men retired, the home team struck in waves as five consecutive Orioles proceeded to reach base. Elrod Hendricks was the first. He singled to right field; it was the Orioles' first hit since the first inning. Dave Johnson then walked on Seaver's first base on balls of the game. Mark Belanger, a .287 hitter in 1969, singled to right field scoring Hendricks. Johnson advanced to third base when Ron Swoboda threw to the plate.

Pitcher Mike Cuellar, a .117 hitter, helped his own cause. Cuellar blooped Seaver's first pitch just beyond the infielders into center field for an RBI single. Johnson scored as Belanger stopped at second base. (Cuellar, standing on first base, declined a warmup jacket when offered it.) Don Buford troubled Seaver for the second time in Game #1 by hitting a double into right field. Buford slid safely into second base on a close play. Belanger scored while Cuellar stopped at third base. Suddenly Baltimore was comfortably ahead by four runs. Action began in the Mets' bullpen. A visit from pitching coach Rube Walker got Seaver refocused. He got Paul Blair, the eighth Oriole to bat in the bottom of the fourth inning, to ground out to third baseman Ed Charles to end the inning, but the damage was done: three Baltimore runs courtesy of four hits and a walk. The Mets walked to the visitors' dugout in deep trouble, trailing the hometown Orioles, 4–0.

Cuellar kept his command over the Mets in the top of the fifth inning. Ed Charles grounded to the sure-handed Brooks Robinson who gracefully fielded the ball and threw him out at first base. Robinson—known as "the human vacuum cleaner" to his fans—recorded his fourth assist of the afternoon. Jerry Grote flied out to shallow right field. Al Weis then hit a tricky grounder, on a 3–2 pitch, toward Robinson. Living up to his nickname, Robinson deftly handled it and retired Weis with a strong, accurate throw to complete the inning. Halfway through the game, Baltimore, according to expected form, led New York by a comfortable 4–0 score.

At this point in NBC's television broadcast, Baltimore announcer Bill O'Donnell took over from Curt Gowdy as play-by-play man. This was typical for the time. NBC, which televised 30 consecutive World Series from 1947 to 1976, had a long-standing policy of blending its *Game of the Week* crew with local broadcasters from the two World Series participants. The low-key O'Donnell was very professional in his methods, seldom becoming overly dramatic in delivering his descriptions. This was completely by design. He once logically explained to a reporter, "If you're always getting excited, you will lose your credibility when it is time to be excited."[14]

The bottom of the fifth inning was uneventful. Frank Robinson flied out to Tommie Agee. Boog Powell sharply hit a ground ball to the right side of the infield, but it was knocked directly at Met second baseman Al Weis. The slow-moving Powell was an easy out at first base. Weis got a putout on the next batter, Brooks Robinson, who smacked a line drive directly at him. Weis made the chest-high catch with no difficulty.

Before the top of the sixth inning began, a Memorial Stadium tradition that began in 1969 took place: Linda Warehime, a 12-year-old member of the grounds crew, did her shtick. Known as "the Baltimore broom girl," Warehime entered the field. Armed with a corn broom, she dutifully swept the plate, the pitcher's rubber, all three bases, the shoes of the Oriole infielders—and those of New York third-base coach Eddie Yost. Sometimes Warehime swept the shoes of the third-base umpire too. (For levity, she occasionally gave the visiting coach or the ump a playful whack on the fanny with her broom or swept dirt onto the coach's feet.) Warehime was paid $5 per game for her services.

With the Mets trailing by four runs and Tom Seaver slated to lead off the top of the sixth inning, New York manager Gil Hodges lifted Seaver for right-handed pinch-hitter Duffy Dyer. Dyer was retired after just one pitch. He grounded to shortstop Mark Belanger for a quick out. (That at-bat would be the only appearance the 24-year-old Dyer made in the 1969 Fall Classic.) Mike Cuellar looked especially sharp in whiffing the next Met to come to bat, Tommie Agee. He got three called strikes on looping curve balls. All of them seemed to freeze Agee. (Bill O'Donnell described Cuellar's strikes as "rainbow breaking balls."[15]) Bud Harrelson, a switch-hitter batting right against the Baltimore left-hander, drew a walk on four pitches. Plate umpire Hank Soar seemed indecisive on the fourth ball. Soar began to raise his right hand to signal a strike, stopped abruptly, and then used the same hand to point Harrelson toward first base. It was hardly a display of textbook umpiring mechanics, causing some ticketholders to mildly jeer. It mattered little as Cleon Jones ended the inning by popping out in foul territory to first baseman Boog Powell.

Before the bottom of the sixth inning, NBC's Tony Kubek, tracked down Detroit Tigers manager Edward (Mayo) Smith for a brief interview. Smith's team had won the previous season's Fall Classic. Detroit finished in second spot in the AL East in 1969—a whopping 19 games behind Baltimore. The 54-year-old Smith generously heaped praise on the Orioles. "This ball club does just what it has to do," he admiringly declared. "If it has to have a good-pitched [*sic*] ballgame, it gets it. If they don't have such a good-pitched game, they score runs. This is one of the finest, well-balanced clubs I've seen in years."[16]

Gil Hodges brought in a right-hander, Don Cardwell, from the Met bullpen to replace the removed Seaver in the bottom of the sixth inning. The first batter he faced was Elrod Hendricks. Hendricks grounded to Donn Clendenon at first base for an easy putout. Dave Johnson grounded out to third baseman Ed Charles on the first pitch he saw from Cardwell for the second out of the inning. Mark Belanger popped up to Clendenon in foul territory to end the home half of the sixth. The much-traveled Cardwell, primarily a breaking-ball specialist, had done his job well.

When NBC resumed its coverage in the top of the seventh inning, it showed a graphic with an impressive statistic: Having shut out the Mets through the first six innings, the Baltimore Orioles had not allowed a run in 39 consecutive World Series innings! This streak—easily a Fall Classic record—encompassed the Orioles' only previous appearance in the Fall Classic. In 1966, they had swept the Los Angeles Dodgers in four straight games and only surrendered two runs in the process. The game scores were 5–2, 6–0, 1–0 and 1–0. Los Angeles failed to score any runs after the third inning of the first game; this meant that the Dodgers played the final 33 innings of the World Series while putting up nothing but zeroes. Mike Cuellar, three years later, was simply extending the Oriole shutout streak.

Of course, the string of zeroes ended shortly thereafter.

The top of the seventh began with Donn Clendenon getting his second hit of the game by singling to left field. He had also gotten New York's most recent hit prior to the seventh inning—a fourth-inning double. Cuellar got himself into further trouble by walking Ron Swoboda on five pitches. (Bill O'Donnell correctly described the New York right fielder as "a local product."[17]) Despite the four-run lead, the home crowd was becoming edgy and unnerved, while the traveling and subdued Met fans at Memorial Stadium finally found their voices.

The Oriole supporters became further agitated and began to howl when Cuellar's first delivery to Ed Charles was high for ball one. Pitching coach George Bamberger came onto the field to settle Cuellar down with the help of catcher Elrod Hendricks. (Cuellar and Hendricks often communicated with each other in either English or Spanish.) Properly refocused, Cuellar got Charles to fly out to Frank Robinson in right field. Both runners held their bases. The next Met batter, Jerry Grote, got ahead in the count against Cuellar 2–0 and singled into left field. Clendenon made a wide turn around third base, but he thought better of testing the arm of Don Buford in left field and quickly retreated back to the bag. Buford had aggressively charged at the ball once it had eluded the grasp of shortstop Mark Belanger. With the bases now loaded, suddenly the Mets had the tying run coming to bat.

Al Weis, sensing that Cuellar was losing his touch, sensibly became extra choosy at the plate. The count on Weis swiftly rose to 3–1. Cuellar threw a strike that caught the inside corner. On the next pitch Weis made good contact in driving the ball to left field. It was hit deep enough to Buford to score Clendenon on a sacrifice fly. The other two New York baserunners held their bases. The surging Mets were now on the scoreboard, trailing Baltimore 4–1. The Orioles' long World Series shutout streak was now gone, however. With the number-nine man in the batting order coming to the plate, Gil Hodges sent up a switch-hitting pinch-hitter in place of Cardwell. Rod Gaspar batted right-handed against lefty Cuellar. On a

1–2 pitch, Gaspar hit a slow chopper toward third base. Brooks Robinson, play-ing shallow as usual—even with a force play available at third base—made easily the best defensive play of the game. He charged the ball, picking it up barehanded, and made an accurate, running throw to Boog Powell at first base. "The play, amaz-ingly, was not even close. Gaspar, who is not all that slow, was out by two steps,"[18] marveled Mark Mulvoy of *Sports Illustrated.* The Mets' promising inning had only amounted to one run.

"Whenever I go after the ball," Robinson later told Mulvoy, "I always think I can get the out. The trick here is to have your left foot in front of your right foot when you bend for the ball. Otherwise you come up off balance and throw the ball away. A lot of third basemen do that."[19] Robinson told another reporter, "I was play-ing back because there were two strikes on Gaspar, but I don't think he got a good jump out of the batter's box."[20]

The Mets' rally had been squelched with panache by the great Brooks Rob-inson. The Orioles ran off the field to resounding cheers, holding a three-run lead heading into the home half of the seventh. Thus far, the 1969 World Series was unfolding according to form.

Right-hander Ron Taylor, a native of Toronto, became the Mets' third pitcher in the bottom of the seventh inning. (Bill O'Donnell quaintly used the term "reliefer" to describe Taylor—and any other substitute coming from either bullpen.) Taylor was the only Met with any previous World Series experience, having pitched 4⅔ innings for the St. Louis Cardinals in their seven-game triumph over the New York Yankees in 1964. Taylor's best weapon was a sinking fastball.

Mike Cuellar led off for Baltimore and worked Taylor to a full count before striking out swinging on the seventh pitch he saw. Next, Don Buford came up and got a warm welcome from the crowd for his two extra-base hits in the game. This time Buford flied out to center fielder Tommie Agee. Paul Blair drew a walk, becoming the first Oriole to reach base since the fourth inning. He wasn't on base very long, however. With Frank Robinson batting, Blair broke for second base on what looked to be a hit-and-run play. However, Taylor saw Blair head for second and simply stepped off the rubber and threw to first baseman Donn Clendenon. Blair froze on the base path and was quickly involved in a rundown. He was tagged out by Al Weis on a play that went into the books as "caught stealing 1–3–4." The score remained 4–1 in Baltimore's favor with two innings left to play.

After the slight hiccup in the seventh inning, Mike Cuellar continued to roll along for the Orioles in the top of the eighth. He struck out Tommie Agee on three pitches. Bud Harrelson gave the Mets a glimmer of hope. He reached base by slap-ping a single into left field past the outstretched glove hand of shortstop Mark Belanger. It was New York's fifth hit of the game. The next batter, Cleon Jones, hit a sinking line drive that landed near the feet of Oriole second baseman Dave John-son. Johnson had some difficulty corralling it, but he did retire Harrelson at second on the force play with an accurate sidearm toss to Belanger. Belanger's throw to first baseman Boog Powell was far too late to complete a double play. Jones was safe at first base on the fielder's choice. There he remained as Donn Clendenon—who had doubled and singled already—struck out swinging. It was Cuellar's seventh strikeout of the afternoon.

When NBC resumed its coverage, a graphic appeared on the screen, courtesy of statistician Alan Roth, indicating how important a win in the opening game of a World Series had been historically. It noted that in the previous 65 World Series of the modern era, the team that won the first game had gone on to win the Fall Classic 39 times—exactly a 60 percent success rate.

Ron Taylor remained on the mound for the Mets. The first batter he faced was the hitless Frank Robinson who had batted .308 in 1969. (In the NBC booth, Bill O'Donnell and Curt Gowdy discussed Robinson's desire to someday become a major league manager. With Robinson's obvious baseball smarts, both announcers agreed he had the qualifications to be a very good one. Robinson, it was noted by O'Donnell, would be managing a team in the Puerto Rican Winter League once the World Series concluded.) On a full count, Taylor struck out would-be manager Robinson swinging. The next batter, Boog Powell, hit an 0–2 pitch just inside first base. It was easily scooped up by Donn Clendenon who stepped on the bag himself for the second out of the inning. Brooks Robinson received a long ovation when he strode to the plate with two out, undoubtedly because of his fine defensive play. He too struck out swinging, ending the frame. Taylor had been excellent in relief for New York, striking out three Orioles in two solid innings of work in which he had faced the minimum six Baltimore batters.

With only three outs left to work with, the Mets gave their fans a modicum of hope to start the top of the ninth. With the count 2–2, Ron Swoboda hit a sharp, high-bouncing grounder back to the mound. Cuellar got his glove up to face level, but he only knocked the ball down. It rolled toward third base. By the time Cuellar retrieved the ball, he knew he had no play at first base and did not attempt a throw. Swoboda was properly credited with a base hit by the committee of official scorers. The Mets, desperate for baserunners, had one to start the ninth inning.

Baltimore manager Earl Weaver had had little to do thus far in the game, but he now decided to activate his bullpen in case the Mets mounted a late rally. Pete Richert, a left-hander, and Eddie Watt, a righty, began to warm up. Cuellar got back to work. Ed Charles flied out to Paul Blair in center field. Jerry Grote struck out looking. Thinking the third strike was both low and outside, Grote grumbled to umpire Hank Soar as he strode back to the visitors' dugout. It was Cuellar's eighth strikeout of the game. However, Cuellar found himself suddenly facing adversity after walking Al Weis on four pitches. It was the fourth base on balls allowed by the Baltimore left-hander. As in the seventh inning, the Mets had the potential tying run stepping into the batter's box.

Baltimore pitching coach George Bamberger again came to the mound to settle Cuellar. Catcher Elrod Hendricks joined them. Bamberger was satisfied that

Cuellar was strong enough to try for the game's final out. "I told him he was trying too hard," Bamberger later elaborated. "I told him to forget the men on base, get the batter, and walk off the field a winner."[21]

The number-nine spot in the Mets' batting order was filled by left-handed pinch-hitter Art Shamsky, who was three days shy of his 28th birthday. Shamksy had batted exactly .300 during the 1969 regular season, but he caught fire versus Atlanta in the NLCS, going seven for 13 at the plate in New York's three-game sweep. On the second pitch Shamsky saw from Cuellar, he softly grounded to second baseman Dave Johnson. Johnson made the routine throw to Boog Powell at first base. Frank Secory signaled the out. Powell gave a celebratory pump with his right fist as he jogged toward the mound to congratulate Cuellar on his complete-game victory. Baltimore, as predicted, had won the opener of the 1969 World Series, by a convincing 4–1 score. The home crowd roared its approval. Game #1 had sped by, taking just two hours and 13 minutes to complete.

In an on-field, postgame interview with Tony Kubek immediately afterward, Cuellar credited the control he had with his screwball as the reason he had been successful in generally shutting down the Mets. Cuellar also complimented his infielders, specifically singling out Brooks Robinson. "He's the best third baseman I've ever seen in my life,"[22] the winning pitcher proudly said. Few people in Baltimore would disagree with Cuellar's assessment.

On the reverse side of the coin, it was the first loss absorbed by Tom Seaver in more than two months since the Cincinnati Reds beat him on August 5 in the first game of a doubleheader at Crosley Field.

Seaver blamed his subpar outing on a calf muscle injury that he developed during his NLCS start versus Atlanta six days earlier—a revelation to baseball fans and journalists everywhere. "I haven't been able to run in the outfield all week," he said. Seaver admitted to "running out of gas" in the fourth inning when Baltimore scored three runs off him, but he insisted, "I don't think the long layoff meant as much as not running. Buford's homer didn't shake me. I think I had really good stuff for the first 3⅔ innings, but then my legs just seemed to get tired. They wouldn't normally."

Seaver added, "I'm not trying to alibi, though. In spite of it all, playing in my first World Series game has to be a fine experience—something I will always remember. I hate to have to remember it as such a miserable performance. But we will get another shot."[23]

In summarizing the contest with Bill O'Donnell, Curt Gowdy conceded that Game #1 was a rather tame affair that did not feature very many exciting plays. Gowdy declared Brooks Robinson's charging, bare-handed scoop and throw to quash the Mets' rally in the top of the seventh inning to be its deciding point. He pointed out that Robinson had been flawless at the hot corner for Baltimore, recording six assists without an error. That view was echoed by an unnamed correspondent for United Press International. He noted that while Cuellar outpitched

Seaver, the lingering impression of Game #1 was "Brooks Robinson, who seems to have a patent on outstanding defensive plays at third base. [He] made a spectacular play on pinch-hitter Rod Gaspar to end the seventh."[24]

Donn Clendenon humorously said Gaspar's knocking a ground ball at Robinson "wouldn't have happened to me [because] I'm not hitting the ball to Robinson in this Series. He's the vacuum cleaner, don't you know that? I'm hitting it towards center. Like I did today. I got two hits today. You don't get any hits going toward third base."[25]

In his postgame summary, one Associated Press reporter agreed that Clendenon had the right idea. He commented, "It's obvious the Mets didn't follow the book on Brooks Robinson. The National League champions kept trying to hit the ball past the stellar third baseman of the Baltimore Orioles on Saturday. They failed."[26]

After the New York loss in the opener, Las Vegas bookmakers installed the Mets as even longer longshots to win the World Series, shifting the odds from 2–1 to 3–1. The general feeling among the baseball scribes covering the Fall Classic was that everything in Game #1 had generally unfolded as they had expected. Jack Hand of the Associated Press wrote,

> Mike Cuellar and the Baltimore Orioles brought the giddy New York Mets back to Earth on Saturday with a 4–1 victory over Tom Seaver in the opening game of the World Series.
>
> Seaver had not lost a game since August 5 when the Cincinnati Reds beat him.
>
> Don Buford's leadoff homer in the first inning and a three-run fourth inning ruined Seaver, who had finished the National League season with 10 straight victories and added another in the [NLCS].
>
> Cuellar, a fast-working Cuban left-hander with a darting screwball pitch, mastered the Mets except for a few brief moments in the seventh inning when they loaded the bases with one out and scored a run on Al Weis' sacrifice fly.
>
> A total of 50,429 tickets were sold, but only 48,400 [spectators] showed up, leaving gaps in the upper stands of Memorial Stadium despite the warm sunshine and clear skies. It was an orderly crowd with only a smattering of the wild banners that always decorate Shea Stadium for Met home games.
>
> It was a routine game with Buford's leadoff homer on Seaver's second pitch providing the most excitement.[27]

The media generally saw the outcome of Game #1 as an indication that the Miracle Mets had finally bitten off more than they could chew with the Baltimore Orioles. It was, in a way, the Mets' comeuppance. The *Tuscaloosa News* ran a story in its sports section titled "And Where Were Met Fans?" In it, an unnamed AP correspondent noted, "It was strictly an Orioles day—and a crowd to match. Where did all the Mets fans go? There were no flying banners and no ear-splitting calls of 'Let's go, Mets!' as the Baltimore Orioles clobbered destiny's darlings. It was so dignified you'd have thought it was the opera."[28]

Tom Loomis of the *Toledo Blade* concurred that the staid crowd in Baltimore was a stunning opposite of what the Orioles could expect to experience at Shea Stadium. "At times you got the impression it was a tennis match they were watching," he wrote in his column. "Oh, there were moments when they yelled. There was even polite applause when the opposition did something commendable. But there was no hysteria."[29]

Some Orioles took the opening game victory as a matter of course, too. Frank Robinson told reporters that the Mets seemed lifeless on their bench during the game. That comment irked the New Yorkers. Upon hearing what Robinson had to say, Gil Hodges quipped, "I am very happy Frank is watching us," he said. "I hope he continues to watch us. Who knows what will happen in right field?"[30] In response to what the Mets' manager had to say, Robinson retorted that he could take care of right field and Hodges should take care of the Mets' bench.

Frank Robinson was also outspokenly critical about the teams' World Series shares, despite them being record highs. For the 1969 World Series it had been predetermined that the players on the winning team would get $15,000 apiece, while the losers would get $10,000. The Associated Press called it "the biggest pot of gold in baseball history."[31] Under the old system, based solely on gate receipts from the first four World Series games, the record high had occurred in 1963 when the Los Angeles Dodgers had each collected $12,794 after sweeping the New York Yankees. With the advent of divisional play in 1969—and an extra tier of playoffs that came with it—Robinson figured the players were being shortchanged out of some of those new MLB revenues.

"What we wanted was $25,000, but the owners wouldn't go for it,"[32] declared Robinson, who figured the World Series winners ought to be paid more than the Super Bowl champions, who each got $23,000 for the past season—a figure that included a share of the pro football leagues' playoff games. "The owners basically collected money off the [two league championship series]. We got nothing."[33]

New York could take some solace in some recent World Series history. The previous year's World Series winners, the Detroit Tigers, had also lost Game #1 on the road before winning Game #2 in St. Louis and rallying for an eventual seven-game triumph over the Cardinals. From experience, Ralph Kiner warned the Orioles and their fans not to become overly confident based solely on the results of Game #1. "This is a resilient Mets team,"[34] he informed the NBC radio audience in the postgame show.

In its coverage of Game #1, *The Sporting News*, a periodical that once proclaimed itself as "The Bible of Baseball," was fixated on the less than capacity crowd at Memorial Stadium. One scribe disgustedly wrote, "Game #1 tickets, in every available price range, had been available in abundance around Baltimore's downtown hotels—and it wasn't a scalper's market. A fan could buy as many tickets as he needed for the established price."[35]

Despite the empty seats, at least one Met appeared to be awed by the occasion.

Roy McHugh of the *Pittsburgh Press* wrote, "Ron Swoboda ... epitomizes the Mets. Out in right field he kept turning around and looking at the scoreboard. 'When I saw our game was the only one up there,' he [later] said, 'I knew we were definitely playing in the World Series.'"[36]

The Mets being in the World Series was affecting other professional sports teams in the Big Apple. The defending Super Bowl champion New York Jets, who shared Shea Stadium with the Mets, had played their first five games of the 1969 season on the road to avoid scheduling conflicts with the baseball team. They announced that their American Football League game on October 19 versus Houston—the team's home opener—had been moved 32 hours to the evening of Monday, October 20. No reason was given, but it was obvious to anyone who knew the baseball schedule: Had the game not been rescheduled, there was the distinct possibility it would have been in direct competition with Game #7 of the World Series in Baltimore that afternoon.

During the 1969 World Series, many newspapers across North America carried an uplifting human-interest story about Baltimore's 16-year-old bat boy, Jay Mazzone. The remarkable youth had captured the attention of many TV viewers who saw him handle his duties for the AL champs with hooks at the ends of his arms instead of hands. Curt Gowdy briefly mentioned Mazzone during NBC's telecast of Game #1, citing him as an inspiration for anyone who had suffered a setback in life.

"It happened near Atlantic City, NJ," Mazzone explained about the life-altering accident that occurred when he was just two years old. "I was burning some stuff in the back yard and playing with a can of kerosene. I must have got some kerosene on my [snowsuit.] It caught fire. My mother tried to help me. Her clothes caught fire too."

He continued, "Then a neighbor ran across the field and threw dirt on us and put out the fire. But for me it was too late."[37] His hands had been burned off at the wrists, leaving him with two charred stubs.

Despite his handicap, Mazzone won a contest to be the Orioles' bat boy in 1966—the season Baltimore won its first AL pennant—and he had held the position ever since. To do his job, Mazzone strapped metal claws to his arms. "He handles bats as easily as some might handle toothpicks," marveled a scribe, "and [he] can catch and throw balls with the best of them."[38]

The Orioles regularly traveled with about 500 bats, according to Mazzone, and each of the regulars has five or six dozen personal models. Eight or ten dozen bats were cared for by Mazzone at each game. Mazzone missed plenty of school because of his unusual job, but he said he still maintained an overall B average. For his labors, Mazzone was paid $5 per game.

"They're all great fellows," Mazzone said of the Baltimore players. "[At first] I thought they might be stuffy and tough, but they're not at all. They treat me like a prince."[39]

Mazzone told the reporter that Elrod Hendricks swung the heaviest bat—even weightier than Boog Powell's. Mike Cuellar, he stated, was the most superstitious of the Baltimore players while Brooks Robinson was the most finicky.

1969 World Series, Game #1

New York Mets 1, Baltimore Orioles 4
Game played on Saturday, October 11, 1969, at Memorial Stadium

New York Mets	ab	r	h	rbi	Baltimore Orioles	ab	r	h	rbi
Agee cf	4	0	0	0	Buford lf	4	1	2	2
Harrelson ss	3	0	1	0	Blair cf	3	0	0	0
Jones lf	4	0	1	0	Robinson F. rf	4	0	0	0
Clendenon 1b	4	1	2	0	Powell 1b	4	0	1	0
Swoboda rf	3	0	1	0	Robinson B. 3b	4	0	0	0
Charles 3b	4	0	0	0	Hendricks c	3	1	1	0
Grote c	4	0	1	0	Johnson 2b	2	1	0	0
Weis 2b	1	0	0	1	Belanger ss	3	1	1	1
Seaver p	1	0	0	0	Cuellar p	3	0	1	1
Dyer ph	1	0	0	0	**Totals**	**30**	**4**	**6**	**4**
Cardwell p	0	0	0	0					
Gaspar ph	1	0	0	0					
Taylor p	0	0	0	0					
Shamsky ph	1	0	0	0					
Totals	**31**	**1**	**6**	**1**					

New York	0	0	0		0	0	0		1	0	0	–	1 6 1
Baltimore	1	0	0		3	0	0		0	0	x	–	4 6 0

New York Mets	IP	H	R	ER	BB	SO
Seaver L (0–1)	5.0	6	4	4	1	3
Cardwell	1.0	0	0	0	0	0
Taylor	2.0	0	0	0	1	3
Totals	**8.0**	**6**	**4**	**4**	**2**	**6**

Baltimore Orioles	IP	H	R	ER	BB	SO
Cuellar W (1–0)	9.0	6	1	1	4	8
Totals	**9.0**	**6**	**1**	**1**	**4**	**8**

E—Weis (1). **DP**—Baltimore 1. **2B**—New York Clendenon (1, off Cuellar), Baltimore Buford (1, off Seaver). **HR**—Baltimore Buford (1, 1st inning off Seaver 0 on, 0 out). **SF**—Weis (1, off Cuellar). **U**—Hank Soar (AL), Frank Secory (NL), Larry Napp (AL), Shag Crawford (NL), Lee Weyer (NL), Lou DiMuro (AL). **T**—2:13. **A**—50,429.

8

World Series Game #2

Koosman Is Masterful

"The Mets can take heart from how Seaver and the reliefers [*sic*] handled the power of the Orioles here yesterday—namely Blair, Frank Robinson, Powell and Brooks Robinson—limiting those four power boys to only one base hit in 15 times at bat."[1]—Oriole broadcaster Bill O'Donnell, prior to Game #2

"This Mets team has shown a great amount of bounce-back. I think you'll see it again."[2]—Commissioner of Baseball Bowie Kuhn, prior to Game #2

Date: Sunday, October 12, 1969
Site: Memorial Stadium, Baltimore, Maryland

Sun-splashed weather again blessed Memorial Stadium in Baltimore on Sunday, October 12 for Game #2 of the 1969 World Series. An Associated Press correspondent accurately called it "a beautiful fall day."[3] It certainly was. The temperature hovered near 80 degrees, even warmer than it had been for Saturday's Game #1. Sunday's contest began at 2 p.m.—one hour later than Saturday's starting time. There was no assigned vocalist for the national anthem this time, but the crowd was invited to sing "The Star-Spangled Banner" as the Suburban High School band of York, Pennsylvania, played the tune. Many people did.

During the pregame player introductions, the loudest and most prolonged cheers from the confident Oriole fans descended upon manager Earl Weaver, Don Buford and Brooks Robinson.

Claire Ruth, the 72-year-old widow of Babe Ruth, threw out the ceremonial first pitch. It was an appropriate choice on two levels: The late Babe had been born in Baltimore and, as part of the centennial celebrations for professional baseball earlier in the season, he had been voted the greatest ballplayer of all time. In a brief interview during the game, Mrs. Ruth told NBC's Tony Kubek that, despite residing in suburban Boston and New York City for most of his adult life, the Babe "had always considered Baltimore to be his hometown."[4]

Former Yankee great Joe DiMaggio, who was employed by the Oakland A's in 1969, was interviewed prior to Game #2 by Tony Kubek, another former Yankee. He ranked Brooks Robinson as the equal of Ken Boyer at third base "if not possibly a little bit better."[5] He attributed the Orioles' overall dominance in the AL to being a mature club that seldom made mental errors on the field.

Apart from the starting pitchers for both teams, there was only one change in the lineups from Game #1: Andy Etchebarren replaced Elrod Hendricks as the Baltimore catcher. Etchebarren caught all four games for the Orioles during their 1966 World Series triumph over the Los Angeles Dodgers. Etchebarren was also Dave McNally's preferred catcher.

Umpire Frank Secory of the NL was behind the plate for Game #2. The Port Huron, Michigan, resident had not only umpired in three previous World Series, he had also played in one. As a member of the 1945 Chicago Cubs, Secory rapped a key pinch-hit single in the 12th inning of Game #6 that led to the winning run being scored in an 8–7 Cubs victory at Wrigley Field. After Secory's batting heroics, the Cubs would not win another World Series game for 71 years.

Dave McNally was the Game #2 starter for Baltimore. The 26-year-old left-hander from Billings, Montana, had won his last World Series start, shutting out the anemic Los Angeles Dodgers 1–0 in Game #4 in 1966. He was one of three Oriole pitchers to hurl whitewashes consecutively at the NL champs three Octobers earlier. McNally had gotten off to a fabulous start in 1969, having won his first 15 decisions before suffering a defeat on August 3 at Minnesota. He cooled off slightly the rest of the way and finished the regular season with a 20–7 mark. He had also thrown an 11-inning, 1–0 shutout versus the Twins in Game #2 of the ALCS exactly one week earlier at Memorial Stadium. He was clearly at the top of his form.

McNally started well in the top of the first inning. Leadoff hitter Tommie Agee fouled off several 1–2 pitches before going down on strikes to start the game. The second Met batter, shortstop Bud Harrelson, hit a slow chopper to the left side of the mound. McNally scurried off the rubber and made a fine defensive play to nip the speedy Harrelson at first base by less than a step. Cleon Jones made the third out of the opening frame, lofting a high pop-up to first baseman Boog Powell who made the catch very close to the box seats. The confident home crowd cheered the play.

When the bottom of the first inning began, NBC flashed a graphic across its telecast informing viewers that the Orioles had never lost a World Series game. It was accurate; the Orioles were a perfect 5–0 in World Series play. Since the former St. Louis Browns had relocated to Baltimore in 1954, they had swept four games from the Los Angeles Dodgers in 1966 and had taken the opener of the 1969 Fall Classic the day before in the only two World Series appearances in the club's relatively brief history.

Jerry Koosman, a 6'2" left-hander, began his Game #2 outing manicuring the mound to his liking. His labors were fruitful. Don Buford went down swinging on an inside fastball. Paul Blair, a .285 hitter in 1969 who failed to connect in Game #1, flied out to Cleon Jones in left field. Frank Robinson, who struck out twice in Saturday's contest, excited the crowd with a long drive to right-center field, but it was hauled in by Ron Swoboda on the warning track directly in front of the 390-foot sign. A strong breeze may have kept the ball from being a home run. Instead it was merely a loud out that retired the Orioles.

Dave McNally, who had pitched four shutouts in 1969, got himself into a bit of a jam in the top of the second. Donn Clendenon led off for New York with a base on balls. Mets fans seemed to be more plentiful as a noticeable cheer greeted Clendenon's walk. Ron Swoboda followed by becoming the second Met to pop out to Boog Powell in foul territory. Powell employed sunglasses on the play. Baltimore second baseman Dave Johnson made an excellent play on Ed Charles' ground ball. It was a sinking line drive that the Oriole second baseman short-hopped. He made the throw to Belanger covering at second base to force out Clendenon as Charles reached first base on the fielder's choice.

With Jerry Grote batting, McNally hurled a wild pitch into the dirt. Catcher Andy Etchebarren had difficulty corralling it. Charles broke for second base. Etchebarren's throw was high and slightly off the mark, but shortstop Belanger did well. He knocked it down, preventing Charles from advancing to third. Baltimore manager Earl Weaver bolted from the dugout to mildly argue that Grote has impeded Etchebarren's throw to second base. Umpire Secory disagreed. Weaver did not press the issue too long. Nevertheless, he got an appreciative hand from the Baltimore faithful as he headed back to the home team's dugout. (NBC's Curt Gowdy commented that Weaver possessed an "angelic smile"[6] that frequently irked umpires during arguments.) It turned out to be much ado about nothing when Grote flied out to center fielder Paul Blair to end the top of the second inning.

Working fast, as was his style, Koosman handled the Orioles well in the home half of the second inning. Boog Powell led off for Baltimore and went down swinging on a breaking ball. That was Koosman's second whiff of the game. Next up was Brooks Robinson. He hit a potentially dangerous high fly ball to shallow center field, but shortstop Bud Harrelson backpedaled to make the catch in front of teammate Tommie Agee. Dave Johnson became the first Oriole to reach base when he drew a base on balls on a full count. He was stranded on first base, however, when Andy Etchebarren flied out to Agee in deep center field. Agee, covering a lot of ground, made the catch look easy.

Light-hitting Al Weis, who batted just .215 in the regular season, led off the top of the third inning against McNally with a base hit to center field. He may have been the beneficiary of a generous non-call. On the previous pitch, a 1–2 offering, Weis appeared to barely restrain swinging on a pitch that looked to be in the strike zone, but the plate umpire called the pitch a ball. The pro–Baltimore crowd strongly disagreed. "About 20,000 umpires are behind umpire Frank Secory,"[7] Bill

O'Donnell wryly commented on NBC's telecast. Pitcher Jerry Koosman was the next Met batter. Not much of an offensive threat, Koosman tried to advance Weis to second base with a sacrifice bunt. He failed. With two strikes and Weis running, Koosman fouled a bunt downward that painfully struck Oriole catcher Andy Etchebarren on his throwing arm. By rule, Koosman was called out on strikes. Baltimore trainer Ralph Salvon and Earl Weaver both came to the plate area to check on Etchebarren's fitness. The meeting was short; Etchebarren stayed in the game.

Tommie Agee was up next. He hit a ground ball to Belanger. Moving to his right, Belanger—a onetime high school basketball star at Pittsfield, Massachusetts—fielded the ball and, against his momentum, made a fine, leaping throw to second baseman Dave Johnson for the force out on the sliding Weis. Agee reached first base on the fielder's choice without drawing a throw from Johnson. McNally, who had been consistently getting ahead of New York's hitters, faltered slightly as Bud Harrelson walked on four pitches. (During the at-bat, McNally threw once to first base to keep Agee close. It was something the Oriole starter seldom did.) Agee moved to second base. McNally fell behind Cleon Jones in the count 3–1, causing the home crowd to grumble. The Mets' threat evaporated, however when Jones flied out on a 3–2 pitch to Don Buford in left field. Buford misjudged the well-struck ball initially, but he recovered in plenty of time to make a running, stretching catch near the warning track. "That ball was really ripped!"[8] commented Curt Gowdy. The relieved crowd at Memorial Stadium applauded Buford's play loudly. The score was still 0–0 heading into the home half of the third inning.

Only one of seven Oriole batters had reached base in the first two innings and Koosman continued his strong and efficient work in the bottom of the third frame. Mark Belanger made good contact with a Koosman offering and drove center fielder Tommie Agee nearly to the warning track in straight center field. Agee made the tricky catch comfortably. Baltimore pitcher Dave McNally, who batted an unthreatening .085 in 1969, struck out swinging on five pitches. Back at the top of the batting order Don Buford hit Koosman's first pitch. It was a sinking line drive to the left side of the infield. Shortstop Bud Harrelson made a terrific defensive play, moving swiftly to his right and diving at the ball. He caught it about six inches off the ground, crashed heavily, but managed to retain control of the ball. Third baseman Ed Charles approved of what his infield teammate had done and raised his arms in celebration. Harrelson's catch, described twice by Bill O'Donnell as "magnificent," elicited a long round of applause from the knowledgeable and fair-minded home crowd at Memorial Stadium. O'Donnell's broadcasting partner, Curt Gowdy wholeheartedly agreed. "We've seen brilliant plays by the shortstops, first Belanger and now Harrelson.... A sensational stab by Harrelson!"[9] In retrospect, Harrelson's terrific catch was perhaps a turning point of the entire World Series. Game #2 remained scoreless after three innings.

When New York's Donn Clendenon stepped into the batter's box to lead off the top of the fourth inning, a prescient television graphic noted that he had averaged a home run every 16.8 at-bats during the 1969 season. On cue, Clendenon smacked a knee-high, 0–1 McNally pitch for a home run. It chased Frank Robinson to the warning track, but the ball flew over the right-field fence not far from where Don Buford's home run had departed in Game #1. Prior to the pitch, McNally was riding a personal 14-inning shutout streak and a 12-inning World Series scoreless streak. There seemed to be more Mets fans in attendance at Memorial Stadium in Game #2 compared to Saturday's game. They let out a loud cheer as Clendenon circled the bases. New York took their first lead in the 1969 World Series as they jumped out to a 1–0 advantage. The home run also marked the first time the Orioles had ever trailed in any of their six World Series games. The Mets were clearly making better contact off McNally than the Orioles were making off Koosman.

McNally fought back to strike out Ron Swoboda swinging for his third whiff of the game. Ed Charles hit a high chopper to shortstop Mark Belanger whose long throw narrowly nipped the 36-year-old Charles at first base. Jerry Grote was the next Met to bat. After a slight delay in which a curious bird was shooed from the infield, Grote hit a slow bouncer near the third-base line. Brooks Robinson charged and made another gem of a play. Similar to his assist in the seventh inning of Game #1, Robinson fielded the ball with his bare hand, fired the ball on the run, and retired Grote at first base by less than half a step. The Baltimore crowd roared its approval of the trademark Robinson assist. Game #2 of the 1969 World Series was turning into a stellar defensive showcase, but the visitors were on top, 1–0.

Paul Blair led off the bottom of the fourth inning. During his at-bat the home crowd began rhythmic clapping, but it did Blair no good. He flied out to second baseman Al Weis in shallow center field. Next up was Frank Robinson who grounded out to shortstop Bud Harrelson. Harrelson moved nicely toward second base to spear the bouncing ball. His throw to first base was a smidgen off target, but Donn Clendenon made the catch and kept his foot on the bag to retire Robinson. Clean-up hitter Boog Powell concluded the inning by grounding out to Weis at second base. The Orioles had not yet managed to get a hit off a very dominant Jerry Koosman.

In the top of the fifth inning Dave McNally was superb in retiring the side entirely on strikeouts. He struck out Al Weis on a called third strike for the first out of the inning. Pitcher Jerry Koosman was the next batter. He got a loud round of applause from the Met supporters when his name was announced. Curt Gowdy noted that Koosman had a personal cheering section of about a dozen rooters inside Memorial Stadium from his hometown of Morris, Minnesota (population 4,100), who had made the thousand-mile journey to Baltimore to see him pitch in the World Series. One was his father. Nevertheless, Koosman—who was born in even tinier Appleton, Minnesota—struck out swinging. (It was the second time in the game the Mets left-hander had gone down on strikes.) Tommie Agee took a called third strike, raising McNally's strikeout total to six.

Baltimore again did nothing offensively when they batted in the bottom of the fifth inning. Brooks Robinson grounded out sharply to his third-base counterpart Ed Charles. Dave Johnson, the only Oriole to reach base thus far in the game (on a walk in the second inning), worked Koosman to a full count but then harmlessly flied out to Ron Swoboda in right field. Swoboda employed his sunglasses to assist him in finding the ball. Andy Etchebarren, the next Baltimore hitter, also drove a ball to right field that Swoboda, with a slight leap, caught at the base on the wall. It was now conceivable that Jerry Koosman might possibly throw a World Series no-hitter.

In the top of the sixth inning, Dave McNally, who was also pitching a fine game, had little difficulty setting down the Mets. Bud Harrelson tried to bunt for a base hit, but he gently popped up to catcher Andy Etchebarren to the right of home plate for an easy out. Cleon Jones flied out to Paul Blair in center field and Donn Clendenon grounded out to second baseman Dave Johnson. It was the first time in Game #2 that the productive Clendenon had not reached base.

Koosman continued to stymie the Orioles in the bottom of the sixth inning. Mark Belanger flied out to Ron Swoboda in right field. Swoboda battled the sun but still made the catch. Belanger was the 11th consecutive Oriole to not reach base. Dave McNally grounded back to Koosman who needed good reflexes to make the play at his waist. Don Buford, a switch-hitter, was the third Oriole batter of the inning. His ground ball to Bud Harrelson took a bad hop, but the New York shortstop deftly fielded it and threw to Clendenon at first base to retire the side. In the NBC broadcast booth, as the network led into a commercial break, Curt Gowdy—going somewhat against baseball tradition and superstition—openly acknowledged that a Koosman no-hitter was in the offing.

Ron Swoboda led off the top of the seventh for New York. His long fly ball to right-center field gave Frank Robinson some trouble. Even with his sunglasses down, Robinson seemed to struggle to find the ball. Nevertheless, Robinson made a two-handed, football-style catch at the wall for the first out of the inning. Ed Charles was the next Met batter. He ripped a McNally pitch just inside the third baseline into left field. Don Buford played the carom well, but Charles made it easily to second base with a stand-up double. Catcher Jerry Grote was the next hitter. He popped up to shortstop Mark Belanger in shallow center field. With two Mets out, Oriole manager Earl Weaver employed some strategy by intentionally passing Al Weis, the number-eight hitter, so McNally could face the weak-hitting Jerry Koosman. The maneuver was roundly booed by the Met supporters. "I guess I've only been walked intentionally a few times in my life," Weis conceded afterwards, "and that's only when it's been done for a [strategic] purpose."[10] Weaver's ploy worked as Koosman quickly grounded out to second baseman Dave Johnson. Despite squandering Charles' double, the Mets still led the Orioles 1–0.

Koosman's bid for a no-hitter vanished in the bottom of the seventh inning. He had set down 13 consecutive Orioles, but leadoff hitter Paul Blair slapped a solid single into left field. The fair-minded Baltimore fans responded with a long ovation for both their team's first hit of the afternoon and for Koosman's impressive six innings of no-hit pitching.

The next two Baltimore batters, however, failed to advance Blair. Frank Robinson lined out to Tommie Agee in center field; Agee only had to retreat a couple of steps to haul it in. Boog Powell popped out to Bud Harrelson at shortstop who caught the ball a few feet onto the outfield grass. Harrelson later told the press that it had briefly crossed his mind to let Powell's pop up fall to the ground—and then make a force play at second base to remove the fast Blair from the base path and replace him with the lumbering Powell. It may have been a costly non-decision.

With Brooks Robinson batting, Paul Blair—still the runner at first—broke for second base. Catcher Jerry Grote made an accurate throw, but Blair slid in safely, just under Al Weis' tag. (Blair had stolen 20 bases in 1969 to lead the Orioles in that category.) It was the first stolen base of the World Series by either team. Shortly thereafter, Robinson made the most of Blair's stolen base. On Koosman's first pitch, Robinson drove Blair home with a single to center field. Game #2 was suddenly level at 1–1—and Memorial Stadium was noticeably louder and more confident than it had been since Clendenon had hit his home run for New York in the fourth inning. A fine defensive play by Mets third baseman Ed Charles concluded the bottom of the seventh. He ventured far to his left to corral a hard and low-bouncing Dave Johnson grounder. Charles threw to Weis at second base to easily retire Brooks Robinson on a force play. "There's been sensational infielding [sic] today on the part of both ball clubs!" declared an impressed Curt Gowdy. "Pitching and defense have sparkled today."[11]

Jerry Koosman averaged just over 7½ innings per start during the 1969 campaign in a 17-win season. However, in his two World Series starts, Koosman was on the mound for all but one out. He allowed a mere seven hits and four bases on balls in 17⅔ innings (National Baseball Hall of Fame and Museum, Cooperstown, NY).

Right-hander Dick Hall was warming up in the Baltimore bullpen in case he was needed, but Dave

McNally required no help to set down the Mets quickly and quietly in the top of the eighth inning. Tommie Agee—who had set a Met scoring record with 97 runs in 1969—grounded out to Mark Belanger. Bud Harrelson grounded out to Brooks Robinson, who made another excellent defensive play in covering plenty of ground. Robinson was almost directly in front of shortstop Belanger—at about the same location where Ed Charles had made his fine play the previous inning—when he fielded the ball. Cleon Jones lofted a fly ball on a 2–2 pitch to Frank Robinson deep in right field. He made a routine catch to end the New York half of eighth.

In the bottom of the eighth inning, Jerry Koosman was as workmanlike as McNally as he stifled the Orioles efficiently. He faced the bottom of the Baltimore order and encountered no serious trouble. Andy Etchebarren lined out to Al Weis at second base. Mark Belanger was called out on strikes by plate umpire Frank Secory. (Belanger griped at Secory momentarily, believing the third strike was off the plate.) Dave McNally, on the first pitch, surprisingly hit a ball to deep left field, but it was not deep enough as Cleon Jones tracked it down for the third out. The home crowd let out a collective groan when the catch was made. Heading to the top of the ninth inning, the score of Game #2 dramatically remained tied, 1–1.

The ninth inning provided plenty of excitement and drama in both halves—but it did not start out that way. The first two batters to face Dave McNally were retired in short order. Donn Clendenon struck out swinging on five pitches. Ron Swoboda grounded out to Boog Powell. Powell, a good-fielding first baseman despite his imposing 240-pound size, scooped the ball up nicely and tossed it underhand to McNally who was covering the bag well ahead of Clendenon. Then things got interesting.

Ed Charles kept the Mets' ninth alive by singling into left field just beyond the reach of Brooks Robinson. On a hit-and-run play, Jerry Grote singled into left field. Because Charles was on the move as McNally delivered the pitch, he made it to third base easily. Oriole pitching coach George Bamberger came to the mound to briefly talk to McNally. New York had runners on the corners with two out. Al Weis, who had batted just .215 during the regular season, was the next batter. After Weis was Jerry Koosman in the number-nine spot. Weis could have been intentionally walked—as he had in his previous time at bat—to force Gil Hodges into a decision about leaving Koosman in the game or removing him for a pinch-hitter, but Hodges was spared that dilemma as Baltimore curiously chose to pitch to Weis. It was a bad move. On McNally's first offering, a high, hanging slider, Weis lined a single into left field. Charles trotted in with the go-ahead run while Grote scampered to second base. The Mets took the lead for the second time in Game #2, 2–1. The traveling New York rooters celebrated loudly. "I wasn't surprised they pitched to me," Weis declared afterward, "but I didn't expect to see that good a pitch—not with Koosman coming up next. He's not a very good hitter. He's proven it this year."[12]

"There was no discussion about walking Weis," McNally told reporters afterward, "although I didn't care if I did. I just wanted to make good pitches. I saw soon enough that I didn't make the one I wanted."[13]

Jerry Koosman batted in the ninth spot as scheduled—and promptly grounded out to Oriole shortstop Mark Belanger to end the inning.

Koosman took the mound for the bottom of the ninth. Leadoff hitter Don Buford flied out to Ron Swoboda in right-center field. Paul Blair, on a 3–1 pitch, grounded out to shortstop Bud Harrelson. With Koosman needing just one more out for a complete-game victory, NBC's Curt Gowdy noted that Koosman had only thrown 90 pitches thus far. However, like his counterpart McNally, a tidy third out of the ninth inning proved to be elusive.

Power-hitting Frank Robinson was the next batter. Manager Gil Hodges decided to employ a defensive tactic he had used occasionally in the regular season in such situations against Richie Allen, Willie McCovey and Hank Aaron when there had been two outs and no runners on first base: He shifted second baseman Al Weis to left field as a fourth outfielder! Hodges figured the pull-hitting Robinson

would not likely hit to the gap to the right of second base that Weis' absence had just created. He also wanted an extra man in the outfield to prevent a possible extra-base hit. A buzz went through the crowd as most of the Oriole fans in Memorial Stadium for Game #2 had never seen this type of shift used against Robinson. Robinson had seen it before, though. Hodges had previously used it against him occasionally while managing the Senators.

The strategy was rendered moot when Robinson drew a walk. As Weis moved back to his usual position at second base, Earl Weaver made a move. Robinson had been noticeably limping in the outfield, so Weaver sent substitute Merv Rettenmund to first base to pinch-

Dave McNally racked up his second consecutive 20-win regular season for Baltimore in 1969 en route to becoming a dominant pitcher in the postseason. His nine-inning, complete game in Game #2, in which he took the loss, was an example of how close the World Series really was (National Baseball Hall of Fame and Museum, Cooperstown, NY).

run for Robinson. (The 26-year-old Rettenmund was a fast, versatile athlete who had been drafted by the Dallas Cowboys in 1965. He would have been a starting outfielder for most MLB teams in 1969.) It was later revealed that Robinson had suffered a painful bruise on his left foot when he fouled off a pitch during pregame batting practice. Boog Powell was the next Baltimore hitter. Koosman lost his control again and walked Powell on a 3–2 pitch. Suddenly Baltimore had both the tying and winning runs on base.

Gil Hodges entered the field and signaled for Ron Taylor to come out of the Mets' bullpen to replace Koosman and face Brooks Robinson. The 31-year-old Taylor had retired Robinson in his two-inning stint in Saturday's game. Koosman got a long round of applause from both teams' fans as he departed. "I never like to leave a game," Koosman said later, "but Gil hasn't been wrong all year. I wasn't about to argue with him."[14]

Taylor fell behind in the count, 3–1, to Robinson as the excited crowd roared with every pitch. On the fifth pitch Taylor threw, Robinson swung awkwardly at a pitch that appeared to be out of the strike zone and fouled it off. With the count now full, the runners would be running on Taylor's next pitch.

Given a bit of a reprieve, Taylor got Robinson to hit a grounder to 36-year-old Ed Charles at third base. It took a wicked bounce. Charles snared it as it bounced off his chest. For just a moment, Charles, who was playing well behind the bag, thought about trying to outrace Rettenmund to third base for the force play. He took two steps toward the bag, but quickly realized he would lose that contest, so he fired a throw across the diamond as Rettenmund passed directly in front of him. The throw was on time and on target to first baseman Donn Clendenon. Robinson was retired for the third out. The Mets had won a nail-biter, 2–1. One reporter noted, "The drama of the brilliantly played game … played in warm sunshine, went down to the last pitch."[15] On NBC radio, Ralph Kiner, displaying a touch of hyperbole, declared it to have been "one of the most exciting games you could ever imagine."[16]

The dramatic bottom of the ninth inning had taken 20 minutes to play. Even so, the total game time was just 140 minutes.

The 1969 World Series was now tied at a game apiece. This guaranteed the Fall Classic would need at least five games to decide a winner. The Series would now shift to New York City for the next three games, scheduled for Tuesday, Wednesday, and Thursday afternoon at raucous Shea Stadium. Each game would start at 1 p.m. Whether the World Series would return to Baltimore was yet to be decided.

Attendance at Memorial Stadium for Game #2 was officially 50,850, based on ticket sales. There were far fewer no-shows than in Game #1, giving the ballpark a better atmosphere for a World Series contest. Still, it was disconcerting to see any empty seats whatsoever for a World Series game.

The Game #2 loss at Memorial Stadium was a rarity for Baltimore. The Orioles had won 60 of 81 regular-season games at home plus three additional post-season games in 1969. It also snapped their five-game World Series winning streak dating back to 1966.

The Orioles' output of just two hits in Game #2 was their smallest of the whole season. Their previous low was three hits—and that only happened twice to the powerful Baltimore hitters.

Frank Robinson told reporters at the end of the game that if he had been the runner at second base on the game's final play, he would have taken a more aggressive approach than Rettenmund had. He said, "My first reaction probably would have been to slide and try to knock Charles off his feet." Robinson then quickly added, "But I'm not knocking Merv."[17] Pinch-runner Rettenmund said he thought the smart play in that situation was to stay on his feet. He sensed Charles might bobble the ball off his chest. If that happened, Rettenmund explained, he might be able to score the tying run all the way from second base on such a misplay.

Winning pitcher Jerry Koosman told the media he was somewhat worried before he threw his first pitch of the game. "I was concerned that my control would be off because I hadn't pitched in a week,"[18] he noted. Indeed, Koosman's last pitching assignment was a no-decision versus Atlanta in Game #2 of the NLCS the previous Sunday. He had been replaced in the fifth inning of that game after allowing six earned runs and nearly blowing a huge New York lead against the Braves.

Koosman elaborated. "With that kind of rest, you build up a lot of strength—sometimes too much," he said. "Pitching batting practice in New York during the week, my fastball kept tailing and I couldn't control it. But I took my time warming up [before Game #2], and everything worked out for me."[19]

Koosman admitted that a possible no-hitter was running through his mind as he routinely mowed down the Orioles over the first six innings. "When was I thinking about a no-hit game? About the second inning," Koosman stated. "I thought about the no-hitter early," Koosman told reporters, "because it's always been my dream to pitch one in the World Series. I also have an ambition to get four hits in a game. I think I'll fulfill the first dream before I do the second."[20] Koosman humorously knew his limitations. He had managed only four hits in 84 at-bats during the 1969 regular season—all of them singles—in compiling a pitiful .048 batting average.

As for the two walks he issued in the bottom of the ninth inning that caused his manager to pull him, Koosman had a ready explanation: "I was trying to be too fine."[21]

Gil Hodges praised the solid relief pitching of Ron Taylor. "He's a very valuable man," Hodges declared of his rangy Canadian right-hander. "He's an individual [whom] you can pitch two days in a row and [he'll] save ball games for you."[22] Since 1969 was the initial season in which saves became an official MLB pitching statistic, Taylor's one-batter save in Game #2 was a World Series first.

Frank Robinson's unusually silent bat was duly noted by an unnamed Associated Press correspondent in an article that appeared in newspapers across the continent. The scribe wrote, "[Frank] Robinson has taken care of right field extremely well in the first two games of the Series, but has done nothing at the plate, failing to collect a hit in seven trips."[23] Frank Robinson had some notable teammates who were also enduring offensive woes. He, Boog Powell and Brooks Robinson were a combined 2-for-22 (.091) in the first two games of the 1969 World Series.

New York Mets owner, Joan Payson, could not bear to watch the bottom of the ninth inning unfold when the Orioles threatened to erase the Mets' lead. Payson was described by the AP as "a 66-year-old dowager who is one of the wealthiest women in the world." A report declared she "was in such a tizzy she couldn't watch Mets reliever Ron Taylor's final ninth-inning pitch to Brooks Robinson with two out and two on."[24] Instead she placed her scarf in front of her eyes and thus missed the ground ball and Ed Charles' throw to Donn Clendenon for the last out of the game. When told the Mets had safely gotten the third out—and the win—the excited Payson kissed Gil Hodges' wife, Joan, who was seated nearby among other Mets VIPs.

"Oh, it was frantic!"[25] she told a reporter with great relief. Her husband, industrialist Charles Shipman Payson, took it all in stride, happily claiming he won a $40 wager on Game #2. "We'll win the next three at home,"[26] he stated with absolute confidence. Sportswriter Red Smith liked to refer to Shea Stadium as "Payson Place."

Also exuding confidence was Donn Clendenon. "I'm tired of hearing how great [the Orioles] are," he snapped at one journalist. "We're the National League champions and we'll find a way to beat them." Clendenon then repeated himself for effect: "I'm sick and tired of hearing how great they are."[27]

In Las Vegas, the odds on the Mets winning the World Series dropped from 3–1 to 2–1 after New York's tight victory in Game #2. Still, the supposed smart money was on Baltimore. Brooks Robinson, who got Baltimore's only RBI in Game #2, was unperturbed by the setback. He insisted the Orioles would prevail in the Series "because we're a better balanced team."[28]

It was revealed afterward that a handful of Mets wives paraded through Memorial Stadium with a large "Let's Go Mets" banner to inspire the visitors when the game was in the balance. With the score tied 1–1, the banner was unfurled and carried through the stands by "mini-skirted cuties—a real eyeful,"[29] according to Lawrence M. Stolle of the *Youngstown Vindicator*. "[They] received a mixture of cheers and catcalls" from the Baltimore fans, he reported. Few of the gawkers realized the gals were New York players' wives.

Lynn Dyer, wife of Duffy Dyer, pilfered a hotel bedsheet to create the banner. She used shoe polish for the dark lettering. "Our guys were dead out there, so we wanted to shake them up," she noted. "So we paraded, catcalls and all."[30] Accompanying Dyer were Ruth Ryan, Nancy Seaver, and Melanie Pfeil. (Bobby Pfeil was the Mets third-string third baseman. He played 62 games in the regular season, but he was not included on New York's 25-man World Series roster.)

Optimism about the Mets' chances was suddenly growing across North America. Across the border from Detroit in Canada, Jack Dulmage, the sports editor of the *Windsor Star*, hinted that the World Series might not return to Baltimore because "the Mets now have three straight home games at Shea Stadium where madness and incredibility beset all those who enter the portals."[31] Dulmage noted that Oriole rooters were in scarce supply in Windsor—except for the Butcher family of nearby St. Clair Beach. One of the Butcher clan, Connie, was the wife of Brooks Robinson. Dulmage reported that Brooks' father-in-law and a friend were attending the World Series as guests of the Baltimore third baseman and Connie.

Reports of baseball's demise as America's favorite sport were proving to be utterly false. Viewership stats for the first two games of the 1969 World Series were more than impressive, reported Will Grimsley of the Associated Press. He wrote, "An early sampling of the television ratings showed the national pastime clobbering the sport which critics predicted would bury it—pro and college football."[32]

The National Broadcasting Company reported that 51.5 million people watched Game #1. That figure jumped to 58.5 million viewers for Game #2. The highest-rated NFL game on that same Sunday did not draw one-fourth the viewers of the Mets-Orioles clash.

A spokesman for NBC told Grimsley, "If the World Series goes seven games, with the final game next Sunday, we expect to have 90 million people watching. It would be the biggest sports audience ever."[33]

What was driving this stupendous interest in the World Series? That answer was obvious, according to one pollster. "It's the amazing Mets," he insisted. "They have captivated everyone. They have brought baseball interest to an all-time high."[34]

1969 World Series, Game #2

New York Mets 2, Baltimore Orioles 1
Game played on Sunday, October 12, 1969, at Memorial Stadium

New York Mets	ab	r	h	rbi	Baltimore Orioles	ab	r	h	rbi
Agee cf	4	0	0	0	Buford lf	4	0	0	0
Harrelson ss	3	0	0	0	Blair cf	4	1	1	0
Jones lf	4	0	0	0	Robinson F. rf	3	0	0	0
Clendenon 1b	3	1	1	1	Rettenmund pr	0	0	0	0
Swoboda rf	4	0	0	0	Powell 1b	3	0	0	0
Charles 3b	4	1	2	0	Robinson B. 3b	4	0	1	1
Grote c	4	0	1	0	Johnson 2b	2	0	0	0
Weis 2b	3	0	2	1	Etchebarren c	3	0	0	0
Koosman p	4	0	0	0	Belanger ss	3	0	0	0
Taylor p	0	0	0	0	McNally p	3	0	0	0
Totals	**33**	**2**	**6**	**2**	**Totals**	**29**	**1**	**2**	**1**

New York	0	0	0	1	0	0	0	0	1	–	2	6	0
Baltimore	0	0	0	0	0	0	1	0	0	–	1	2	0

w

New York Mets	IP	H	R	ER	BB	SO
Koosman W (1–0)	8.2	2	1	1	3	4
Taylor SV (1)	0.1	0	0	0	0	0
Totals	**9.0**	**2**	**1**	**1**	**3**	**4**

Baltimore Orioles	IP	H	R	ER	BB	SO
McNally L (0–1)	9.0	6	2	2	3	7
Totals	**9.0**	**6**	**2**	**2**	**3**	**7**

E—None. **2B**—New York Charles (1, off McNally). **HR**—New York Clendenon (1, 4th inning off McNally 0 on, 0 out). **IBB**—Weis (1, by McNally). **SB**—Blair (1, 2nd base off Koosman/Grote). **WP**—McNally (1). **IBB**—McNally (1, Weis). **U**—Frank Secory (NL), Larry Napp (AL), Shag Crawford (NL), Lou DiMuro (AL), Hank Soar (AL), Lee Weyer (NL). **T**—2:20. **A**—50,850.

9

World Series Game #3

Agee Steals the Show

"This will be the first time I've ever been in Shea Stadium. One time a bus driver took the team there by mistake, but we didn't go inside."[1]—Jim Palmer, Baltimore's starting pitcher for Game #3

"Playing in a World Series is much more difficult than managing in one. As a manager you don't have to worry about going 0-for-21."[2]—New York Mets manager Gil Hodges, who infamously went 0-for-21 as a Brooklyn Dodger in the 1952 World Series

Date: Tuesday, October 14, 1969
Site: Shea Stadium, Borough of Queens, New York City

Game #3 of the 1969 World Series began shortly past 1 p.m. on Tuesday, October 14. World Series games in the daytime—even on weekdays—were still a cherished tradition in 1969. Night games at MLB's showcase event were still two Octobers away. People in the workforce and schoolchildren made do as best they could with portable televisions and transistor radios wherever possible.

Those who could watch the NBC telecast, heard the folksy southern voice of 50-year-old Mets broadcaster Lindsey Nelson alongside that of Curt Gowdy. A beloved character, Nelson's trademark was not his Dixie charm nor his aphorisms, but instead his sartorial splendor. He possessed a vast wardrobe of loud, gaudy, plaid sports jackets. According to Nelson, they were designed to capture the attention of color-TV viewers and give them something to discuss. (Nelson allegedly started his collection by going into a men's clothing store and asking a salesman for all the jackets he had been unable to sell. At one point he reputedly owned 335.) The likable Nelson, a native of Pulaski, Tennessee, had a long and varied sportscasting résumé. Above all else, Nelson preferred calling college football games, but he had been with the Mets since their first spring training in 1962.

The weather in New York City that day was a little bit threatening. Rain was in the forecast, but it was an otherwise pleasant day, a mixture of sunshine and clouds. It would become windy at times too. At one point in the afternoon game, the floodlights were turned on as cloud cover became heavy. Baseball history buffs noted that it was the first time since Game #7 of the 1956 World Series that a World Series game had been played in New York City in a National League ballpark. Gil Hodges had played in the last one. His team, the Brooklyn Dodgers, had lost badly to the New York Yankees that day, 9–0.

The Mets, who won just 27 of their first 52 home games in 1969, had vastly improved to 25–5 over their final 30 regular-season games at Shea Stadium.

Excitement gripped the ballpark as it prepared to host its first World Series game. Unlike in blasé Baltimore, Shea Stadium was sold out and was buzzing in anticipation. Curt Gowdy reported that the Mets could have sold 150,000 tickets to Game #3 if the facility had somehow been three times its actual size. It was no exaggeration. It had become more fashionable than ever for all New Yorkers to go gaga over the Mets. Accordingly, celebrities aplenty were scattered around the ballpark for the Series games at Shea Stadium: Jerry Lewis, Louis Armstrong, Earl Warren, Pearl Bailey, Jackie Onassis, to name a few. Even 79-year-old Casey Stengel was present in a field-level seat. (The Mets' aging ex-manager remained the long-winded Casey of old. Between innings, he gave a rambling answer in Stengelese to a simple question asked by NBC's roving reporter, Tony Kubek.)

But it was not the famous folks who best represented Met fandom; it was the ordinary New Yorkers. Amid the lively atmosphere at Shea Stadium, Lindsey Nelson amusingly declared before the start of Game #3, "They used to say if the Mets ever advanced to mediocrity, they'd lose their fans. They got around that by never being mediocre. They went from being very bad to very good."[3]

Still, a showbiz touch to the proceedings seemed appropriate. Accordingly, recording artist Steve Lawrence sang the national anthem. However, he was barely audible on both radio and TV performing in front of the booming military brass band that accompanied him. Former Brooklyn Dodger catcher Roy Campanella, paralyzed in an automobile wreck in 1958, received a predictably warm greeting as he threw out the ceremonial first pitch from his wheelchair. (Like Gil Hodges, Campanella had also played in the last World Series game hosted by a New York–based NL club.) During the player introductions there were more boos directed at the visiting Orioles by far than had greeted the Mets at Baltimore's Memorial Stadium.

The New York Mets made four changes in their starting lineup. Gil Hodges, an avid practitioner of platooning players based on the opposition's starting pitcher, severely revamped his starting nine as he had done all season. Since the right-handed Jim Palmer would be the Baltimore hurler, Hodges countered with a Met lineup heavy with left-handed hitters. Ed Kranepool was now at first base. Ken Boswell occupied second base. Wayne Garrett was at third base. Only Bud Harrelson and Jerry Grote retained their infield positions from Game #2. In the Met outfield, Art Shamsky replaced Ron Swoboda in right field. Tommie Agee and Cleon Jones were the outfield holdovers from Sunday's game in Baltimore.

Rookie hurler Gary Gentry warmed up to the strains of "Let's Go Mets" played by Shea Stadium organist Jane Jarvis—who composed the tune herself. In 1965, Gentry compiled a 17–1 seasonal mark pitching at Arizona State University, a team that won the NCAA baseball championship. The plate umpire for Game #3 was Larry Napp of the American League. He got a rude welcome to the game when the second pitch thrown by Gentry was fouled off by Don Buford and struck him squarely on the mask. Buford went down swinging on four pitches. Paul Blair, who was once part of the Met farm system, batted second. He tried to bunt one of Gentry's offerings that was eye-high; he fouled it back. Blair eventually flied out harmlessly to Tommie Agee in center field. Frank Robinson was lustily booed when he stepped into the batter's box, presumably for his ongoing war of words with beloved Mets manager Gil Hodges and his general belief, given wide circulation in the New York City dailies, that most teams in the AL would surely beat the Mets. The home fans roared when he swung and missed at two pitches, but Robinson patiently drew a base on balls from Gentry. Boog Powell, who was introduced by Mets P.A. announcer Jack Lightcap as "John Powell," failed to bring Robinson home. He grounded to second baseman Ken Boswell. Boswell threw to Kranepool at first base to retire the side.

In the bottom of the first inning, leadoff hitter Tommie Agee faced Oriole starter Jim Palmer, who was a day shy of his 24th birthday. Nine days before his 21st birthday in 1966, the right-handed Palmer became the youngest man to pitch a World Series shutout. He had told reporters after Game #2 that he planned to throw mainly fastballs to the Mets. He had the best record by winning percentage (.800) of any AL starter in 1969 with his 16–4 mark. His four losses were by a combined six runs. Injured for a large part of the season, Palmer nevertheless won 11 consecutive decisions at one point. He had also thrown an 8–0 no-hitter versus the Oakland Athletics on August 13—the only one tossed by any AL pitcher during the 1969 regular season. That was not going to happen on this day.

On a high 2–1 pitch, Agee launched a line-drive home run over the center-field fence to give the Mets a fast 1–0 lead and the partisan crowd of 56,335 at Shea Stadium something to cheer loudly about. (Despite Shea Stadium's scoreboard declaring Agee's homer to be the fifth leadoff round-tripper he had hit in 1969, it was actually the sixth time he had done it—all of them occurring since July 3.) Ironically, Agee's home run came mere seconds after Curt Gowdy had commented that the top of the Mets' batting order had been stifled during the first two games of the World Series. "It was a high fastball," Agee said after game. "They've been pitching me high and I was looking for it. Luckily, I got it."[4] In Jim Palmer's terrific 19-year MLB career, comprised of 536 regular-season and postseason starts, Agee's solo blast was the only leadoff home run that he ever surrendered.

Palmer recovered to strike out Wayne Garrett looking. (NBC's Curt Gowdy offered the comical opinion that the red-haired Garrett, who was 21 years old and looked his youthful age, resembled the fictional Huckleberry Finn. Indeed, some of his Met teammates called Garrett "Huck." He hated the nickname.) Cleon Jones flied out to Frank Robinson in deep right field. Art Shamsky, celebrating his 28th birthday, also flied out to Robinson to end the bottom of the first. Shamsky's milestone was duly acknowledged on the Shea Stadium scoreboard while he batted.

Baltimore mustered no offense in the top of the second inning. Brooks Robinson grounded a Gentry curveball to Bud Harrelson for a 6–3 putout. Elrod Hendricks lofted a pop-up to Wayne Garrett at third base. Dave Johnson—who had batted sixth in Game #2 but had been demoted to seventh spot in the Orioles' batting order—followed by flying out to Harrelson. The Met shortstop had to drift back into

In what would be a career shortened by injuries, Gary Gentry's 1969 rookie season would be his finest. Compiling a 13–12 record, Gentry pitched a 6–0 shutout to clinch the National League East title for the Mets. In pivotal Game #3 of the World Series, Gentry tossed 6⅔ innings of shutout ball for the victory (National Baseball Hall of Fame and Museum, Cooperstown, NY).

shallow left field to make the catch. He did, with Cleon Jones close behind him. Two pitches before Johnson was retired, a fan made a splendid one-handed snag on a foul ball hit into the stands along the third-base side of Shea Stadium, earning plaudits from the TV broadcasters and a cheer from the impressed crowd.

The bottom of the second inning provided another indication that it would be the Mets' day. It did not start out that way, though, as the first two New York batters made outs. Boswell grounded to Powell (who flipped the ball to Palmer who was covering first base). Ed Kranepool then harmlessly popped out to Oriole shortstop Mark Belanger. Jerry Grote was the next Met batter. He drew a walk from Palmer on five pitches. Bud Harrelson kept the rally going with a single to center field. Grote advanced to second base. Pitcher Gary Gentry, who batted .081 in the regular season—and had not gotten a hit in his previous 27 at-bats—stepped to the plate. He slashed a double into right-center field alley, well over the head of outfielder Paul

Blair who was understandably playing Gentry quite shallow. It rolled to the wall. Both Met baserunners crossed the plate. The two RBI on one stroke of the bat doubled Gentry's seasonal output. The home team now led 3–0, much to the delight of the boisterous crowd. Baltimore pitching coach George Bamberger decided to have a chat with Jim Palmer, but he let him remain in the game. Palmer responded by coaxing Agee to ground out to Brooks Robinson at third base to retire the side.

Baltimore did nothing in the top of the third inning. Mark Belanger grounded out to Bud Harrelson; the Met shortstop made a fine play to retire his counterpart. Jim Palmer popped out to Ed Kranepool in foul ground. (Kranepool and catcher Jerry Grote, each seemingly unaware of the other's presence, lunged simultaneously for the ball near the Mets' dugout. The taller and better positioned Kranepool made the catch.) Another pop-up, this time by leadoff hitter Don Buford, was caught in foul territory beyond third base by Harrelson. Baltimore's offense, which had been largely held in check for the first two World Series games, was again noticeably sputtering in Game #3.

Jim Palmer continued to find control to be an elusive entity. He walked Wayne Garrett to start the home half of the third inning. Coach Bamberger again entered the field to attempt to get Palmer focused. Palmer responded well. He struck out Cleon Jones swinging for the first out of the frame. With Art Shamsky batting, the Mets tried a hit-and-run play. Garrett ran and Shamsky grounded to Powell. Powell had no chance to retire Garrett at second base, so he took the simple out at first base. Garrett was left stranded at second base when Ken Boswell flied out to Frank Robinson in right field for the inning's third out.

The Orioles mounted a threat in the top of the fourth inning. Gentry struck out Paul Blair on a slider that froze him. Frank Robinson finally got his first hit of the Fall Classic. He singled to left field in front of Cleon Jones who attempted to make a sprawling catch. Many Met fans thought Jones had made the catch as a roar rose from the spectators. However, left-field umpire Hank Soar was positioned well on the play; he clearly saw the ball bounce in front of—and then into—Jones' glove. Soar quickly and correctly gave the palms-down signal to indicate no catch. Boog Powell then singled into right field, moving Robinson over to third base with just one out. A worried murmur crept across Shea Stadium. Gentry responded by promptly whiffing Brooks Robinson for the second out of the inning. Robinson was overpowered by Gentry's fastballs in his unproductive at-bat.

Elrod Hendricks was the next Oriole batter. With Hendricks batting left, Met center fielder Tommie Agee had shifted toward right-center field in anticipation of the ball being pulled. Hendricks crossed him up by hitting a drive into center field. (On the radio Bill O'Donnell called it a "wind-blown fly ball."[5]) Agee had to run madly, changing directions slightly along the way. But he got to the ball—just barely—with a backhanded stab in front of the 396-foot sign on the outfield wall. There was also the real danger of Agee slamming into the wall and jarring the ball loose. However, Agee used his bare hand to brace himself for a softer impact. It was a classic snow-cone catch with the ball partially sticking out of Agee's glove. "The ball landed in the webbing; it almost got through,"[6] Agee would later tell the media. "What a grab by Agee!"[7] shouted Curt Gowdy as the crowd erupted with cheers. With both Baltimore baserunners on the move, the New York center fielder had surely saved two runs. The score was still 3–0 in favor of the Mets as Agee and company trotted off the field to their dugout to riotous applause.

As the wind picked up to start the bottom of the fourth inning, Ed Kranepool led off for the home team and flied out to Frank Robinson who was the busiest Oriole outfielder by far. Jerry Grote then grounded out to Dave Johnson at second base. As Bud Harrelson walked to the left-side batter's box, the wind increased noticeably, blowing dirt around the infield, especially near home plate. Harrelson drew a walk from Jim Palmer. With Gary Gentry batting, Harrelson took a big lead off first base and drew a pickoff throw from Palmer. The toss eluded Boog Powell at first base. Powell attempted to chase the loose ball as Harrelson tried to advance to second base. The two men became entangled well off first base. Plate umpire Larry Napp immediately called obstruction on Powell and awarded Harrelson second base. (Napp's call was correct: A defensive player cannot impede a baserunner's attempted advancement in any way, even accidentally, if he does not possess the ball.) Catcher Elrod Hendricks was livid. He began an argument with Napp as did manager Earl Weaver. The Baltimore manager was of the opinion that Harrelson and his burly first baseman were equally at fault. Napp was unmoved and Harrelson trotted down to second base. Palmer was charged with an error for the bad throw. Nothing came of Harrelson being in scoring position, however, as Gentry struck out swinging to end the bottom of the fourth inning.

The Orioles endured another quiet inning in the top of the fifth. Dave Johnson, who batted .280 in the regular season but had not yet managed a hit in the World Series, grounded out to shortstop Bud Harrelson, as did Mark Belanger, as did Jim Palmer. Of the three assists that Harrelson recorded, the one on Johnson was the most eye-catching. Baltimore's offense was unexpectedly being stifled for the second consecutive game. They did not look like the second-highest scoring team in the AL.

Tommie Agee started the bottom of the fifth inning by lining out to shortstop Mark Belanger who caught the ball just above his shoes. Wayne Garrett drew his second walk of the game off Palmer on just four pitches. Cleon Jones made the second out of the frame by flying out to Frank Robinson in right field. Art Shamsky, the birthday boy, grounded out weakly to Dave Johnson to conclude the inning.

The top of the sixth inning saw Don Buford go down swinging followed shortly thereafter by Paul Blair popping up to the shortstop. Frank Robinson walked on four Gary Gentry pitches to extend the inning. Boog Powell singled to right field sending teammate Robinson to third base. Brooks Robinson failed to drive anyone home when he flied out to Art Shamsky in right field. The Mets retained their 3–0 lead. It appeared to be a solid one.

The Mets opened the bottom of the sixth inning with an unusual infield hit by Ken Boswell. The ball bounced past a lunging Boog Powell who moved well off first base in an attempt to field it. The ball was fielded by second baseman Dave Johnson who covered plenty of ground to get it. Johnson's throw to pitcher Jim Palmer covering the bag was just a smidgen high. Palmer's foot came off the bag as he reached for the ball. Palmer never did regain control of the ball and the base simultaneously. First-base umpire Shag Crawford decisively ruled Boswell safe. (First-base coach Yogi Berra had also helpfully made the safe sign.) It was the correct decision; no Oriole complained about the call.

The action had to be paused before Ed Kranepool could bat. A contraption, somewhere between a kite and an airplane, bearing a pro–Mets banner descended to field level. It crashed near the Baltimore dugout as the hometown fans cheered the brief diversion. "Such sights are not unusual at Shea Stadium,"[8] Lindsey Nelson calmly informed NBC's viewing audience.

When play resumed, Kranepool hit a slow roller to second baseman Dave Johnson. Kranepool was retired at first base, but Boswell moved to second base on the out. Catcher Jerry Grote tagged a hanging curve ball from Jim Palmer to left field, just inside the foul line. His double scored Boswell. The feisty Mets now led 4–0. No further damage occurred as Bud Harrelson was called out on strikes and Gary Gentry struck out swinging.

Before the top of the seventh inning began, Tony Kubek interviewed Nelson Rockefeller, a passionate Mets fan who was also the governor of New York state. Rockefeller erred in calling Kubek "Tommy," but he was wholly correct in saying how much the Mets had unified New York with their remarkable season. He also praised the batting exploits of Tommie Agee and Gary Gentry thus far in Game #3.

Elrod Hendricks flied out to Tommie Agee to begin the Orioles' seventh inning. Dave Johnson also flied out to Agee. This putout was a bit of an adventure, though. Agee slipped for a moment in pursuing the routine fly ball. The crowd gasped, but Agee still had ample time to regain his footing and make the catch for the second out of the inning. As in the top of the fourth inning and the top of the sixth, the Orioles mounted a charge. Mark Belanger drew a walk off Gary Gentry. Earl Weaver opted to pinch hit for Palmer with Dave May. Gentry fell behind 2–0 to May, prompting a visit from Mets pitching coach Rube Walker. Walker failed to settle Gentry down. May walked, advancing Belanger to second base. Gentry then walked Don Buford, loading the bases. That was the end of the line for Gentry. Manager Gil Hodges took the ball from him and summoned Nolan Ryan from the bullpen.

Ryan, a 22-year-old smoke-thrower from Alvin, Texas, had been the winning pitcher in the Mets' pennant-clinching game versus Atlanta in the NLCS. Lindsey Nelson noted that Ryan had been blessed with a tremendous fastball from the day he joined the Mets, but he had become more dominating after he developed a breaking ball as a second weapon to keep opposing batters guessing. Paul Blair was the next Oriole batter. Ryan quickly got ahead of him 0–2. Instead of wasting a pitch, Ryan challenged Blair. Blair timed a Ryan fastball and launched it into right-center field. Tommie Agee, already with one spectacular catch in the game, sped to his left and made another dazzling play, spearing the ball just below knee level as he sprawled to the ground.

"Tommie Agee has made two outstanding, fabulous catches,"[9] gushed Bill O'Donnell once NBC radio returned from a commercial break.

On the television broadcast, Curt Gowdy commented that Agee's two sparkling defensive plays may have prevented five Baltimore runners from scoring. Earl Weaver agreed. Later the Baltimore skipper would tell reporters, "If Agee had an ingrown toenail, we've got five runs. No center fielder in the American League came up with two catches like that in one game all season."[10] Agee got a deserved standing ovation as he left the field. "Words can't describe how that made me feel,"[11] Agee later confessed about the crowd's response.

Afterward Agee said, "I thought right from the start I could catch [the ball hit by Blair]. The wind was blowing, and as I got to the ball it changed, causing the ball to sink. So I had to dive for it."[12] Although Agee was sure he was going to make the catch, there were many doubters. In the Mets bullpen, coach Joe Pignatano was highly skeptical. He later told reporters, "When I saw the look on [Agee's] face, I thought he was going to miss it. I don't think that he knew himself that he caught the ball."[13]

Dave Leonhard, a 28-year-old right-hander, replaced Jim Palmer on the mound for Baltimore. Tommie Agee led off the bottom of the seventh and got another standing ovation from the crowd when he

Tommy Agee led the Mets in home runs (26) and RBI (76) during the 1969 regular season, but his two game-saving catches in Game #3 are the reason he is most remembered. Agee belted a leadoff home run in the same game and was the only Met who stole a base during the five-game World Series (National Baseball Hall of Fame and Museum, Cooperstown, NY).

was introduced. Agee drew a base on balls. Wayne Garrett laid down a sacrifice bunt that Leonhard fielded. Garrett was retired at first base as Agee moved to second base. Agee advanced no farther. Cleon Jones flied out to Frank Robinson in right field and Art Shamsky flied out to Don Buford in left field.

New York made two defensive substitutions before the start of the top of the eighth inning. Both were designed to put better glove men in the Met lineup. Al Weis replaced Ken Boswell at second base. Rod Gaspar took over in right field from Art Shamsky. (Weis was slotted into Shamsky's number-four spot in the batting order. Gaspar took Boswell's number-five spot.) Frank Robinson drove a Nolan Ryan pitch to deep center field, but it was hauled in by the omnipresent Tommie Agee. Boog Powell watched a third strike sail into catcher Jerry Grote's mitt. It was a knee-high fastball that looked to have painted the outside corner. Nevertheless, Powell did not like Larry Napp's call and barked at the plate umpire. Brooks Robinson, having a poor day at the plate, struck out swinging. It was his second time striking out in Game #3. Once again, the Orioles had failed to make a dent in the Mets' four-run lead.

Dave Leonhard was still the Baltimore pitcher in the bottom of the eighth inning. Rod Gaspar led off. He quietly flied out to Don Buford in left field. Ed Kranepool did much better. He followed with a home run to dead center field that Paul Blair could only watch sail over his head. A smile graced Kranepool's face as he circled the bases. Jane Jarvis happily played another chorus of "Let's Go Mets" on the Shea Stadium organ. The solo home run extended the Mets' lead to a secure 5–0.

The inning continued with Jerry Grote flying out to Frank Robinson. It was Robinson's seventh putout of the game. That tied a single-game World Series record for right fielders. Bud Harrelson ended the home half of the eighth by striking out swinging.

The Orioles were down to their final three outs. Nolan Ryan got Elrod Hendricks to fly out to Rod Gaspar in right field. Dave Johnson also hit a fly ball directly to Gaspar who did not have to move more than a step to make the catch. With only one out left, Baltimore showed they still possessed a bit of fight. Mark Belanger walked. Pinch-hitter Clay Dalrymple batted for pitcher Leonhard. He reached first base on a hit that Al Weis dived to corral behind second base. Weis had no play anywhere, however. Manager Earl Weaver sent in pinch-runner Chico Salmon to run for Dalrymple. With runners on second and first base, Don Buford hit a long fly ball down the left-field line that veered out of play as it approached the foul pole. Buford eventually drew a walk too. Courtesy of two walks and a hit that never left the infield, the bases were full of Orioles.

Gil Hodges trudged to the mound to check on Ryan's confidence level. He was satisfied to let Ryan continue with the five-run lead. "I just told [Ryan] there was nothing to be concerned about," Hodges said afterward. "I had no intention of taking him out in that spot."[14] Ryan proceeded to freeze Paul Blair on a looping curve ball that bent over the plate to get a called third strike. The game was over. Ryan picked up the save in the 5–0 New York victory in Game #3. Nolan Ryan would pitch in the major leagues until 1993, setting fabulous lifetime records for strikeouts and no-hitters, but his 2⅓ innings of shutout relief on Tuesday, October 14, 1969, constituted his only career World Series appearance.

Game #3 was played at the same swift pace as the opening two games in Baltimore were. Its length was two hours and 23 minutes. Baltimore only managed four hits all game—and each one was a puny single. The Orioles did draw seven walks, but they left 11 runners stranded on base. Second baseman Dave Johnson was still looking for his first World Series hit, having failed to connect in eight at-bats so far. The two leading RBI men in the Series thus far, each with two, were unlikely ones to be sure: the light-hitting Al Weis and the even-lighter hitting Gary Gentry.

Tommie Agee had endured an awful 0-for-34 batting slump and the wrath of the New York fans during the 1968 season. "I felt like jumping off a bridge,"[15] Agee recalled about those difficult days from the previous season. Those troubles were ancient history in the aftermath of Game #3, however, as Agee was suddenly the toast of New York City and beyond. The Associated Press sang the praises of the Met center fielder in one of its detailed game reports. "Move over Al Gionfriddo, Willie Mays and Sandy Amoros," Jack Hand's report began. "Make room for Tommie Agee who saved five runs for the New York Mets Tuesday afternoon with two of the greatest catches ever made in World Series play."[16]

Those allusions put Agee in fine company. Gionfriddo of the Brooklyn Dodgers had made a fine catch to rob Joe DiMaggio of an extra-base hit in the 1947 World Series. Mays of the New York Giants had outrun and hauled in Vic Wertz' massive 460-foot blast to the deepest reaches of the Polo Grounds in the opener of the 1954 Fall Classic. The following season Amoros, another Dodger, had run seemingly forever to corral Yogi Berra's dangerous fly ball in the deciding game of the 1955 World Series and turned it into a rally-killing double play. Were Agee's catches comparable? Gil Hodges, who witnessed two of the others up close from field level thought so, especially his first catch, off the bat of Elrod Hendricks. "It was better than Gionfriddo's and as good as Amaros's,"[17] according to the Mets manager.

Jack Hugerich, the sports editor of the *Schenectady Gazette*, concurred. "[Agee] guarded center field like a store detective,"[18] he wrote. Hugerich rated Agee's second catch to be the better of the two. A correspondent from United Press International declared, "There is little doubt both grabs will go down as among the best in Series history."[19]

Perhaps the best comment about Agee's defensive wizardry came from NBC's Joe Garagiola. He told Agee after the game, "You caught everything in the air today but the helicopter."[20]

It is almost impossible to understate the importance of Agee's defensive wizardry in Game #3. A Baltimore victory would have given the Orioles a 2–1 advantage in games and they would have seized the momentum of the 1969 World Series on that Tuesday afternoon—a World Series they were supposed to win handily. A Baltimore win in any game at Shea Stadium would have deprived the Mets from any opportunity of winning the Series at home. Instead, Agee's two stellar catches prevented five Oriole runs, and the Mets won Game #3 by a shutout to assume a 2–1 lead themselves. One can only speculate about what might have happened in the remainder of the World Series if either of those balls had fallen to the turf instead of Agee's outstretched glove. Clearly the Met center fielder was pivotal in keeping the momentum firmly on the side of the underdog New Yorkers instead of the favored Baltimore Orioles.

Somewhat ungenerously, Paul Blair downplayed the excellence of Agee's snags. He basically accused Agee of showboating, especially on the second one. "Great catches?" he said with an incredulous tone when asked by reporters about them. "Hell, I know he timed mine. The ball wasn't hit that hard; he should have had it easily. When he dove, I thought maybe he slipped."[21]

Baltimore manager Earl Weaver was considerably more magnanimous on the subject of Agee's defense than his own center fielder was. "I've always said [Agee] can play center field,"[22] noting that Agee had first caught his attention when he was playing in the low minors. Weaver also praised the pitching of Gary Gentry. "Gentry is a lot better than I thought he was. He throws harder than their first two starters [Seaver and Koosman]."[23]

With the Mets now holding an unexpected 2–1 edge in the Series, the betting odds in Las Vegas shifted to 6–5 in favor of the NL champions. Tough, unflattering questions were starting to be asked about the AL pennant holders who had won 109 games in the regular season. The mighty Orioles had only managed to score five runs and get 12 hits in the first three games versus New York. Had Baltimore been overrated by the baseball pundits? Gary Gentry, basking in his first World Series win, put a swift stop to that discussion. "I think the Orioles are as close to a perfect ball club as they can be," he politely insisted. "They have everything. But luck has a lot to do with winning ball games. We had the luck."[24]

When a reporter slyly asked Gentry if his two-run double off Jim Palmer in the second inning was part of the luck he had just mentioned, the winning pitcher gave his reply without saying a word: He burst out laughing.

The bottom line from Game #3 was that the 1969 Mets were surely for real and bore little resemblance to their bungling forebears. "Stress the superlatives— amazing, incredible, implausible, magical, phenomenal—all fit the New York Mets," wrote Lawrence M. Stolle in the *Youngstown Vindicator*. "One has to become a believer after watching Gil Hodges' 'Destiny's Darlings' take a 2–1 lead in the World Series."[25]

"We just picked up some more non-believers," Hodges gleefully proclaimed in the boisterous home team's clubhouse. "Somebody must be rooting for us to win [the Series] after seeing what we did in this one." Hodges was not one to count his chickens in advance, but he did say he liked the Mets' chances in the next two games, but not in so many words. "With Seaver and Koosman all set, I couldn't plan for anything better," he told the press. "I'd have to say we're in good shape."[26]

Years later Frank Robinson said, "I thought the third game of the Series was the most important. We had Palmer going against Gentry. I didn't even think about losing. It was the perfect matchup for us."[27]

Columnist Jim Murray of the *Los Angeles Times* figured the Mets were benefiting from the "superiority complex" that, he said, naturally came along with being a New Yorker or an athlete that played for a New York–based team. He opined, "There are probably only a handful of Mets fans who even know which direction Maryland is. If you can't get there on a token, why should you want to go there?" Murray wrote that stats do not discourage the Mets nor their rabid fans. "[The Mets] came into this World Series with a team that can't hit as well, field as well, and scored fewer runs [than the Orioles]. They scored 147 fewer runs than that funny little team from Maryland, wherever that is. They struck out 265 more times and hit almost 70 fewer home runs. No matter. It says 'New York' on their suits, right? All right, run those other bums out of here. Back to the sticks, bushers!"[28]

1969 World Series, Game #3

Baltimore Orioles 0, New York Mets 5
Game played on Tuesday, October 14, 1969, at Shea Stadium

Baltimore Orioles	ab	r	h	rbi	New York Mets	ab	r	h	rbi
Buford lf	3	0	0	0	Agee cf	3	1	1	1
Blair cf	5	0	0	0	Garrett 3b	1	0	0	0
Robinson F. rf	2	0	1	0	Jones lf	4	0	0	0
Powell 1b	4	0	2	0	Shamsky rf	4	0	0	0
Robinson B. 3b	4	0	0	0	Weis 2b	0	0	0	0
Hendricks c	4	0	0	0	Boswell 2b	3	1	1	0
Johnson 2b	4	0	0	0	Gaspar rf	1	0	0	0
Belanger ss	2	0	0	0	Kranepool 1b	4	1	1	1
Palmer p	2	0	0	0	Grote c	3	1	1	1
May ph	0	0	0	0	Harrelson ss	3	1	1	0
Leonhard p	0	0	0	0	Gentry p	3	0	1	2
Dalrymple ph	1	0	1	0	Ryan p	0	0	0	0
Salmon pr	0	0	0	0	**Totals**	29	5	6	5
Totals	31	0	4	0					

```
Baltimore   0  0  0    0  0  0    0  0  0  –  0  4  1
New York    1  2  0    0  0  1    0  1  x  –  5  6  0
```

Baltimore Orioles	IP	H	R	ER	BB	SO
Palmer L (0–1)	6.0	5	4	4	4	5
Leonhard	2.0	1	1	1	1	1
Totals	**8.0**	**6**	**5**	**5**	**5**	**6**

New York Mets	IP	H	R	ER	BB	SO
Gentry W (1–0)	6.2	3	0	0	5	4
Ryan SV (1)	2.1	1	0	0	2	3
Totals	**9.0**	**4**	**0**	**0**	**7**	**7**

E—Palmer (1). **2B**—New York Gentry (1, off Palmer); Grote (1, off Palmer). **HR**—New York Agee (1, 1st inning off Palmer 0 on, 0 out); Kranepool (1, 8th inning off Leonhard 0 on, 1 out). **SH**—Garrett (1, off Leonhard). **U**—Larry Napp (AL), Shag Crawford (NL), Lou DiMuro (AL), Lee Weyer (NL), Frank Secory (NL), Hank Soar (AL). **T**—2:23. **A**—56,335.

World Series Game #4

The Ejection, the Catch and the Bunt

"For seven long and ghastly years [the Mets] had been beating themselves. The balls bounced wrong for them and the breaks invariably went to the other team. But this season they were hearing for the first time the moan that complaining losers fired at them: 'the lucky stiffs.' Now it appears the Mets may be starting to have a similar effect on the powerhouse Baltimore Orioles..."[1]—*New York Times* baseball columnist Arthur Daley

"In the third inning they threw the Baltimore Orioles' manager out of the game. He will shortly be followed by the rest of the team, it appears."[2]—Jim Murray, *Los Angeles Times* sports columnist

Date: Wednesday, October 15, 1969
Site: Shea Stadium, Borough of Queens, New York City

Politics, the Vietnam War, the meaning of patriotism in America, and sports all clashed on October 15, 1969. That Wednesday had been declared Vietnam Moratorium Day by antiwar advocates and was observed by thousands of people in the United States. Those who sought an immediate end to hostilities in southeast Asia insisted on flying the American flag at half-staff as a form of protest and to mourn the 40,000 American servicemen who had died in the war thus far. In contrast, veterans' groups, Boy Scout troops, and assorted counter-protesters showed their opposition to Vietnam Moratorium Day and their support of President Nixon's policies by making a point of flying the flag at full-staff as usual and engaging in various patriotic activities. The profound difference of opinion spilled over to Game #4 of the World Series.

New York City mayor John Lindsay had ordered the American flag to be flown at half-staff at all public buildings—including Shea Stadium. However, Mayor Lindsay had not figured on the reaction of the military commander in charge of a color guard that was to parade the flag before that day's World Series game. Under no circumstances would he permit his men to parade with the Stars and Stripes at half-staff. Baseball Commissioner Bowie Kuhn, after consulting with both the military and the mayor's office, ordered the flags at Shea Stadium to be flown at full-staff. Kuhn later said Lindsay allowed him to make whatever decision he thought "would most allow respect and quiet" in the ballpark. "There were no protests on the field from moratorium supporters," declared the Associated Press. "Some dark armbands and buttons were seen in the crowd, but there were no demonstrations."[3] About 200 antiwar activists carried placards outside Shea Stadium. One was obviously a Mets fan. His sign read, "Bomb the Orioles not the peasants!"

The temperature at Shea Stadium for Game #4 was "topcoat weather,"[4] according to Jim Simpson on NBC radio. It was 57 degrees when Tom Seaver threw the first pitch of the game to Don Buford shortly past 1 p.m. Screen and stage star Gordon MacRae sang the national anthem. Before breaking into song, MacRae addressed the crowd and made a veiled reference to Steve Lawrence's rendition being drowned out by the brass band the previous day. MacRae acknowledged he was going to perform *a capella*, but he encouraged the fans at Shea to sing along with him. Many did.

Casey Stengel, prominently wearing a World Series VIP ribbon, threw out the ceremonial first pitch from the commissioner's box with an exaggerated windup followed by a gentle left-handed toss to Mets catcher Jerry Grote. Stengel was a good choice for the honor. He, of course, had been the manager of the Mets from 1962 to 1965. He had also been a World Series hero both as a manager with the New York Yankees, but also as a player with the New York Giants. Stengel had hit two home runs against the Yankees in the 1923 World Series—including a game-winning, inside-the-park round-tripper at Yankee Stadium in Game #1. No player other than Stengel has ever managed that same feat.

Both teams' managers opted to use their Game #1 pitchers a second time in the Series rather than give the ball to their usual fourth starters from the regular season. Thus Tom Phoebus (who won 14 games and lost seven in 33 starts for Baltimore in 1969) and Don Cardwell (who had a record of 8–10 in 21 starts for the Mets) were both bypassed. With New York facing the left-handed Mike Cuellar for the second time in the World Series, Mets manager Gil Hodges went back to his Game #1 lineup that was heavily laden with right-handed hitters. Henry C. (Shag) Crawford of the National League, whom *Sports Illustrated* called "our favorite umpire"[5] in a 1956 issue because of his unceasing hustle on the diamond, was behind the plate. He would become the center of attention on more than one occasion during this memorable game.

With the pitching matchup a rematch of Game #1 in Baltimore—Tom Seaver versus Mike Cuellar—there was ample opportunity to speculate if the outcome would change this time. During the NBC-TV pregame show, Sandy Koufax predicted Seaver would bounce back from the loss in the opening game and have a dominant outing. On NBC radio, Bill O'Donnell suggested that Cuellar, a Cuban, might be uncomfortable in the cool New York City weather. Accordingly,

O'Donnell thought Cuellar might not do as well as he had in the World Series opener in balmy Baltimore four days before.

"The first thing I noticed when I went to warm up before the fourth game of the Series was that the bullpen was in the shade and the pitching mound on the playing field was in the sun," Seaver later wrote. "I would have preferred both exactly the same, but if there had to be a difference, I was glad that I'd be moving from the cooler spot to the warmer, an easier adjustment than the opposite."[6]

Don Buford had homered to start the Orioles first inning in the first game, but he went down swinging against Seaver in Game #4. Paul Blair came up next and lashed a single to center field. Frank Robinson was predictably booed when he stepped into the batter's box. He responded by hitting a long drive to center field that was chased down and caught by Tommie Agee a couple of feet from the wall. Boog Powell was called out on strikes by umpire Crawford. Seaver looked composed and confident as he walked off the mound. Unlike in Game #1, this time he was not trailing after his first inning of work.

Play in the bottom of the first inning was delayed for a few moments while Oriole left fielder Don Buford was tended to by the Baltimore trainer Ralph Salvon. Buford seemed to be favoring his right leg. With umpire Crawford closely observing the goings-on in the Baltimore dugout, it was decided that Buford was fit to continue. He trotted out to his position in left field.

The first Met batter of the game was Tommie Agee. He received an especially large cheer for his all-around heroics in Game #3. Agee did nothing wonderful in his at-bat, grounding out to Brooks Robinson at third base. Bud Harrelson, after bunting one pitch foul, lined a single into left field. Like the Orioles, the Mets' second batter of the game had reached first base on a base hit. His stay there was brief as Cleon Jones hit into a 6–4–3 double play to end the inning. "The Oriole infield doubles its pleasure to wrap up the home half of the first inning!"[7] declared Bill O'Donnell with a phrase he commonly used. Mike Cuellar appeared to be in fine form too.

Brooks Robinson led off the top of the second inning by grounding out to shortstop Bud Harrelson. Catcher Elrod Hendricks worked Seaver for a walk after falling behind 1–2 in the count. The next Oriole batter, Dave Johnson, hit a high, bounding ball to Bud Harrelson, the Met shortstop. Harrelson threw to second baseman Al Weis to force out the sliding Hendricks. There was no time to turn a double play, though. Johnson was easily safe at first base on the fielder's choice. Mark Belanger was the next Oriole batter. Bill O'Donnell told his listeners that Belanger had markedly improved his batting average from 1968. After hitting a long foul ball near the left-field foul line, Belanger took a high, inside pitch as Johnson broke for second base on an attempted steal. Jerry Grote, who possessed one of the best arms in the NL, made an excellent throw to Harrelson. The throw was a bit high, but Johnson was still out by a considerable margin. Umpire Lee Weyer emphatically made the appropriate signal with his right fist.

Donn Clendenon led off the bottom of the second inning for New York. He was the only Met to get two hits off Cuellar in Game #1. Cuellar got ahead of the Met first baseman 0–2, but the Baltimore left-hander faltered. With the count at 2–2, Cuellar threw a pitch that he thought caught the inside corner. Umpire Crawford called it a ball. Clendenon homered on the next pitch, the ball falling deep into the Orioles bullpen in left field. That was a rare sight for Met fans to see at Shea Stadium. Since coming from Montreal in June, Clendenon had clouted 12 home runs, but only four of them had occurred at home. (Amusingly, Tom Seaver later wrote that he did not see Clendenon's homer give him a 1–0 cushion; he only heard the crowd's excited roar after the ball cleared the fence. Seaver had quietly slipped into the clubhouse during Clendenon's at-bat to get himself a soft drink.) "The home run smacked by Clendenon has really put this Met crowd alive,"[8] said O'Donnell, who also commented that Cuellar was not throwing as many screwballs as he had in Game #1. "The Mets are not supposed to be a hitting club,"[9] Jim Simpson said on the radio broadcast as he noted that the Mets had now outhomered the Orioles by a surprising 4:1 ratio. Cuellar retired the next two Mets without much difficulty. Ron Swoboda grounded out to shortstop Mark Belanger as did third baseman Ed Charles. Jerry Grote, who had two hits thus far in the Series, struck out looking.

The game took a bizarre and unexpected twist with Mark Belanger batting in the top of the third inning. Belanger took a borderline pitch on (or near) the outside corner for a called strike. The next thing television viewers saw was umpire Crawford marching steadfastly toward the Baltimore dugout to angrily confront a prominent heckler—Oriole manager Earl Weaver. Catcher Elrod Hendricks was yelling at Crawford too. Crawford turned around and Weaver followed him toward home plate. When Weaver elected to continue his griping, he was ejected for arguing balls and strikes. Weaver claimed he had followed Crawford back onto the field because he had not heard what the umpire had said to him.

"I told him to shut his damned mouth," Crawford bluntly told reporters after the game. (His comment was clearly audible on the NBC radio broadcast.) "If he didn't hear me, then his ears are as bad as he thinks my eyes are!"[10] "It's funny," Weaver told reporter Gordon Beard afterward, "but before the Series, Commissioner Kuhn told us at a meeting the umpires would bend over backwards to keep us in the game. He told us to inform our players, however, not to use profanity. I didn't use any profanity."[11]

Although Jim Simpson told his listeners that no one in the press box could remember a manager being ejected from a World Series game before, it had happened. In the days before instant information, it took until the eighth inning until a previous example was found by NBC's resident statistician, Alan Roth. He passed along a note to the network's radio and TV crews saying that Weaver was the first manager to be ejected from a World Series game since Charlie Grimm of the Chicago Cubs in Game #3 of the 1935 Series. ("How's this for research!"[12] exclaimed the impressed Simpson.) It was true, although there was a similar, more recent example. In the 1959 World Series, a coach—Chuck Dressen of the Los Angeles Dodgers—had been given the thumb in Game #6 by Umpire Ed Hurley for arguing balls and strikes. (Interestingly, Hurley was the first-base umpire in that game.) Further research found that Weaver was just the fifth player, coach or manager to be tossed from a Fall Classic contest.

After the game, Weaver explained the origin of his ejection. "I had hollered on a pitch to Clendenon just before he hit the homer in the second. Then when Crawford called the strike on Mark, I yelled, 'Hey, we want that pitch too!'"[13] The combative Weaver had been ejected four times during the 1969 regular season. Jim Simpson explained to the radio audience that Crawford, as a National League umpire, positioned himself

National League umpire Henry Charles (Shag) Crawford officiated more than 3,100 games over a 20-year career. The 1969 World Series was the third time (along with 1961 and 1963) that Crawford had worked the biggest games of the sport. His notable ejection of Earl Weaver in Game #4 was the first time anyone had been thumbed out of a Fall Classic since 1935 (National Baseball Hall of Fame and Museum, Cooperstown, NY).

on the inside corner of the plate and generally gave the pitcher the benefit of the doubt on anything close to the outside corner. AL umpires, said Simpson, tended to stand more directly over the catcher to call balls and strikes and were not so generous on borderline pitches.

With Weaver now residing in the visitors' clubhouse and third-base coach Billy Hunter now serving as Baltimore's manager, Mark Belanger continued his at-bat and singled into right field. Next up was pitcher Mike Cuellar. He squared around to bunt, then pulled the bat back and dropped a single into left field over the charging Met infielders. Belanger glided into second base. The Orioles had two runners on base with none out. Don Buford was the next Oriole to bat. Anticipating a bunt, New York first baseman Donn Clendenon was playing in front of first base. Buford hit a high chopper that the lanky Clendenon had to spear above his head. Clendenon threw to second base to force out Cuellar, but Belanger advanced to third base and Buford reached first base on the fielder's choice.

Next up was Paul Blair. He tried to score Belanger with a squeeze bunt but popped up the ball near the mound. Belanger froze at third base, fully expecting Seaver to catch the ball. Seaver instead deliberately let the ball fall to the right of the mound. He fielded it and threw to first base to retire Blair as Clendenon moved to second base. Blair was charged with an at-bat on the play; no sacrifice was given. Seaver's odd decision was a head-scratcher—and he knew it. Afterwards he told reporters, "If I had to do it over again, I'd catch it. I was thinking about a double play."[14] With two out and two Orioles in scoring position, Frank Robinson popped out to Clendenon in foul territory. Despite his mental error on Blair's bunt, Seaver had gotten himself out of trouble after allowing two Baltimore hits to start the inning. The Mets still led 1–0.

In the bottom of the third inning, Al Weis led off for New York and was generously credited with an infield hit when Brooks Robinson, playing well in, could not handle Weis' sharp grounder that struck his chest and rolled down his arm. He made no play to first base knowing his throw would not beat Weis there. Even some Mets fans loudly booed when the play was curiously scored as a hit rather than an error. Tom Seaver was up next. He struck out trying to bunt. Tommie Agee then singled to the alley in center field. Don Buford did an excellent job in getting to the ball quickly, preventing the lead runner, Weis, from advancing no farther than second base. The Baltimore bullpen sprung into action, but Bud Harrelson grounded out to Dave Johnson at second base who had to cover a lot of territory to his left to make the play. He barely retired Harrelson. The two Met baserunners advanced into scoring position with two out. The New York threat died when Cleon Jones grounded out to Brooks Robinson at third base. This time Robinson reverted to his usual fine defensive form to record the assist.

Baltimore went down quickly in the visitors' half of the fourth. Boog Powell grounded out to Al Weis at second base on a high chopper. Brooks Robinson fouled out to Ed Charles near the tarpaulin on the third-base side of the infield. Elrod Hendricks' ground ball to Donn Clendenon forced the Met first baseman to veer to his right and toss the ball to Seaver who was alertly covering the bag. Seaver stepped on the bag awkwardly with his right foot causing him to lose his balance slightly. Hendricks then accidentally stepped on Seaver's left foot, spiking his ankle and landing on his baby toe.

"I let out a little scream; I felt a sharp pain, and for a moment, I feared I might be seriously hurt, that I might not be able to continue pitching," Seaver wrote after the Series. Hendricks, for his part, was apologetic. "You all right?" he asked Seaver. "You okay?"

"I didn't say anything to him," Seaver continued. "I thought he might have been going after me, and I was angry. Hendricks probably didn't mean to spike me, but with the sudden pain and the tenseness of the situation, I wasn't about to be polite."[15]

Seaver's wound was examined by the Mets trainer Gus Mauch between innings. Hendricks' spikes had pierced Seaver's shoe and ripped the skin off the back of his ankle. Mauch swabbed the surface of the cut and covered it with a gauze pad while NBC's cameras looked in. (The Seaver-Hendricks collision was shown in slow motion when the broadcast resumed after a commercial break.) The toe was only bruised, but Seaver noted, "I was afraid it might bother my pitching more than the cut."[16] Seaver, who had spent $2,500 on game tickets for his family and friends, was not about to leave the game because of such a trivial matter.

Clendenon stuck out looking at a knee-high fastball in the top of the fourth inning. The last pitch was borderline on the outside edge of the plate. He did not like Shag Crawford's call. Ron Swoboda singled into center field on an 0–2 pitch. The Mets felt aggrieved by a non-call by Shag Crawford when Ed Charles batted. On the second pitch, the right-handed hitting Charles hit the deck when Cuellar's pitch veered inside. The ball ricocheted toward the Mets dugout. Crawford ruled it to be a foul ball while Charles maintained it had hit his hand first. (Charles stuck out his left pinkie for effect.) Trainer Gus Mauch—who was getting a lot more TV time than usual—and Gil Hodges both came onto the field to check on their third baseman's left hand. When Hodges calmly asked Crawford about the ruling, the umpire said the ball had hit the knob of Charles' bat before striking his hand, making the play a foul ball. With the crowd booing, Charles resumed his at bat and struck out on a play where Swoboda was caught stealing. Hendricks threw to Dave Johnson for the putout.

Seaver, showing no signs of discomfort from his collision with Hendricks in the fourth inning, promptly set down the Orioles with little difficulty in the top of the fifth inning. Dave Johnson popped out to Cleon Jones in shallow left field. Jones had to make a sprawling catch for the putout. Jones displayed the ball to left field umpire Frank Secory who signaled the out. "Cleon Jones has just made the fielding gem of this ballgame!"[17] exclaimed Bill O'Donnell on NBC radio, who described the putout as a "fabulous catch."[18] Mark Belanger attempted to bunt his way onto first base, but Grote alertly made the play to retire the Baltimore shortstop. Cuellar struck out, missing on three cuts. "Seaver's fastball is humming here in the top of the fifth inning,"[19] said O'Donnell. The Mets still led 1–0—and Baltimore had not scored a run in their last 16 innings. The first four batters in the Orioles lineup were a collective 7-for-52 thus far in the World Series.

Jerry Grote led off the home half of the fifth by whiffing, giving Mike Cuellar his fifth strikeout of the game. Al Weis continued his unexpected hot hitting. He knocked an 0–2 pitch from Cuellar into left field for his fourth hit of the World Series. Tom Seaver grounded to Mark Belanger who started a 6–4–3 double play to retire the Mets. It was the first time in 1969 that Seaver had hit into a twin killing.

The top of the sixth began with switch-hitting Don Buford (batting left-handed against the right-handed Tom Seaver) grounding to first baseman Donn Clendenon who flipped the ball to Seaver at the bag for the out. There was no collision this time. Paul Blair, who was 1-for-14 in the World Series thus far, drew a base on balls. It was Seaver's second walk of the game. The struggling Frank Robinson lofted a high pop-up to shortstop Bud Harrelson for the second out of the inning. With the Orioles searching for offense, Boog Powell was given the green light to swing away on a 3–0 pitch. He painfully fouled it off his right foot. Paul Blair was running on the next pitch, which Powell also fouled off. Powell eventually flied out to Tommie Agee in center field.

Agee led off the bottom of the sixth inning, swinging on Cuellar's first offering. He grounded out to Brooks Robinson at third base. Jim Simpson informed his NBC radio audience that it was the first time in the game that a Met batter swung at the first pitch. Bud Harrelson popped out to Dave Johnson for the second out. Cleon Jones, who had just one hit in the Series, grounded out to Belanger at shortstop as the Mets went down quietly.

Brooks Robinson, with just one hit in the Series, came up empty again by grounding out to Ed Charles at third base to start the top of the seventh inning. Elrod Hendricks grounded out to Harrelson. After mildly arguing a called second strike called by Shag Crawford, Dave Johnson struck out swinging. Johnson—who had finished third in the AL in doubles—had yet to register a single hit in the World Series. "Another perfect inning for Tom Seaver,"[20] noted Jim Simpson as the frame ended.

In the bottom of the seventh inning, Donn Clendenon hit an easy bouncer to Mike Cuellar who leisurely tossed the ball to Boog Powell for the first out. Ron Swoboda got his second hit of the game by lining Cuellar's first pitch into left field. Ed Charles lined out to Don Buford in left field. Cuellar threw to first base twice as Swoboda increased his lead. Grote grounded out to shortstop Mark Belanger who made the throw to first base for the third out.

Leading off the top of the eighth inning, Mark Belanger popped out to fellow shortstop Bud Harrelson. Acting Oriole manager Billy Hunter lifted Mike Cuellar for pinch-hitter Dave May who had batted .242 in the regular season. In the same role in Game #3, May had worked Nolan Ryan for a walk. Seaver struck him out. Don Buford, whose home run in the first inning of Game #1 was the Orioles' only extra-base hit thus far in the 1969 World Series, feebly popped out to third baseman Ed Charles. The Orioles had only managed three hits—all singles—off Seaver in the first eight innings. Their scoring drought had now been extended to 19 innings. The Met fans roared their approval as their team jogged off the field still holding a 1–0 edge.

In the bottom of the eighth inning, Eddie Watt, a 28-year-old right-handed pitcher from Iowa, took the mound for Baltimore. He shut down the Mets effectively. Al Weis flied out to Don Buford in left field. Tom Seaver got a standing ovation when he batted second in the inning, but he grounded out to Dave Johnson at second base. (Jim Simpson noted that Seaver did not expend very much energy in running to first base.) Tommie Agee followed Seaver. He struck out swinging.

Trailing 1–0, Baltimore needed a run to stay alive in the top of the ninth. It was not quite 3 p.m.; the swift-moving game was less than two hours old. Baltimore had been shut out eight times during the 1969 regular season, but never twice in a row—an outcome that was now staring the favored Orioles in the face. Paul Blair flied out to Ron Swoboda in left field to start the inning. (It was Swoboda's first putout of the game; it would not be his last.) Frank Robinson broke out of his batting funk by singling to left field. He was the first Oriole in 21 to get a hit off Seaver. Cleon Jones badly bobbled the ball, but Robinson cautiously did not attempt to go to second base. Boog Powell also came to life at the plate. He singled off Seaver to right field. Robinson advanced to third base on the hit. With one out and runners on the corners, the crowd at Shea Stadium grew tense and quiet. Gil Hodges came to the mound. Two Met relievers, Tug McGraw and Ron Taylor, were ready to come into the game if necessary, but Hodges left the ball in Seaver's capable right hand.

Another slumping Oriole—Brooks Robinson—came to bat. Curt Gowdy mentioned that Robinson had not hit the ball out of the infield in his three previous at-bats in Game #4. He did this time. On Seaver's first offering, Robinson drove a sinking fly ball into right-center field. Ron Swoboda made a spectacular running, diving catch inches off the outfield grass to take a hit away from the Baltimore third baseman. Swoboda rolled over once, held the ball up very briefly to indicate to the umpires that he had indeed made the catch, and threw it on target toward home plate despite having no real hope of beating Frank Robinson. (Robinson had smartly tagged up on the play; he raced home with the tying run.) Brooks Robinson was properly credited with a sacrifice fly for his plate appearance—although that was hardly his intention.

Incredibly, the two NBC play-by-play men calling Game #4 severely understated Swoboda's fabulous catch. Curt Gowdy merely said, "Swoboda comes up with it."[21] Jim Simpson, on the NBC radio call, gave it only a little more pizzazz, stating, "Swoboda makes the dive!"[22] Both Gowdy and Simpson seemed more focused on Frank Robinson scoring from third base than what had just occurred in right-center field. In recapping the play a few seconds later, however, Simpson upped it to "Swoboda made a tremendous catch. Had it gotten by him, Powell may have scored all the way from first base."[23] Gowdy added, "Swoboda making another sensational catch for the Mets!"[24] Neither truly comes close to doing justice to it. Four days after Swoboda had awkwardly misplayed Don Buford's home run in Game #1, he dramatically made a jaw-dropping defensive gem for the ages.

Mickey Mantle, who played in 18 regular seasons and 13 World Series as a New York Yankee, was working the 1969 Series as an analyst on NBC's pregame show (alongside Sandy Koufax). He commented to Jim Simpson the next day, "[That's] the best play I've ever seen in my life."[25]

In the next day's *Pittsburgh Press*, sports editor Roy McHugh accurately penned, "Swoboda, celebrated in Met folklore for his atrociously clumsy outfielding [*sic*], had kept the Mets from losing a game by hurling himself at a line drive and making a backhanded catch while parallel to the ground at an altitude of maybe six inches."[26]

In 2019, Ron Cassie of *Baltimore Magazine* wrote with wonderment,

> Watching clips of the game on YouTube a half-century later, it's still hard to believe Robinson's line drive does not hit the turf, skip off the warning track, and bounce to the fence. But out of nowhere, diving headlong into NBC's shot, comes Ron Swoboda, an outfielder nicknamed "Rocky" because of his less-than-smooth reputation with the glove, who proceeds to make what is possibly the greatest catch in World Series history. Certainly, it is the catch of his life—a full-speed, belly-up, lose-your-cap plunge across the Shea [Stadium] grass.[27]

"Oh, I remember the catch," Boog Powell said in Cassie's nostalgia piece. "I can see it like it happened yesterday. What I don't remember is how I reacted. I don't know if I stopped dead halfway between first and second or tried to get back to the bag. I was stunned. Mesmerized."[28]

One statistician, using modern day analytics to examine the catch, outlined his findings on a YouTube video. He calculated that Swoboda had to travel between 52 and 60 feet in 3.4 seconds to catch the sinking ball hit by Brooks Robinson. Based on inputting data on hundreds of MLB catches, the mathematician calculated that similar catches are only made somewhere between eight and 10 percent of the time. However, that does not include considerations for the dive or Swoboda's backhanded reach for it. Those two factors make the odds of a successful catch even longer, of course.

Perhaps the best play-by-play description of the catch is by Swoboda himself, doing it by heart, on a 2016 video, in which he employs the necessary hyperbole that was conspicuously absent in the real-time discourse from 1969. (Swoboda's monologue is amusing—and it can be seen on YouTube.) Swoboda does make one minor error in his commentary, however: He says there was nobody out when Brooks Robinson hit the ball. In truth, one Oriole had been retired before the Baltimore third baseman's plate appearance.

Swoboda himself likes to point out that when one watches the clip of his famous catch, something is missing: Center fielder Tommie Agee is not in the frame of the NBC television picture. He was basically in straight-away center field, thus Swoboda—despite the long run and subsequent dive—was the closest Met outfielder to the ball. After the game, knowing his reputation as a poor defensive player, Swoboda wittily chirped, "It's a little late for the Gold Glove Award."[29]

New York third baseman Ed Charles was not entirely certain that Robinson had properly tagged up at third base, however. When play resumed, he instructed Seaver to step off the rubber and throw the ball to him on an appeal play. Third base umpire Hank Soar gave the palms-down "safe" signal to indicate the tag-up had been valid. Although precious few spectators probably had their eyes on Robinson during that play, the partisan Met fans impulsively booed Soar's call, of course.

Frank Robinson's important run counted and the Orioles were on the scoreboard. Game #4 was now tied 1–1. It was now either team's contest to win.

With two men out and a Baltimore runner (Powell) on first base, Elrod Hendricks very nearly gave the Orioles a 3–1 lead. He slammed a 2–0 Seaver fastball high and long down the right-field line. It just veered to the right of the foul pole for a long strike. He eventually flied out routinely to the suddenly busy Swoboda, who made all the putouts in the dramatic inning. Long afterward, Seaver would write that the most memorable part of Game #4 to him was Hendricks' long foul ball.

The Mets tried their best to win the game in the bottom of the ninth. Watt was still on the mound for Baltimore. A ground ball by Bud Harrelson just eluded Watt's glove, but second baseman Dave Johnson fielded it. His throw beat Harrelson to the bag by a hair. Umpire Lou DiMuro correctly made the "out" call. Cleon Jones excited the home fans with a single to left field just beyond the reach of Brooks Robinson. Donn Clendenon failed to advance Jones; he struck out swinging. Defensive hero Ron Swoboda came up next and appeared to have flied out to Frank Robinson in right field. However, Robinson misjudged the ball off Swoboda's bat and moved backwards when he should have moved forward. By the time Robinson realized his error, the ball had fallen to the grass in front of him. Jones was running on the play and advanced to third base. The Mets had the game-winning run 90 feet from home. Gil Hodges sent up pinch-hitter Art Shamsky to bat for Ed Charles. Shamsky failed to come through, however. He grounded out routinely to Dave Johnson. After nine

Famous for his spectacular catch in Game #4, Baltimore-born Ron Swoboda also batted an impressive .400 during the 1969 World Series after having hit just .235 during the regular season. The 25-year-old Swoboda's average was second only to teammate Al Weis (National Baseball Hall of Fame and Museum, Cooperstown, NY).

innings, Game #4 was deadlocked 1–1. Extra innings would be needed to decide a World Series game for the first time since the Cardinals-Yankees tilt in 1964.

Seaver came out to pitch the tenth inning to great applause. He had already thrown 135 pitches, but few people paid much attention to that statistic in 1969. It did not merit a mention on either the NBC television or radio broadcasts.

Gil Hodges summoned Wayne Garrett, a good glove man, to play third base in the top of the tenth inning. He immediately drew action when Dave Johnson slammed a hard ground ball that caromed off his arm in rolled into foul territory. Johnson was standing on first base with nobody out. The play was initially scored as a hit, but upon further reflection it was later ruled to be an error. It was the first error committed by either team in Game #4. Another would come later.

With the score tied in extra innings, it was an obvious bunt situation. The next Baltimore hitter was Mark Belanger. He attempted to lay down a sacrifice, but he popped it up to catcher Jerry Grote in foul territory near home plate. Grote made the easy play for the first out of the inning. Pinch-hitter Clay Dalrymple batted for pitcher Eddie Watt. He singled to center field off the tiring Seaver. (That base hit gave the seldom-used Dalrymple a perfect 2-for-2 batting average in the 1969 World Series.) Johnson advanced to second base. Mets pitching coach Rube Walker came to the mound to assess Seaver's ability to continue. Seaver frankly told Walker he was tired but still had a few pitches left in his right arm. Walker was satisfied with the reply and left Seaver in the game. Don Buford, the next Oriole to bat, lofted a fly ball to deep right field. Swoboda drifted back and made the catch. Johnson advanced to third base with two out. Seaver coolly struck out Paul Blair swinging on a 1–2 breaking ball to end the Baltimore threat. Blair was slumping at the plate as badly as any Oriole.

The oldest player on either team's roster, 39-year-old Dick Hall, became the third Baltimore pitcher of the afternoon. Hall had begun his professional baseball career as a third baseman in the Pittsburgh Pirates' farm system in 1952. This was his first World Series appearance. On the NBC television broadcast, Lindsey Nelson amusingly declared Hall's quirky delivery to be akin to "a beach chair unfolding."[30]

Hall appeared to have things well under control as leadoff hitter Jerry Grote hit a lazy fly ball to left field; Grote's bat broke upon contact. But there was immediate trouble. Left fielder Don Buford lost the ball in the sun and retreated when he should have rushed forward. He hollered for help. Shortstop Mark Belanger scrambled from his position deeper and deeper into left field. With his back to the plate, Belanger lunged for the ball—and just missed. "I nearly had it,"[31] Belanger lamented afterward. It was thought by some journalists that the ball, in its descent, had actually ticked the edge of Belanger's glove before dropping to the outfield turf. After the game Belanger maintained it had not. Jack Hand of the Associated Press later commented, "Buford, Blair and Belanger could have shaken hands with one another as the ball fell in behind Belanger's outstretched glove."[32]

Some writers thought Buford was at fault for positioning himself far too deep in left field before the ball had been hit. Jim Murray of the *Los Angeles Times* was one such critic. He humorously declared, "[Buford] was on the outskirts of Waterbury when Grote came to bat. It would have been a drive and a three iron for Arnold Palmer."[33]

Grote, who had alertly hustled on the play, ended up sliding into second base with a fortuitous two-bagger. The Mets had the potential game-winning run in scoring position with nobody out.

The game quickly turned into a chess match. Gil Hodges sent in Rod Gaspar to pinch-run for the slower Grote. Al Weis, hitting in the eighth spot, was the next Met scheduled to bat. Acting Baltimore manager Billy Hunter forced Hodges to make a strategic decision of his own by signaling Hall to intentionally walk the New York second baseman. "Weis wasn't accustomed to being treated with such respect,"[34] Seaver later wrote understatedly in a book about Game #4. Hodges opted to replace Tom Seaver with a pinch-hitter, J.C. Martin. Hunter waited for Martin to be officially announced; he then countered by bringing left-hander Pete Richert from the bullpen to face Martin, who batted left.

In the Mets' NLCS victory over Atlanta, Martin had smacked a key two-run single in Game #1, but he was not permitted to swing freely versus Richert. With nobody out and two runners on base, Martin was ordered by Hodges to lay down a bunt with one restriction: He was to aim it far away from where Brooks Robinson might field it. A United Press International correspondent wrote, "Every one of the record 57,367 fans knew what was going to happen, and so did Richert—Martin was going to sacrifice."[35]

On Richert's first pitch, Martin dropped an excellent bunt along the first-base side of the diamond between Richert and catcher Elrod Hendricks. After the game Casey Stengel commented that Martin's bunt was so good it looked like he had placed it "with a pool cue."[36] Both Orioles charged for the ball—and both arrived at it almost at the same time. First baseman Boog Powell moved in on the play too.

"Richert got there about the same time as the catcher," said Martin in an interview 50 years later. "They may have had a bit of thing about who was going to take the ball."[37] Years later Richert admitted there was "some indecision" about whether he or Hendricks would make the play.

Although the catcher would later tell reporters, "I was calling for it all the way,"[38] Richert picked the ball up as Hendricks shied away from it. His throw, intended for second baseman Dave Johnson who was covering first base for Powell, smacked Martin on his left wrist. (Lindsey Nelson initially—and wrongly—told his television viewers that Martin had been struck on his back. On NBC radio, Bill O'Donnell reported that Martin had been hit on the leg.) The ball rolled "somewhere in the vicinity of second base," according to the esteemed Jim Murray. Gaspar scored quite easily on what was ruled a sacrifice bunt and a throwing error. Half a century later Gaspar remembered, "I hesitated a little bit until I turned and saw where the ball was, then I took off. I probably could have walked home."[39] New

A 25-game winner for the Mets in 1969, future Hall-of-Famer Tom Seaver was dominant in Game #4 of the World Series. Seaver tossed a masterful 10-inning, complete game in which he surrendered just six hits to the potent Orioles (National Baseball Hall of Fame and Museum, Cooperstown, NY).

York's third-base coach Eddie Yost, who had just had his 43rd birthday, told reporters, "I was running with [Gaspar]. I think I could have beat him to the plate I was so excited. But I stopped three-quarters of the way."[40] Fifty years later, Gaspar recalled that Tom Seaver was the first Met to rush onto the field to greet him after he crossed home plate with the game-winning run.

The Mets quickly emptied from the dugout to celebrate their thrilling 2–1 victory. "Good gosh, it was utopia!"[41] Martin remembered. Tom Seaver, who threw a 10-inning complete game, deservedly picked up his first World Series win. The tense, incident-filled, extra-inning game had taken two hours and 33 minutes to play.

With New York now ahead three games to one, even the most skeptical baseball fans were becoming believers in the 1969 Mets. The odds were now solidly against a Baltimore comeback in the Series. In Fall Classics that had been best-of-seven affairs, only three teams had rallied from a 3–1 deficit to win in seven games. Optimistic Oriole supporters could easily recall that the 1968 Detroit Tigers had achieved the feat just the previous October, however.

In describing his bunt just minutes later to reporters, Martin declared, "The pitch was in on me. I tried to bunt it to first to keep it away from [Brooks] Robinson. I don't even know who threw the ball, but he made a good play [fielding it] because the ball had backspin. I knew they had no play on the bases, so my job was to get to first base."[42] Martin happily showed his bruised wrist to reporters to pinpoint exactly where Richert's wayward throw towards first base had struck him.

"J.C. has been a valuable man all this year and all last year," Gil Hodges noted after the game. "He's done some other things that won ball games for us. He got a big hit in our first playoff game in Atlanta." Hodges added, "Is he a good bunter? I really don't know."[43]

Strangely, no one on the Orioles complained about how the game ended—at least initially. Replays of Richert's throw to first base seemed to indicate that Martin was running in fair territory instead of within the three-foot lane mandated by the rules for such a play. Martin could have—and probably should have—been called out for interference in accordance with Rule 6.05k. Here is what the *Official Rules of Baseball* says:

> A batter is out when ... in running the last half of the distance from home base to first base, while the ball is being fielded to first base, he runs outside (to the right of) the three-foot line, or inside (to the left of) the foul line, and in the umpire's judgment in so doing interferes with the fielder taking the throw at first base, in which case the ball is dead; except that he may run outside (to the right of) the three-foot line or inside (to the left of) the foul line to avoid a fielder attempting to field a batted ball.

On such a play, it is almost always the plate umpire's call as he has the best and clearest view of the entire baserunning lane. As former AL umpire Bill McKinley commented, "If the first-base umpire is watching first base as DiMuro is doing, it should be up to the plate umpire to make the call."[44]

Shag Crawford, by saying nothing, tacitly ruled that Martin had not violated the baserunning rule. Only after they had seen television replays and still photos of the incident long after the game was over did the visitors start to squawk about Crawford's non-call in earnest. The October 27 issue of *Sports Illustrated* had a dandy color photo of J.C. Martin being indisputably in fair territory while running toward first base.

Richert himself was one of the first Orioles to question the legality of Martin's baserunning on the play—albeit way too late. "I'd like to see the video replay," he said to reporters in the Baltimore clubhouse immediately after the game. "I don't know if Martin was inside the foul line while running towards first. I was trying to throw the ball inside the line." When told that his throw had struck Martin's left wrist, Richert tersely replied, "I hope it's broken." Upon later seeing the photographic evidence, Richert was furious. "[Crawford] didn't have guts enough to call the play in the first place and now he doesn't have enough to admit he blew it."[45]

A United Press International story that widely ran in the next day's newspapers across North America backed up Richert's assertion. It began, "One picture is worth—what? Pictures of J.C. Martin of the New York Mets racing towards first base in the 10th inning of Wednesday's 2–1 Met victory over the Baltimore Orioles show J.C. where he shouldn't be, according to the rules of baseball."[46]

During NBC's pregame show for Game #5, Jim Simpson, Sandy Koufax and Mickey Mantle all agreed that Martin had violated the baserunning rule, but each man said he had not noticed it until the controversy became a hot topic in the newspapers. Koufax stated, "I didn't see it yesterday; I don't know if anyone saw it yesterday. I just know that I'd hate to be the umpire that had to make that decision yesterday at Shea."[47]

Earl Weaver had basically said the same thing to reporters. "It's the plate umpire's call," said the ejected Oriole manager. "It's just like calling a ball or a strike. It takes a lot of guts to call it, but Martin appeared to be out of the [lane]." He then added. "Gee, I wish I had not seen the newspaper picture at all."[48]

In a 2019 *Newsday* interview about the play, several Orioles who were close to what happened when it happened were still perturbed about the lack of an interference call from the umpiring crew. "Martin definitely was inside that line," Dave Johnson stated without hesitation. "That's why I couldn't catch it. He definitely impeded the throw to me. To me, that's the home plate umpire and the first base umpire's call. They should know that."[49]

Pete Richert concurred with his second baseman. "Davey would have caught the ball for the out if I hadn't hit [Martin] on the wrist, which means he was inside. They blew the call—without a doubt."[50]

Boog Powell too could not understand how the critical call was missed by the umpires. He asked, "How could they not get that right? If it was a question of judgement, the umpires' judgement was screwed up."[51]

In that same *Newsday* interview, Jerry Crawford, Shag's son—who became a longtime MLB umpire himself—said his father did admit to him that the call had been missed.

Prior to Game #5, Commissioner Bowie Kuhn felt compelled to make a formal statement saying that such a play is totally a judgment call for an umpire. "It's not protestable," Kuhn noted. "The game is over."[52] Crawford himself explained that he thought Martin's right foot was on the baseline at the moment he was struck by Richert's throw, which, for the purpose of the rule, put him inside the lane. Crawford was mistaken.

Earl Weaver summarized the game in very simplistic terms. "They laid down a bunt. We didn't. I'm not blaming anyone for the loss."[53] With all the hullabaloo about the ejection, the bunt controversy, and Swoboda's catch, Weaver did not want the performance turned in by #41 of the Mets to be ignored or shortchanged by the reporters. To his credit he said, "Seaver pitched a real [*sic*] good ballgame. I hope he gets his name in the paper."[54]

New York City was now fully anticipating a Mets Series-clinching triumph in Game #5 the following day—and a raucous celebration at the venue and beyond.

"Now [the Mets] feel everything else will be anticlimactic. That they will win the world championship of baseball is a certainty,"[55] wrote Fred Girard of the *St. Petersburg Times*. An unnamed scribe from the Associated Press noted in his summary of Game #4, "The 57,367 fans, who set a new Shea Stadium attendance record, went home to make plans for dismantling the Flushing ballpark Thursday afternoon if their amazing Metzkies can win one more from the Orioles and close out their greatest year with a World Series success."[56]

Tom Seaver's photogenic wife, 24-year-old Nancy, sporting a jaunty pink tam, became a favorite of the NBC camera crew in the late innings—and the subject of a widely circulated Associated Press sidebar story to Game #4. She nervously agonized as the drama grew exponentially in both the ninth and tenth innings. In a postgame interview with Tony Kubek, Tom Seaver laughed at the attention his attractive blonde spouse was getting and agreed she was more jittery than he was during his pitching assignments. Once the final out was made, Nancy Seaver fell into the arms of a friend and cried. "I feel like I pitched the game myself,"[57] she told a reporter. After regaining her composure, and apparently a New York celebrity in her own right, she accommodated several fans' autograph requests. According to security personnel at Shea Stadium, they had been given special instructions to keep gawkers and autograph-seekers away from her box as much as possible during the game.

Seaver himself said it was the happiest day of his life, having wanted to win a World Series game since about the age of nine. He further stated he had never seen a team anything quite like the 1969 Mets before and he was proud in every way to be associated with them. When Tony Kubek asked him if he thought the World Series would return to Baltimore, Seaver chuckled and said he hoped not.

Down three games to one, the Orioles were now in deep trouble. When he could not identify which Met had scored the winning run, Frank Robinson was informed by a journalist that it was Rod Gaspar. Robinson did not need to be reminded that before the World Series he had dismissed Gaspar by saying "...whoever the hell he is."[58]

Cumulative offensive stats from the first four games proved that pitching was thoroughly dominating hitting in the 1969 World Series. The Mets were batting .220, while the Orioles' average was only .144.

Gil Hodges was asked by a reporter what he thought of his team's chances of winning the World Series now that they held a 3–1 advantage in games won. Always logical, Hodges coyly replied, "Much better than yesterday."[59] Hodges had cause for optimism: His team had not lost at Shea Stadium since Bob Moose no-hit the Mets on September 20—a home winning streak of eight games.

In the Mets' clubhouse, Seaver accepted congratulations from teammates and other members of the team's staff. "That was the real Seaver today," pitching coach Rube Walker informed him—within earshot of reporters. Seaver made a point of seeking out Jerry Koosman, New York's scheduled starter for Thursday afternoon's game. He wanted to give him some extra encouragement to pitch well in Game #5. "Wrap it up, tomorrow, Koos," Seaver implored. "I don't want to go back to Baltimore. That place makes Fresno look like Paris."[60]

"I will," Koosman assured his teammate. "I don't want to go back there either."[61]

Amidst the postgame tumult in the lively New York clubhouse, Seaver proudly spoke to Hal Bock of the Associated Press, "I'm a believer in this club," he said. "The way we've been playing for the last three games, in here are a lot of believers now. We're slowly making believers out of everybody."[62]

1969 World Series, Game #4

Baltimore Orioles 1, New York Mets 2
Game played on Wednesday, October 15, 1969, at Shea Stadium

Baltimore Orioles	ab	r	h	rbi	New York Mets	ab	r	h	rbi
Buford lf	5	0	0	0	Agee cf	4	0	1	0
Blair cf	4	0	1	0	Harrelson ss	4	0	1	0
Robinson F. rf	4	1	1	0	Jones lf	4	0	1	0
Powell 1b	4	0	1	0	Clendenon 1b	4	1	1	1
Robinson B. 3b	3	0	0	1	Swoboda rf	4	0	3	0
Hendricks c	3	0	0	0	Charles 3b	3	0	0	0
Johnson 2b	4	0	0	0	Shamsky ph	1	0	0	0
Belanger ss	4	0	1	0	Garrett 3b	0	0	0	0
Cuellar p	2	0	1	0	Grote c	4	0	1	0
May ph	1	0	0	0	Gaspar pr	0	1	0	0
Watt p	0	0	0	0	Weis 2b	3	0	2	0
Dalrymple ph	1	0	1	0	Seaver p	3	0	0	0
Hall p	0	0	0	0	Martin ph	0	0	0	0
Richert p	0	0	0	0	**Totals**	34	2	10	1
Totals	35	1	6	1					

```
Baltimore    0  0  0     0  0  0     0  0  1     0  –  1   6   1
New York     0  1  0     0  0  0     0  0  0     1  –  2  10   1
```

Baltimore Orioles	IP	H	R	ER	BB	SO
Cuellar	7.0	7	1	1	0	5
Watt	2.0	2	0	0	0	2
Hall L (0–1)	0.0	1	1	0	1	0
Richert	0.0	0	0	0	0	0
Totals	**9.0**	**10**	**2**	**1**	**1**	**7**

New York Mets	IP	H	R	ER	BB	SO
Seaver W (1–1)	10.0	6	1	1	2	6
Totals	**10.0**	**6**	**1**	**1**	**2**	**6**

E—Richert (1), Garrett (1). **DP**—Baltimore 3. **2B**—New York Grote (2, off Hall). **HR**—New York Clendenon (2, 2nd inning off Cuellar 0 on, 0 out). **SF**—B Robinson (1, off Seaver). **SH**—Martin (1, off Richert). **IBB**—Weis (2, by Hall). **CS**—Johnson (1, 2nd base by Seaver/Grote); Swoboda (1, 2nd base by Cuellar/Hendricks). **IBB**—Hall (1, Weis). **U**—Shag Crawford (NL), Lou DiMuro (AL), Lee Weyer (NL), Hank Soar (AL), Larry Napp (AL), Frank Secory (NL). **T**—2:33. **A**—57,367.

11

World Series Game #5

Shoe Polish and Sweet Victory

"The fact that Ron Swoboda is a hero in the World Series may even be more implausible than the fact that the New York Mets are in one."[1]—excerpt from an October 16, 1969 United Press International story about the Mets right fielder

"I think the Orioles are in the position about like [General] Custer was when he told his men he'd take no prisoners."[2]—Mickey Mantle on NBC's pregame show prior to Game #5

Date: Thursday, October 16, 1969
Site: Shea Stadium, Borough of Queens, New York City

Thursday, October 16, 1969—an afternoon that will live forever in the hearts of New York Mets fans—was a cool and overcast day at Shea Stadium. Win or lose, the Mets would be playing their final game of 1969 at home. They were very comfortable there, having only lost five of their previous 33 home games. There were no political sideshows or peripheral distractions on this day. Baseball, as is should have been, was front and center at the ballpark.

The temperature when the first pitch was thrown was a comfortable 61 degrees. There was a noticeable wind blowing across the diamond from third to first base. Pearl Bailey, star of *Hello, Dolly* on Broadway, a prominent Mets fan, and a frequent patron of Shea Stadium throughout the 1969 season, sang the national anthem. (Over the years, some avid Met supporters have questioned the true level of Bailey's fandom during that historic year, describing her somewhat unkindly as a fair-weather fan. "Where was she when the Mets were 10–14 in May?" one skeptic asked on an internet post.)

The stately, 54-year-old Joe DiMaggio, who played in 10 World Series as a New York Yankee and batted .271 in those games, got a huge cheer when he threw out the ceremonial first pitch. (As part of professional baseball's centennial celebrations in 1969, the magnificent Yankee Clipper had been voted the greatest living ballplayer.) In a pregame interview with Tony Kubek, DiMaggio praised Ron

Swoboda for his terrific diving catch late in Game #4. He said it surpassed the one that Brooklyn's Al Gionfriddo had famously made against him at Yankee Stadium 22 Octobers before in Game #6 of the 1947 World Series.

With left-hander Dave McNally pitching for the Orioles, Gil Hodges opted to pencil in his predominantly right-handed batting lineup again; in fact, it was a wholly right-handed lineup. For Baltimore, the only change was at catcher. Andy Etchebarren replaced Elrod Hendricks. In a pitching rematch of Game #2 starters, Jerry Koosman would be McNally's opponent again.

The Orioles' offensive woes continued in the top of the first inning as Koosman looked sharp. Switch-hitter Don Buford, batting right, grounded out to New York shortstop Bud Harrelson who made the play to first baseman Donn Clendenon with ease. Paul Blair, who had broken up Koosman's no-hitter in Game #2, flied out to Tommie Agee in center field on the first pitch he saw. Frank Robinson also flied out, as Ron Swoboda made a running catch in right field.

As Dave McNally warmed up to face the top of the Mets' lineup, NBC's Curt Gowdy reminded viewers that McNally had begun the 1969 season by winning his first 15 decisions before suffering his first defeat. It was a statistical feat that had last been achieved by Johnny Allen of the Cleveland Indians in 1937.

McNally, who had averaged 2.8 walks per game during the regular season, had wildness trouble immediately. Tommie Agee drew a base on balls with a full count. The count on Bud Harrelson also reached 3–2. On the next pitch, McNally may have gotten a favorable strike call from plate umpire Lou DiMuro. Agee broke for second base on the pitch and probably should have been retired. Catcher Andy Etchebarren's throw was ahead of Agee, but shortstop Mark Belanger couldn't quite grasp the ball at ground level. Agee was safe and was credited with a stolen base— the first by a Met in the World Series. Cleon Jones flied out to Frank Robinson in right-center field. It was deep enough to allow Agee to advance to third base. Donn Clendenon also walked, putting New York runners at the corners. The Mets' first-inning threat died, however, when Ron Swoboda struck out swinging.

Koosman retired the first two Orioles in the top of the second frame. Boog Powell flied out to Cleon Jones. Brooks Robinson grounded out to shortstop Bud Harrelson. (During the at-bat Curt Gowdy mentioned that Robinson had driven in the only two Baltimore runs during the past three games.) Dave Johnson, who was badly struggling at the plate, finally got his first hit of the World Series with a single to left field. Johnson was forced out at second base when the next batter, Andy Etchebarren, grounded to New York third baseman Ed Charles.

McNally looked better in the second inning. He had no control problems as the Mets went down in order. Ed Charles grounded out to Brooks Robinson at third base. Jerry Grote flied out to Paul Blair in center field. Al Weis lined out to Mark Belanger at shortstop, who had to leap slightly to make a fine one-handed catch. After two innings, Game #5 was still tied at 0–0.

Mark Belanger led off the top of the third inning with a bloop single that dropped into right field. Proving that pitchers are not necessarily offensive alba-trosses, Dave McNally surprisingly launched a home run into the Orioles' bullpen in left field. He had hit one round-tripper in 1969 and just four in his career. Bal-timore led 2–0. It was the first lead they had held in any game since Game #1. The clamor at Shea Stadium declined by a few decibels.

Don Buford came up next and grounded out to Bud Harrelson at shortstop. Paul Blair's at-bat was painful for plate umpire Lou DiMuro. Twice foul balls rattled off his mask. Blair went down swinging for the second out. Frank Robinson then hit a bomb to left field. It majestically sailed over the bullpen for another Baltimore home run. The Orioles' dormant bats had suddenly come to life. The solo homer extended their advantage to 3–0. Boog Powell struck out swinging to end the top of the third inning, but the damage had been done. Koosman seemed unfazed by the score when he took a seat on the New York bench. "Let's score some runs, boys," he confidently bellowed to his fellow Mets. "They will not get another run off me."[3]

Koosman decided he ought to do something about the three-run deficit him-self. He led off the bottom of the third inning. He too performed unexpected magic with his bat, hitting a double down the left field line. He got no farther than sec-ond base, however. Tommie Agee flied out to Paul Blair in center field. Bud Har-relson struck out swinging. Cleon Jones popped out to Boog Powell. Any one of four Oriole infielders could have caught the ball, but Baltimore's first baseman took charge. Powell was closer to second base than first base by the time the ball settled in his mitt.

The Orioles went down quickly in the top of the fourth inning. Brooks Rob-inson flied out to Tommy Agee in left-center field. On a check swing, Dave John-son tapped the ball back to the mound. Koosman fielded it and made the easy play to Donn Clendenon at first base. Catcher Andy Etchebarren grounded out to sec-ond baseman Al Weis.

Donn Clendenon struck out looking to begin the home half of the fourth inning. Clendenon did not agree with the second and third strikes called by umpire Lou DiMuro—and he let him know it before marching back to the New York dug-out. Ron Swoboda singled up the middle. Ed Charles hit a towering pop-up behind home plate. Catcher Andy Etchebarren had to wait an unusually long time before it descended. His catch retired Charles for the second out of the inning. Jerry Grote hit a sharp ground ball to Mark Belanger. He fielded it cleanly and beat Swoboda in a footrace to second base for the force out to end the inning. Baltimore still led Game #5, 3–0.

Baltimore mustered no offense in the top of the fifth inning. Mark Belanger flied out to Ron Swoboda in left field. Pitcher Dave McNally could not duplicate his earlier home run. He struck out swinging on three pitches. Don Buford flied out to Swoboda who made a fine, running backhanded catch in left-center field.

The Mets put another zero on the scoreboard in the bottom of the fifth inning. Al Weis grounded out to Brooks Robinson at third base. Like his Baltimore counterpart in the top of the inning, Jerry Koosman struck out swinging. Tommie Agee surprised the Orioles with a bunt single toward third base. Brooks Robinson made a desperate charge for it. He tried to stab it with his bare hand but missed it. In all likelihood, Agee would have beaten the play at first base had Robinson corralled his bunt, so the play was properly ruled a base hit. Agee was stranded at first base when Bud Harrelson flied out to Paul Blair in center field. Associated Press scribe Jack Hand would later state, "Clouds blew across the darkening skies and the lights were on as McNally continued to put down the Mets, clinging to that 3–0 lead. Mets fans who had come to celebrate … were beginning to wonder if they were to be denied a final victory at home."[4]

The top of the sixth inning began with Paul Blair flying out to Tommie Agee. Agee made the play a bit of an adventure by nearly turning the wrong way on the ball as he backed up. He corrected himself in time and hauled in the ball for the first out.

Umpire Lou DiMuro became the center of attention for the first time in the game—but certainly not the last—when Frank Robinson batted. It looked like Robinson had clearly been struck on the hip by an 0–2 Koosman fastball—the game film shot from center field later confirmed this to be so—and he took a couple of steps toward first base. DiMuro called him back. Robinson was more than familiar with being hit by stray pitches; seven times in his career he had led his league in being awarded first base in that category. He was both angry and incredulous when DiMuro ruled it to be a foul ball and waved him back in the batter's box. (The ball had ricocheted off Robinson's hip before striking his bat.) Earl Weaver sprinted out of the visitors' dugout to complain. He asked DiMuro to seek help from Lee Weyer, his first-base umpire. Oddly, DiMuro said no. "The ball hit the bat—and that's it,"[5] he informed Weaver and Robinson.

In an act of both showmanship and gamesmanship, Robinson headed down the steps into the Baltimore clubhouse. Some fans assumed he had been ejected. He had not. Everyone, including DiMuro, wondered what had happened to Robinson. The Orioles' star right fielder had his hip examined by team trainer Ralph Salvon, who later said there was indeed a prominent goose egg. (During the long lull, NBC radio aired a ginger ale commercial!) Robinson, with his pants still unbuckled, made his way back to the bench and continued to further argue with DiMuro about his decision. Sitting on the bench, Dave McNally was furious at the umpire. "You showed no guts. The crowd must be getting to you!"[6] he screamed at DiMuro.

Witty Jim Murray of the *Los Angeles Times* was astonished that DiMuro had neither seen the play accurately nor sought help from his colleagues. He wrote, "Robinson was hit by a fastball that is likely to give him a blood clot on the thigh. He had to go to the clubhouse to get it iced or it would have put a hole in his pants. He got the swelling down in less than a half hour."[7]

With the New York crowd becoming agitated by the lack of action on the field, Robinson eventually resumed his at-bat, with an 0–2 count, after a considerable delay. (If one listens carefully to the NBC-TV audio, the faint voice of a heckler can be heard shouting, "What the hell was that, Frank?")[8] On the radio broadcast, Jim Simpson said that it was well known in baseball circles "that the one man you don't want to get mad when he has a bat in his hands is Frank Robinson."[9] Robinson did not channel his anger productively this time. He struck out looking on a dandy Koosman curveball for the second out of the inning. The hometown fans derisively hooted and waved handkerchiefs at him as he walked back to the Baltimore dugout without expression.

The baseball gods gave the Orioles a kind break on the very next batter to even things out. Powerful Boog Powell got an excuse-me single when a check swing produced a base hit that somehow found its way past shortstop Bud Harrelson and into left field. Powell seemed amused and embarrassed by the dinky hit. Nevertheless, he was standing safely at first base. That is where he remained when Brooks Robinson flied out to Cleon Jones in left field to end the visitors' sixth inning.

The home team finally made a breakthrough in the bottom of the sixth. The inning opened with another incident that baseball fans are still discussing half a century later. With Cleon Jones batting for New York, McNally threw a poor first pitch that was destined for the dirt, but also headed toward Jones in the right-handed batter's box. Jones thought the ball struck his foot—or he gave a tremendous acting job—and trotted toward first base. (In the NBC radio booth, Bill O'Donnell was unsure. He said Jones "must have skipped rope on a low pitch in the dirt."[10]) As in the previous inning, DiMuro did not think the play was a hit-by-pitch. Jones turned to complain. He was joined by first base coach Yogi Berra and then by manager Gil Hodges who coolly strolled toward home plate. "Lou, the ball hit him,"[11] Hodges calmly said to the plate umpire. Hodges had retrieved the ball, which had conveniently rolled into the home team's dugout, and asked DiMuro to examine it. Hodges had integrity and reputation on his side, according to author Wayne Coffey:

> [Hodges] was a man who had never been ejected from so much as one game in a playing career that had spanned 18 years and 2,071 games. He was almost universally regarded as a complete gentleman who respected umpires and the game and would not argue if he did not believe he was in the right.[12]

"We might have another shoe polish play!"[13] Lindsey Nelson stated on NBC's TV broadcast. Nelson had said "another" because a remarkably similar play had happened in the 1957 Braves-Yankees World Series. In the tenth inning of Game #4 in Milwaukee, Vernal (Nippy) Jones of Milwaukee was awarded first base when he proved to umpire Augie Donatelli, by showing him a shoe-polish smudge on the ball, that a Warren Spahn pitch had hit his foot. It was the start of a three-run, game-winning rally for the Braves. Indeed, proving that history does repeat itself, Hodges asked DiMuro to look for evidence of Jones' shoe polish on the baseball. The plate umpire dutifully examined the ball. Eureka! It was 1957 all over again: DiMuro saw a tiny black spot on the ball and pointed Jones toward first base.

"The ball did hit me," Jones insisted afterwards. "Then it bounced into our dugout."[14] Afterward, when he was told about the Nippy Jones shoe polish play from the 1957 World Series, Cleon amusingly quipped, "We Joneses have to stick together!"[15]

"Jerry Grote was sitting on the bench and he caught it," Hodges later explained. "I was going to go up and talk to the umpire. Grote tossed me the ball. He said to show [DiMuro] the shoe polish on it. There's your turning point."[16]

Columnist Jim Murray was a little bit more skeptical and cynical about the entire sequence of events. He was one of the few writers who thought Jones had faked being hit. Murray wrote,

> A fastball does not hit Cleon Jones. Jones knows this. I know this. The umpire knows this. I'm just guessing, of course, but there is no blood on the ball. But there is shoe polish. Now, who put it there is known but to God. And we're beginning to figure out whose side He's on, aren't we? It's for sure it wasn't put there by Cleon Jones' shoes. It's the sixth inning, right? The only guy whose shoes are still shined in the sixth inning is the team's doctor. Cleon Jones has made two putouts and chased a few homers by that inning.[17]

Out came Earl Weaver, to no one's surprise. An argument was bound to ensue considering what had happened in the top of the sixth inning with Frank Robinson's at-bat. Weaver wanted to examine the baseball himself. DiMuro said no. Weaver, irked by the situation, stormed back to the dugout and silently steamed. Weaver later admitted, "The ball hit Jones; DiMuro got that one right. I saw Jones get hit. But Frank was also hit; he got that one wrong."[18] Weaver also said he was arguing only because he did not like the roundabout way DiMuro came to his decision.

Weaver's attitude turned darker moments later when Donn Clendenon homered high into the left field stands on a belt-high, 2–2 pitch for two RBI. It was the Met first baseman's third home run of the World Series. (He had hit 12 for New York in the regular season after joining the Mets on June 15.) With Jones scoring ahead of Clendenon—it was Jones' first run of the World Series—suddenly the Orioles' comfortable 3–0 lead had been whittled down to a tenuous 3–2 edge. The Shea Stadium patrons woke from their slumber and became noticeably louder.

"When I got to the dugout after the home run," Clendenon later told a reporter, "it was like the college rah-rah spirit. It looked like it would be only a matter of time before we'd get them. It's been this way ever since I joined this team."[19]

Outwardly, McNally seemed unrattled by Clendenon's home run and got three quick infield outs: McNally retired Ron Swoboda on a soft line drive to Dave Johnson, Ed Charles on a ground ball to Brooks Robinson, and Jerry Grote on another ground ball hit to Mark Belanger.

Koosman had another strong inning in the top of the seventh, setting down the Orioles in short order. Dave Johnson flied out to Ron Swoboda in foul territory. Andy Etchebarren struck out swinging. Mark Belanger grounded out to Bud Harrelson.

In the bottom of the seventh inning, Al Weis continued his surprising bat work. This time he hit the jackpot, driving a McNally pitch over the wall in left-center field. It was nothing short of astonishing. It was the first home run Weis had ever hit at Shea Stadium. (It would also be the only one.) It was also the first home run Weis had ever hit in the majors in a home game; diligent researchers later found that all six of his previous MLB homers home occurred on the road. "The mighty mite has become the hitting star of the World Series!"[20] declared Lindsey Nelson as Weis was greeted by his happy teammates inside and outside the Mets' dugout. Game #5 of the World Series was now tied, 3–3. William Leggett of *Sports Illustrated* wrote, with only a smidgen of hyperbole, that Weis "hits a home run about as often as Gil Hodges smiles during a World Series game."[21] In a book published shortly after the World Series, Tom Seaver affectionately called his second baseman "Babe Weis." Shea Stadium was now a bedlam. Despite the score being level, the inhabitants could now sense victory would be theirs.

Weis' homer had an unexpected second benefit for the Mets: Had Weis made an out, Gil Hodges would have sent in a pinch-hitter to bat for Jerry Koosman. Now Hodges had the luxury of leaving his starter—who had been consistently mowing down the Orioles since the fourth inning—in the ball game. Koosman struck out swinging for the first out. Tommie Agee flied out to Frank Robinson in right field. Bud Harrelson hit a bullet toward third base directly to Brooks Robinson, but the Baltimore third baseman caught it for the third out.

Koosman looked terrific in the top of the eighth. Again, no Oriole reached first base. Making his Series debut, Curt Motton, a hero from Baltimore's ALCS sweep, batted for McNally. On the first pitch from Koosman, Motton grounded to Harrelson for a quick out. Don Buford lofted a fly ball to Tommie Agee in center field. (Since his home run to start Game #1, Buford was a dismal 1-for-19 at the plate.) Paul Blair put a scare into the excited crowd by hitting a long fly ball down the left field line that veered foul just before the pole. He then grounded out to Harrelson who made a fine play deep on the infield dirt. The score was tied 3–3 heading to the bottom of the eighth inning. Koosman had retired 16 of the last 17 Baltimore hitters, including seven in a row.

With McNally out of the game, Earl Weaver sent in Eddie Watt to pitch for the second time in the World Series. He immediately found himself in trouble when Cleon Jones led off with a double that smacked off the center field wall. It missed being a home run by about three feet. Baltimore center fielder Paul Blair did well to hold Jones to two bases. The crowd at Shea Stadium could smell victory now. Next up was Donn Clendenon, who was already a serious candidate for World Series MVP. After twice fouling off bunt attempts, Clendenon nearly put the Mets into the lead. He drove a fly ball in the opposite direction of his earlier home run. This one stayed inside the confines of the ballpark, but it veered just wide of the foul line in right field. Clendenon eventually grounded out to Brooks Robinson at third base as Jones stayed put at second base.

Ron Swoboda was the next hitter for the Mets. He yanked Watt's second pitch down the left field line. Left fielder Don Buford was not playing Swoboda to pull the pitch. He had a long run and could not make the catch. He ended up short-hopping the ball. Jones scored easily. The Mets led for the first time in Game #5 by a 4–3 score. Swoboda coasted into second base on a play that was debatably ruled as a double. It was Swoboda's second hit of the game and is sixth hit of the World Series. No one on either team had more. During the regular season, right-handed batters had fared poorly against Watt, just batting .140. In this one catastrophic inning, two of them had hit doubles off him.

Joseph Durso of the *New York Times* alluded to the Mets' dismal history when he later wrote, "The deciding run was batted home by Ron Swoboda who joined the Met mystique in 1965 when the team was losing 112 games and was finishing last for the fourth straight time."[22]

The next batter was Ed Charles. He hit a routine fly ball to Buford for the second out of the inning. Swoboda could not advance; he held at second base.

Up came Jerry Grote, who had managed a hit in each of the first four World Series games. He struck what looked to be an inning-ending ground ball towards first base. Instead it turned out to be the death blow for the Orioles. Grote hit a chopper about eight feet wide of first base. The usually sure-handed Boog Powell, playing behind the bag, had trouble fielding the ball on its second bounce. The ball careened off his chest (and perhaps his glove too) and fell in front of him. Pitcher Eddie Watt was late in covering the bag. Powell made an underhand toss to Watt who was clearly going to lose the footrace to the base to Grote. Grote was safe— and Watt misjudged Powell's throw. It was a little bit high and slightly behind him, but certainly catchable. First base coach Yogi Berra saw the ball get away from Watt and excitedly signaled across the diamond for Swoboda to keep running to the plate. He did, scoring easily. (Grote stayed at first base.) The Mets were now in front 5–3. Two errors were charged on the play. One went to Powell for his fielding miscue that allowed Grote to reach base. The other went to Watt for failing to catch Powell's toss, allowing Swoboda to score. There was no RBI awarded on the play.

The next Met batter, Al Weis, watched a two-strike pitch from Watt sail across the heart of the plate for a strikeout. It mattered little to the excited Mets fans buzzing with anticipation at Shea Stadium. They were three outs away from seeing their underdog team win the World Series. Amazing!

In the NBC broadcast booth, Curt Gowdy was by himself for the top of the ninth. Lindsey Nelson was on his way to the Mets' clubhouse in expectation of the home team's victory celebration and trophy presentation. Mets fans had already begun a chant of "We're number one!" before the first Oriole batter of the ninth inning, Frank Robinson, came to bat. "If the Mets do hold onto this lead it will be hard to pick out their hero," Gowdy noted. "There have been so many of them. The Mets, who lost 89 games last year and finished ninth, are three outs away from becoming world champions."[23]

In a 2019 interview, Jerry Koosman recalled two things before he faced the desperate Orioles in the top of the ninth inning: the deafening roar of the crowd; and that he could not control his curve ball during his warmup tosses. Accordingly, he decided to throw just fastballs. Frank Robinson was the first Baltimore batter.

The anticipation of a Mets victory was too much for one teenage fan wearing a beige, turtleneck sweater. With the count 2–0 on Robinson, the youth ran onto the infield to get a head start in congratulating first baseman Donn Clendenon. Two New York City policemen roughly hustled him off the field—but not before he thrust both arms upward in triumph. The crowd cheered the lad's enthusiasm.

But the game was not over yet. Robinson walked on five pitches—the first base on balls surrendered by Jerry Koosman in Game #5. Gil Hodges was taking no chances. Tug McGraw and Ron Taylor were already warming up in the Mets' bullpen in case Koosman faltered. When Koosman fell behind the next Oriole batter, Boog Powell, 2–1, a nervous murmur crept across Shea Stadium. However, Powell could only knock a slow grounder to second baseman Al Weis. He forced out Frank Robinson who slid hard at shortstop Bud Harrelson. Harrelson made the put out and deftly avoided most of Robinson's bad intentions. There was no throw to first base. "They're booing him," Curt Gowdy said of the crowd's reaction to Robinson's malicious slide, "but that's the way you should run the bases."[24]

With the slow-running Powell on first base, Baltimore manager Earl Weaver sent in Chico Salmon to pinch-run for his first baseman. Brooks Robinson came to bat. He hit a gentle fly ball on an 0–2 pitch to Ron Swoboda in right field for the second out. Robinson's parents had made the trip from Arkansas to New York City to watch their son play in his second World Series. On this day they saw him go a disappointing 0-for-4 at the plate.

Victory was now at hand for the Mets. "I think if there's one word that can describe this Mets team," said Curt Gowdy, "it's 'inspired.'"[25]

The last hope for the Orioles was Dave Johnson who had a dismal World Series at the plate. He had recorded just one hit in the five games—and that had come in the second inning of Game #5. Koosman's first pitch to Johnson was a ball. The second was a strike. A breaking pitch wide of the plate made the count 2–1. On Koosman's fourth pitch to Johnson, the Baltimore second baseman made good contact and drove the ball to left field. (Johnson later told reporters he thought he had hit a home run. Fifty years later Koosman said he feared the same thing.) But it was catchable. "There's a fly ball hit out to left. Waiting is Jones," Curt Gowdy reported. Cleon Jones later said he was talking quietly to the ball, saying, "Come on down, baby. Come on down!"[26] Jones had one foot on the warning track and the other foot on the outfield grass when the ball fell securely into his glove. "The Mets are the world champions!"[27] Gowdy announced. The game had taken 134 minutes to play.

Koosman leapt into the arms of catcher Jerry Grote. The players on the field and some in the Mets' dugout rushed out to congratulate their pitcher. "Koosman

Before Dave Johnson's fly ball settled into Cleon Jones' glove for the final out of the 1969 World Series, jubilant Mets fans, overjoyed at their team's improbable championship, began rushing onto the field. They had endured the Mets being the laughingstocks of the National League for the better part of a decade. Now they were at the top of the heap (National Baseball Hall of Fame and Museum, Cooperstown, NY).

is being mobbed!"[28] said Gowdy. That huddle only lasted for a couple of moments as the Mets, fearing the tide of emotion and humanity engulfing the playing field, quickly fled from sight. It was a wise decision. Koosman recalled, "Some of those people might have been Oriole fans, so I ran for my life."[29] Some individuals from the youthful mob were already invading the home team's dugout trying to scoop up souvenirs. Fifty years later Koosman recalled, "stepping on the side of one guy's leg; [I] just tore his leg up with my spikes."[30]

Within seconds, dozens—then suddenly hundreds—of people descended to field level to whoop it up. Some daring and athletic fans jumped from the high outfield seats in left field onto the warning track. Others slid down the foul poles. Shea Stadium's red-coated ushers, badly outnumbered, were helpless to control the mob. They simply gave up trying to prevent the people from celebrating on the infield and outfield. Bases were torn from the infield dirt as souvenirs of the occasion. Home plate disappeared. Huge chunks of sod were ripped off the field too. Flares and firecrackers were thrown. "I never saw anything like it,"[31] marveled Joe DiMaggio to a reporter amid the chaos. The Met players had sensibly hightailed it into the relative safety of their clubhouse where—in those days—the trophy presentation would take place. Fans were still circulating on the field well after the final out had been made. Inside the safety of the home team's clubhouse, Cleon Jones had the chance to present Jerry Koosman with the ball he caught for the final out of the 1969 World Series.

Amid the clamor, Gowdy reported, "*Sport* magazine has declared Donn Clendenon as the Most Valuable Player of the World Series. He wins himself a new Dodge."[32] It was the fifteenth consecutive year that the periodical had determined the MVP of the Fall Classic. Clendenon's three home runs had set a record for the most in a five-game World Series. That stat is even more impressive when one realizes that Clendenon was on the Mets' bench for all of Game #3 because of Gil Hodges' platoon system. Still, nobody would have objected too much if the MVP honor had gone to either Al Weis, Jerry Koosman, Ron Swoboda or Tommie Agee.

Jim Murray chortled,

> Guys who hit three home runs in a short World Series are guys who have their pictures on the wall at the Hall of Fame, Ruth and Gehrig to name a couple. Donn Clendenon is no banjo hitter, but he has trouble hitting three home runs in a month. He has been shipped around the league like a suit that won't sell. The Mets got him at a markdown.[33]

Clendenon graciously and modestly told the media he did not think he— nor any other Met—could be singled out as the 1969 World Series MVP. "We've got no one most valuable player," he said. "We've got many: Swoboda, Harrelson, Agee and lots more."[34] In a strange scene in the victorious dressing room, an unfamiliar gray-haired member of the fifth estate asked the Series MVP to say hello to everyone in Petoskey, Michigan. Clendenon happily obliged. "Hello and goodbye to everyone in Petoskey!"[35] he bellowed into the man's microphone. Later a puzzled Clendenon confessed to a curious reporter that he knew absolutely no one who lived in Petoskey.

As for Gil Hodges' immediate reaction after the final out, coach Joe Pignatano recalled decades later, "Gil was overcome with emotion and started shaking. Rube [Walker] and I took him into another room until he calmed down. He realized what he had done. He had taught these guys how to play. We were 100–1 [longshots] to win the pennant. Now we had won the whole ball of wax."[36]

Decades later, Gil's wife, Joan, remembered her husband's satisfaction when they finally had a few quiet moments alone to talk about the victory and what it meant.

> It was the greatest baseball moment of his life. More than anything, it was for the people of Brooklyn who gave him standing ovations when he went 0-for-21 in the 1952 World Series. He said to me, "I'm so happy to be able to give back to the people of Brooklyn. I was able to bring the championship back to the greatest fans in the world." That was his goal because of how wonderfully they had treated him.[37]

A miniature version of the plundering at Shea Stadium took place at the Hodges residence in Brooklyn too. Gil's daughter, Cindy, remembered in a 2012 interview, "Oh my gosh, what those fans did to our house and the lawn! People stopped their cars in front of the house and went crazy! I have friends that I've made over the years who have grass [taken] from our lawn in 1969!"[38]

Donn Clendenon's home fared far worse than the Hodgeses' abode. The 1969 World Series MVP got a phone call from the police while he was still celebrating in the clubhouse at Shea Stadium. An officer informed him that "fans" had broken into his apartment and cleaned it out, taking literally everything of value—including dishes and wallpaper. He spent the next few days in a hotel while he had his apartment refurnished.

In the raucous New York clubhouse, Bowie Kuhn, the first-year Commissioner of Baseball, made the trophy presentation to Gil Hodges and owner Joan Payson. Kuhn declared the Mets were "a team of destiny" and, in defeating the Baltimore Orioles, they "had beaten the best darn ball club around they could beat."[39]

Mets general manager Johnny Murphy called it "the happiest day of my life"[40] as he held the world championship trophy close to his chest. That was a remarkable statement as he had enjoyed a substantial playing career as a relief specialist with the New York Yankees and Boston Red Sox, winning seven World Series. Not quite three months later, the 61-year-old Murphy would be dead from a heart attack. Bob Scheffing officially succeeded Murphy as the team's general manager in January 1970.

NL president Warren Giles, scheduled to retire once the 1969 season concluded, was surprisingly emotional when Lindsey Nelson asked him for a few comments about the Mets' unexpected triumph. On the verge of tears, Giles said, "This is the greatest thing that's happened to baseball, the greatest thing that's happened to the National League ... and the greatest thing that's happened to me."[41] He punctuated his words with a defiant shake of his fist.

In their clubhouse, the Mets celebrated with "innocent chaos," as one journalist described the scene. "This is the summit," exulted Ed Charles. "We're number one in the world and it just can't get any bigger than this."[42]

Cleon Jones chimed in. "Some people still might not believe in us," he said, "but there are still some people who think the world is flat."[43] Jones earlier took a satisfying jab at the prognosticators when he smugly told Lindsey Nelson, "This is a ball club that didn't belong on the same field with the Baltimore Orioles—but we beat them."[44]

"Let's hear it for Cleon!" added Nolan Rayan. Rod Gaspar humorously added, "and for Frank Robinson."[45]

Coach Yogi Berra, who had been in championship clubhouses more than anyone, said this Mets team was different than the dominant Yankee clubs he knew so well. "This is a club of 25 men all working together," he proudly stated. "That's how we won. Usually there is one standout star, but not on this club."[46]

Pearl Bailey was permitted entry into the Mets clubhouse where she joyfully kissed every player and Gil Hodges. The bubbly performer—who somehow had gotten a prized chunk of Shea Stadium sod too—was asked to repeat her smooch with the manager for the photographers who had missed the first one. Speaking metaphorically, Bailey then told the media, "This is about Gil, not me. Let me get out of the limelight. Gil, it's your spotlight; it's your turn to sing."[47]

Hodges bristled at the notion that his Mets were a "Cinderella team." He gruffly stated, "We're professionals. We do things right."[48] Hodges received congratulations from another tenant of Shea Stadium. He got a congratulatory note from Weeb Ewbank, the coach of the New York Jets. Team owner Joan Payson received a surprise call from President Richard Nixon who also spoke to Gil Hodges for a while. Hodges was surprised that the president remembered that he had made the final putout of the 1955 World Series for Brooklyn.

Payson pooh-poohed the idea that the Mets were a "team of destiny," as some reporters were referring to them. "They're a gutsy bunch of boys, that's all!"[49] she told Sheila Moran of the Associated Press.

The elderly Casey Stengel was brought into the clubhouse too. The usually loquacious ex–Met manager seemed lost for words by the occasion. He repeated, "Yes! Yes! Yes!" over and over. When he finally found words, they were classic Casey. With a straight face, Stengel told a reporter that the Mets' World Series victory was "the best thing that had happened in the last five or six weeks."[50]

Champagne showers splashed all and sundry after the trophy presentations. Mayor John Lindsay was among those who was drenched. He promised a major, official, city-approved celebration of the Mets' thrilling, improbable victory. However, the unofficial championship celebrations began the instant Dave Johnson's fly ball came to rest in Cleon Jones' glove.

In the streets of New York City pandemonium reigned, reminding some people of VJ-Day. Arthur Everett of the Associated Press reported, "An avalanche of ticker tape engulfed Manhattan moments after the once-lowly Mets won the World Series from the Baltimore Orioles. Big, blasé New York went out of its mind with delirium. Ankle-deep paper covered the financial district."[51] One amusing example of spontaneous celebration occurred outside the New York Stock Exchange: a large Mets pennant had been affixed to the hand of the nearby George Washington statue.

"Pedestrian traffic came to a halt in Times Square," Everett continued, "as thousands paused to watch the paper rain down." Even British newsmen in Rockefeller Center, who knew almost nothing about baseball, got into the festive spirit of the occasion "by contributing to the blizzard that sailed down into the plaza."[52]

United Press International described the geographical extent of the merrymaking. "From Fifth Avenue to Wall Street, from Flushing to Staten Island, it was all one big, happy party. Confetti and IBM cards littered Manhattan's streets and sidewalks. Toilet paper festooned skyscrapers as far as the eye could see."[53] One pub, Drake's Drum on 2nd Avenue, unveiled a libation called a "Mets cocktail" containing vodka, gin, Benedictine, lime juice and a touch of sugar.

A random Wall Street secretary, Eileen Nolan, was interviewed. Her reaction was typical. She was overflowing with happiness and superlatives. "It's better than anything we've ever seen here—even better than the [parade for the Apollo XI] astronauts," she joyfully declared. "Everything is covered with snow. It's beautiful."[54]

In the Baltimore clubhouse, the mood was decidedly somber, but Earl Weaver was a gracious loser. "The Mets are a very good team. You sports writers have been downplaying them all season. They have great pitching and they make all the plays. The one thing that suprised me was I didn't think they would make more runs than [we did]."[55]

First baseman Ed Kranepool gives teammate Tug McGraw a traditional celebratory champagne shower. Because of Gil Hodges' platoon system, Kranepool, the all-time Mets leader in games played, only appeared in one game in the 1969 World Series. He had one hit in four at-bats—a home run (National Baseball Hall of Fame and Museum, Cooperstown, NY).

Weaver continued, "The Mets aren't lucky, and they don't need gremlins to win," he said. "We lost because the Mets pitched better than us [*sic*]. No other pitching staff contained us as well during the year. I think we'll be rooting for the Mets next year. If we win our league, we'd like another shot at them."[56] (Indeed, in 1970 the Orioles did not openly discuss their defeat in the 1969 World Series as a motivating factor, but their overall dominance and World Series win over Cincinnati can at least be partially attributed to trying to prove their loss to the Mets was an aberration.)

Later, in a quiet moment, writer Roger Angell of *The New Yorker* asked Weaver if he was surprised the Mets had overcome a 3–0 deficit to win Game #5. "No," he said. "In baseball you can't just run out the clock. You've got to give the other man his chance to bat. That's why this is the greatest game of them all."[57]

Frank Robinson respectfully gave the Mets their due. "I'll give them credit for doing what they had to do," he conceded. "Our scouts said the Mets were a good, solid ball club who could beat us in close games. That's exactly what happened."[58] When prodded to identify the moment the World Series swung towards the New Yorkers, Robinson commented, "If there were any turning points, I'd have to pick the two catches by Agee and the one by Swoboda."[59]

Brooks Robinson was bitterly irked by the loss, but he saw hope on the horizon. "I'm awfully disappointed it all had to end this way for us," he told reporters. "It would be silly to try to take anything away from the Mets because they played just great ball. But don't forget about us. We'll be back!"[60]

Baltimore owner Jerry Hoffberger was less gracious. "[The Mets] got all the breaks and we got none," he moaned. "Our guys gave 120 percent. I still think we have the better team."[61]

Years later, third-string Baltimore catcher Clay Dalrymple theorized that the Mets had peaked at the right time while the Orioles had plateaued long before October and had become blasé in their attitude and too accustomed to easy success. "We played our best [baseball] earlier. The second half was like a cakewalk. There's no doubt that the reason [we lost to the Mets] was a lack of excitement."[62]

Sportswriters who had forecast Baltimore to win in a romp had to admit they were wrong. "Pass the crow, please, with a dab of grits and butter on the side," wrote Brad Willson of the *Daytona Beach Morning Journal*. "The Orioles were the pick here in seven games. Like a lot of other fans, we couldn't believe the Mets had the pitching, power or defense to beat one of the best teams in the American League in modern times. But they did." Despite his incorrect prediction, Willson felt compelled to add, "You'd have to be hard-hearted as well as rock-headed not to have enjoyed, vicariously, the celebration of Gil Hodges and his young team in the clubhouse after the fifth and final game."[63]

The 1969 Mets had done something that only two other MLB teams had done: They won a World Series in five games after losing the opener. That rare achievement matched the feat of both the 1915 Boston Red Sox versus the Philadelphia Phillies and the 1942 St. Louis Cardinals versus the New York Yankees.

Instead of lingering around Shea Stadium, reporter Joe Falls decided to pay a visit to a very quiet Yankee Stadium to see how the team that had dominated MLB for decades was dealing with the sudden ascension of the Mets as New York's team. Falls was invited into the office of Lee MacPhail who handed the scribe a card containing five brief statements:

- Yes, it was amazing.
- Yes, the Mets are No. 1.
- Yes, they did deserve it.
- Yes, it was a truly incredible year.
- Now can we talk about something else?[64]

When all the revenues were counted for the 1969 World Series, both the Mets and Orioles ended up with record shares. Each of the winning Mets got a check for $18,388.18 while every Oriole got $14,904.21.

Three nights after winning Game #5, the Mets made a novelty appearance on *The Ed Sullivan Show*. Decked out in their finest Sunday attire, the World Series champions warbled the tune "Heart" from the musical *Damn Yankees*. Some of the players were clearly more enthusiastic than others; Rod Gaspar appeared to be having the time of his life while Nolan Ryan seemed especially uncomfortable. (The 1969 Mets did have some previous collective singing experience. Earlier in the year they had produced an album featuring 10 musical tracks, including "Heart" and a specialty number titled "The Green Grass of Shea.") Someone at CBS oddly decided that the players' legal names should be shown onscreen rather than their more familiar baseball tags. Thus, Jerry Grote was labeled Gerald, Bud Harrelson was identified as Derrel, and Tug McGraw was called Frank. (Watching at home, perhaps, was McGraw's two-year-old son, Tim. As an adult, Tim would go on to become one of country music's top-selling artists with sixteen #1 albums as of May 2021.) As singers, the Mets were great ballplayers! Nevertheless, a half dozen Mets formed a group and accepted singing gigs in the offseason to squeeze every possible dime from their new national fame.

Lawrence M. Stolle of the *Youngstown Vindicator* cynically wrote, "Even the most devout member of the Audubon Society will have little use for the Birds after this [loss]."[65] He was proven wrong later that day. The Orioles got a pleasant surprise not long after their chartered flight touched down in Baltimore on Thursday night at Friendship International Airport. Much to their astonishment, there were about 4,000 of their most loyal fans assembled to give them a rousing cheer— even after losing four consecutive games in a World Series that most everyone who followed baseball said they were supposed to win with ease. One unconquerable soul proudly held a placard aloft. It declared, "Win or lose, Orioles, we love you." Another sign simply said, "You're still #1 with us." A third proclaimed, "The Orioles are still the class of both leagues."

A reporter noted, "One by one the players approached a wire fence, behind which the crowd stood and cheered—shaking hands, waving, and signing a few autographs."[66] Fan favorite Boog Powell was noticeably tardy in exiting the aircraft. The crowd started a rhythmic chant of "We want Boog!" at which point the husky first baseman finally made his appearance. He raised both arms to wave to the throng, but for some reason he chose not to approach the fence and mingle with the assembled well-wishers. Some of the Orioles' wives, who had flown back to Maryland with their husbands, were brought to tears by the wholly unexpected support from the defeated but diehard Baltimore rooters. The turnout at the Friendship International was greater than when the Orioles came home from Minnesota after sweeping the ALCS.

Team owner Jerry Hoffberger was amazed at what he beheld. "Anybody who would come out here tonight and see us is great," he told the assembled gathering. "I thought we were going to come home to an empty airport."[67]

Earl Weaver addressed the crowd. "There's no way we can explain how sorry we are and how embarrassed we are right now," stated the defeated manager. He then added, "We'll get 'em next year!"[68] as he walked over to thank the fans.

The colorful Jim Murray of the *Los Angeles Times* sympathized with the good but suffering folks of Baltimore, to an extent, in an abrasive sort of way. In his nationally syndicated column for October 17, Murray wrote of Baltimore's sports teams' recent remarkable inability to defeat New York–based sports teams in anything when the results mattered the most:

> [Baltimore] is not a town. It's a hoodoo. It's a show that plays great in the sticks but when they put in on Broadway, they trip over the scenery and start to stutter, and the backdrop falls and hits them on the head.
>
> First the Colts, then the Bullets, and now the Orioles. They should put that town in a padded room and hide the cutlery. It doesn't need players, it needs psychiatry. "Baltimore" is now a transitive verb. "To Baltimore" something means to boglix [*sic*] it up altogether just when everyone is looking. And you say, "But it went so well in rehearsal!"[69]

1969 World Series, Game #5

Baltimore Orioles 3, New York Mets 5
Game played on Thursday, October 16, 1969, at Shea Stadium

Baltimore Orioles	ab	r	h	rbi	New York Mets	ab	r	h	rbi
Buford lf	4	0	0	0	Agee cf	3	0	1	0
Blair cf	4	0	0	0	Harrelson ss	4	0	0	0
Robinson F. rf	3	1	1	1	Jones lf	3	2	1	0
Powell 1b	4	0	1	0	Clendenon 1b	3	1	1	2
Salmon pr	0	0	0	0	Swoboda rf	4	1	2	1
Robinson B. 3b	4	0	0	0	Charles 3b	4	0	0	0
Johnson 2b	4	0	1	0	Grote c	4	0	0	0
Etchebarren c	3	0	0	0	Weis 2b	4	1	1	1
Belanger ss	3	1	1	0	Koosman p	3	0	1	0
McNally p	2	1	1	2	**Totals**	**32**	**5**	**7**	**4**
Motton ph	1	0	0	0					
Watt p	0	0	0	0					
Totals	**32**	**3**	**5**	**3**					

Baltimore	0	0	3	0	0	0	0	0	0	–	3	5	2
New York	0	0	0	0	0	2	1	2	x	–	5	7	0

Baltimore Orioles	IP	H	R	ER	BB	SO
McNally	7.0	5	3	3	2	6
Watt L (0–1)	1.0	2	2	1	0	1
Totals	**8.0**	**7**	**5**	**4**	**2**	**7**

New York Mets	IP	H	R	ER	BB	SO
Koosman W (2–0)	9.0	5	3	3	1	5
Totals	**9.0**	**5**	**3**	**3**	**1**	**5**

E—Powell (1), Watt (1). **2B**—New York Koosman (1, off McNally); Jones (1, off Watt); Swoboda (1, off Watt). **HR**—Baltimore McNally (1, 3rd inning off Koosman 1 on, 0 out); F Robinson (1, 3rd inning off Koosman 0 on, 2 out), New York Clendenon (3, 6th inning off McNally 1 on, 0 out); Weis (1, 7th inning off McNally 0 on, 0 out). **HBP**—Jones (1, by McNally). **SB**—Agee (1, 2nd base off McNally/Etchebarren). **HBP**—McNally (1, Jones). **U**—Lou DiMuro (AL), Lee Weyer (NL), Hank Soar (AL), Frank Secory (NL), Shag Crawford (NL), Larry Napp (AL). **T**—2:14. **A**—57,397.

12

How Did It Happen?

"Had it not been for an amazing catch here or a miraculous stab there, [the Orioles] might have reversed the whole curse of what, mystically, the whole country had begun to regard as inevitable—the triumph of the rankest underdogs. They return to Baltimore where only a million [fans] watched them this year and perhaps fewer will care to view them next year."[1]—William Leggett, *Sports Illustrated*

"The last miracle I did was the 1969 Mets. Before that, I think you have to go back to the Red Sea."—George Burns, from the 1977 movie *Oh, God!*

It has been more than 50 years since the New York Mets won their 1969 miracle pennant (followed by their miraculous World Series). People who witnessed the Fall Classic tend to best remember, and therefore focus on, the heart-stopping catches by Tommie Agee and Ron Swoboda. No doubt they were great and timely defensive plays, and those catches did go a long way in saving Games #3 and #4 for New York, but the main reason the Mets defeated the Orioles was because of their pitching. More harshly, it was the dearth of Baltimore offense that doomed the favored AL champions.

Certainly, the Mets' defense helped when it needed to come to the rescue. Earl Weaver recognized it was the Mets' overall consistency rather than the three spectacular catches that made the difference. The Baltimore manager said afterward of the stellar New York infield and outfield, "We hit the ball right where they could show their defensive ability."[2] He was right. William Leggett of *Sports Illustrated* presented this startling statistic in his coverage of the World Series: After Game #1, almost 50 percent of the outs that Baltimore made (excluding strikeouts) were either hit to Tommie Agee in center field or to Bud Harrelson at shortstop—the two best defensive players the Mets had on their roster. Indeed, before Ron Swoboda made his famous game-saving catch in the ninth inning of Game #4, he had made just one putout all afternoon—and it had come earlier that same inning.

The Mets made just two errors in the whole World Series. The Orioles made two errors on one play late in Game #5 in the sequence where New York scored the final run of the Fall Classic to give them a two-run cushion. (Overall the Orioles made four errors. Generally, the defense was solid by both teams.)

Baltimore managed just 23 hits in five games off the Mets' roster of hurlers. Surprisingly, five of those hits came from the number-nine spot in their batting order! Don Buford, Dave Johnson, Paul Blair and Brooks Robinson were startlingly inept at the plate during the World Series. Altogether they managed just six hits in 75 at-bats. That works out to a pitiful combined batting average of just .080. Only four times did the Orioles lead off an inning with a hit. Baltimore's best hitter was Boog Powell who batted a very quiet .263 (5-for-19). All five of Powell's hits were singles. Of Baltimore's nine RBI in the 1969 World Series, three of them came from the bats of Oriole pitchers (two from Dave McNally and one from Mike Cuellar). Baltimore managed just four extra-base hits in 45 innings. Two of them were struck by Don Buford in the first game. This was truly a Baltimore offense that never got on track despite the promising start early in Game #1. Their team batting average was a lowly .146. The Mets' .220 cumulative batting average, while weak, seems luxurious by comparison.

New York's World Series pitching was quite excellent. The Mets used just six pitchers in the five games. Four of them recorded ERAs of 0.00. Three of the four were relievers, meaning the club's bullpen—and starter Gary Gentry—gave up no earned runs. Jerry Koosman's was 2.00 over 17⅔ innings. Tom Seaver's was 3.00 over 15 innings. The Mets' combined ERA was 1.80. A stingy figure such as that will win most World Series.

In contrast, every Baltimore pitcher in the Series gave up at least one earned run. Mike Cuellar and Dave McNally could hardly be faulted, though. Cuellar's World Series ERA was a terrific 1.13; McNally's was a very good 2.81. Only Jim Palmer's 6.00 ERA, from just one weak, six-inning outing in Game #3, looks bad. Baltimore's bullpen was the opposite of the Mets. While the Met hurlers consistently put up zeroes, the four relievers employed by the Orioles simply could not shut the door on the Mets. Pete Richert's ERA was incalculable because he did not get anyone out. Similarly, Dick Hall's ERA was infinity because he did not retire a batter—and he was responsible for a Met who scored. The ERAs of Dave Leonhard (4.50) and Eddie Watt (3.00) indicate that they were not dominant. Both teams' strikeout-to-walk ratios were similar, but still the Mets had better numbers. The Mets whiffed 35 Orioles while walking 15; the Orioles struck out 28 Mets while issuing 15 passes.

The Mets got offensive heroics from two unexpected sources: Al Weis and Donn Clendenon. Weis was thought to be so weak with his bat that the Chicago White Sox gave up on him after the 1967 season. Somehow Weis ended up as the hitting star of the World Series. Clendenon was not even on the Mets' roster when the season began; he belonged to the Montreal Expos. Had things gone according to plan, Clendenon would have been playing for the Houston Astros in 1969. As it turned out, the Mets picked him up from Montreal near midseason as a part-time first baseman. His .357 batting average in the World Series and three home runs were pleasant surprises for Gil Hodges. The Orioles had nothing comparable. Their stars generally faltered at the plate—and no one stepped forward to pick up the slack. It was fortunate for the Mets that Weis and Clendenon fared so well offensively as some of their regulars suffered through a poor series with the bat. Cleon Jones hit .158, a far cry from his .340 in the regular season. Tommie Agee was not much better with his .167 average. Bud Harrelson hit just .176 while Jerry Grote was teetering on respectable with a .211 average.

Some Oriole fans frequently argue that the Mets got the benefit of bad umpiring. Over the five games of the 1969 World Series, there were only five (perhaps six) substantial talking points involving decisions made by the umpiring crew. Furthermore, only two of the six umpires faced any sort of serious scrutiny for their decisions. The other four fellows in the dark suits handled their assignments with precious little controversy.

During any given MLB game, there will always be a certain amount of squawking about balls and strikes by pitchers, catchers and batters, but egregious umpiring gaffes on any other plays were few. During the entire series there were no debatable safe/out calls at any base. None. There was, however, the play at first base in Game #3 when Jim Palmer attempted to pick off Bud Harrelson. With two out, Palmer made a poor throw that got by first baseman Boog Powell. Harrelson and Powell became entangled as Harrelson attempted to advance on the error. Albeit unintentional, Powell was guilty of obstruction. The Orioles did not like the ruling, but, quite properly, Harrelson was awarded second base by plate umpire Larry Napp who had the best look at the unusual play. Harrelson was stranded at second base when Gary Gentry struck out. Because nothing came of Napp's decision, many of the next day's newspapers did not even bother to mention the obstruction call in their game reports. That was the only rhubarb that Napp endured. Umpires, Frank Secory, Hank Soar and Lee Weyer basically got through the entire World Series without coming under fire for anything they did.

The first true umpiring incident of the World Series did not occur until Game #4 when Earl Weaver was ejected in the third inning by plate umpire Shag Crawford. Did Crawford overreact to the chirping about his strike zone from the Baltimore bench? Yes. Did he have any option other than to eject Weaver? Not really. Once Crawford ordered the Oriole bench to cease complaining about balls and strikes, Crawford's hands were tied when Weaver came out of the dugout to confront him. Entering the field to argue balls and strikes—or giving the appearance of arguing balls and strikes—is an automatic ejection. Some fans were surprised that Weaver did not seriously protest his removal from Game #4. He knew the routine well. The moment Weaver emerged from the visitors' dugout and headed toward the home plate area to continue the discussion with Crawford, he had to know he was done for the day.

An inning later Crawford made a no-hit-batsman call one day before Lou

DiMuro had two such decisions—but hardly anyone remembers Shag Crawford's ruling. That call went the Orioles' way. In the bottom of the fourth inning, New York's Ed Charles thought he should have been awarded first base when a Mike Cuellar pitch hit his hand. Crawford, however, ruled the pitch hit the knob of Charles' bat before striking his pinkie finger. By rule, that is a foul ball. Gil Hodges only mildly complained about Crawford's decision. Instead of being awarded first base, Charles' at-bat continued. He struck out swinging on a pitch where Ron Swoboda was thrown out trying to steal second base.

The next contentious umpire's decision occurred late in Game #4. It was actually a non-decision: Crawford not calling interference on New York's J.C. Martin for running outside the lane on his game-winning bunt play in the bottom of the tenth inning that scored Rod Gaspar from second base. Photographic evidence showed that Crawford clearly missed the call. Martin should have been ruled out for violating rule 6.05k, and the two Met baserunners should have been sent back to their respective bases. That would have been the first out of the inning. How would the bottom of the tenth have unfolded had Crawford called Martin out? Would the Mets have pushed across the winning run anyway? We shall never know, of course. The interesting part of that play was that no one on the Orioles objected to the non-call. The visitors just headed to their clubhouse without complaint, accepting that they had lost Game #4 on Pete Richert's throwing error. Baltimore catcher Elrod Hendricks—who was closer to the play than Crawford was—said nothing. Only Pete Richert, the relief pitcher whose throw struck Martin on his wrist, seemed even slightly suspicious that Martin was not running where he should have been. Still, Richert did not grumble until he spoke to reporters after the game. Only when pictures of the incident were published did Martin's bunt become a controversial play.

In Game #5, plate umpire Lou DiMuro got himself in trouble twice with the two strange hit-by-pitch incidents in the sixth inning.

The first one was a blatantly blown call. Frank Robinson was clearly hit on his left hip by Jerry Koosman's pitch. Umpire Lou DiMuro badly got it all wrong. He claimed the pitch hit Robinson's bat for a foul ball. The view of the pitch captured by a center-field camera leaves little doubt about the matter. The ball struck Robinson and then may have deflected off his bat. By rule, that is a hit-by-pitch and Robinson should have been awarded first base. Looking at the sequence of events more than half a century later, one is struck by the fact that DiMuro did not seek help from his colleagues to make certain his call was right. Both third-base umpire Frank Secory and first-base umpire Lee Weyer had unobstructed views of the play. A plate umpire asking for assistance on such a play would be routine at all levels of baseball today. In 1969, however, it was not quite so automatic. Umpires quite often operated as lone wolves who stuck with their initial calls, rightly or wrongly. DiMuro stuck with his wrongly. He basically told Robinson (and Earl Weaver) that he had ruled the play to be a foul ball—and that was the end of that.

The second incident was the famous (or infamous) series of events during Cleon Jones' at-bat. Dave McNally's first pitch certainly appeared to strike Jones on his foot before bouncing toward the Mets' dugout along the first base side of Shea Stadium. Umpire DiMuro again failed to see it. Author Wayne Coffey, in his book about the 1969 Mets, facetiously asked, "Did Lou DiMuro, a highly respected umpire, have some policy for Game #5 that no batters would be hit by a pitch?"[3]

In the next day's newspapers, Hodges is quoted as saying the ball hit Jones and then rolled into the Mets' dugout. It was picked up by Jerry Grote. Grote handed the ball to Hodges, who then calmly came out to dispute DiMuro's ruling. However, the "shoe polish incident" has expanded into a full-blown conspiracy theory over the years.

On August 22, 2009, at the 40th anniversary celebration of the Mets' 1969 Championship, Jerry Koosman stated in several interviews that it was he who picked up the ball. Furthermore, Gil Hodges instructed him to rub the ball on his shoe to add the polish, which he did. After the dirty deed had been done, Hodges deviously emerged from the Mets' dugout and showed the ball to umpire DiMuro and got him to change his decision to a hit-by-pitch.

Is Koosman's story on the level? There is no video showing what happened to the ball after it rolled towards the home team's dugout. Koosman was well known on the Mets for being a practical joker, so the validity of his claim must be considered with a grain of salt. Perhaps Koosman was just putting everybody on. "Koos likes to tell stories,"[4] Tom Seaver succinctly declared when asked about it. Furthermore, would Gil Hodges have pulled such a stunt? Such shenanigans seem to run contrary to his impeccable character. Nevertheless, Koosman's claim doesn't necessarily mean that the ball didn't strike Cleon Jones' foot. Even if Koosman's yarn is taken at face value, it does not mean that the polish on the ball seen by DiMuro was the polish put there by Koosman. It is quite possible that there was already a genuine spot of shoe polish on the ball.

But wait … there is a completely different story coming from another famous Met. This tall tale comes from Ron Swoboda. In a 1986 interview, Swoboda said that when the ball rolled into the Mets' dugout, it hit an open ball bag under the bench, and several practice balls spilled out on the dugout floor. (That ball must have really been moving with tremendous velocity after it ricocheted from home plate!) According to Swoboda, the actual game ball was indistinguishable from any of the ones that spilled out of the bag. Hodges quickly grabbed a ball that had a noticeable black streak on it and took that one out to show DiMuro the shoe polish "evidence."

Frank Robinson believed to the day he died that something decidedly underhanded had happened in the home team's dugout. "It had to be a [trick]," Robinson insisted in a 2013 interview with a reporter from a website that caters to Met fans. "People forget the length of time the ball went into the dugout before Gil Hodges brought it out to show it to the umpire. That ball didn't go into the dugout with black shoe polish on it, but it came out with black shoe polish on it."[5]

When determining how long it took for Hodges to come out of the New York dugout with the ball, one must take into account when the hit-by-pitch controversy truly started. When Dave McNally's pitch hit (or bounced near) Cleon Jones' foot and the ball caromed away to the right, umpire DiMuro made no signal. He simply threw McNally another ball from his bag so Jones' at-bat could continue. Only when Jones started walking toward first base and DiMuro ordered him back into the batter's box did the dispute begin. The elapsed time from when that argument began until Lindsey Nelson mentioned Hodges was entering the field was 13 seconds. One would have to be a very quick thinker to concoct, attempt, and pull off such an effective ruse that swiftly.

What is generally forgotten is that Earl Weaver freely admitted after the game that *the ball did hit Jones*; he only argued with DiMuro about the roundabout manner by which he came to that conclusion. Jones himself also affirmed that the ball had indeed hit his foot before deflecting into the dugout. If one listens to the NBC audio of the game, the Shea Stadium crowd certainly reacted as if Jones had been hit by a pitch. The evidence seems to indicate that DiMuro made the correct call—shoe polish or no shoe polish. The next Met batter, Donn Clendenon, homered to reduce the Orioles' 3–0 lead in Game #5 to 3–2.

In totality, the umpires missed two calls during the 1969 World Series: J.C. Martin's interference play, and the hit-by-pitch denied to Frank Robinson. How impactful those calls were on the outcome of the series is certainly fuel for debate, but it is largely a matter of opinion and speculation.

Interestingly, Frank Robinson did not think those two umpiring mistakes affected the outcome of the Series. In that same 2013 interview, he told reporter Clayton Collier, "The Mets deserved to win, they did what they had to do to win," said Robinson. "I still watch it on Classic Sports and I still don't believe we lost. They got contributions from everybody—the little guys we used to call them—and they did what they had to do. They also had some great pitching. That's all I have to say about '69."[6]

There was also the novelty factor that was probably driving the Mets to achieve their unlikely October triumph. Most of the 1969 Orioles had already been in a Fall Classic three years earlier against the Dodgers. They had won the World Series quite easily in a bit of an upset that October. That was Baltimore's first thrilling bite at the apple. In 1969, the Orioles were the old hands while the Mets had the enthusiasm of first-time World Series participants. Ron Swoboda recalled something his wife said to him after he insisted that the excitement of the 1969 World Series win would carry over into subsequent seasons for the Mets. She was skeptical. "You can only win it for the first time once,"[7] she noted. She was right. The New York Mets finished third in the NL East in 1970. The more talented (on paper) Baltimore Orioles won 108 games in 1970, captured the AL East again, swept the Minnesota

Twins again in the ALCS—and this time they won the World Series. Baltimore scored just nine runs in the entire 1969 World Series. The following October versus Cincinnati, they scored nine times in Game #1 alone. In total, during the five games of the 1970 Fall Classic, the Orioles scored 33 runs, hit 10 homers, and compiled a team batting average of .292. What a difference a year can make!

In a piece for *The Sporting News*, Melvin Durslag of the *Los Angeles Herald-Examiner* understood that the Mets' triumph in 1969 was a marvelous albeit once-in-a-generation achievement. He wrote, "As leader of the Metropolitans, Gil Hodges has done a rather unusual job this year. And whether he ever matches it is irrelevant. This is like saying Dr. Jonas Salk had a big year with polio, but he couldn't put it back-to-back with cancer."[8]

Sam Lacy of the *Baltimore Afro-American*, who had predicted the Orioles would win the World Series in six games, opined that the Orioles were "snake-bit" and the victims of supernatural goings-on. The renowned journalist had this take on the surprising Fall Classic result:

> The Mets' scouts [submitted] a superb "book" on the Orioles. It was not a "book" in the normal sense in which hitting weaknesses and pitching flaws are meant to be exploited. Rather it was one in which the Met defense was firmed up by being told where to be and when.
>
> Certainly, I'm being facetious, but what else can a Baltimorean turn to after his Colts, Bullets and Orioles have reincarnated the senior citizens' warning that trouble travels in threes?[9]

Since the modern World Series began in 1903, there have been quite a few upsets. (In fact, the Boston Red Stockings' victory over the strong Pittsburgh Pirates in that very first Fall Classic went contrary to what the experts had forecast.) The very nature of deciding a baseball champion in a best-of-seven series goes against the very premise of what gets the two participating teams to the World Series: sustained excellence over a long period of time. In a short series, anything can happen. A team slump—such as what the Orioles experienced in 1969—can be very harmful if not completely fatal. Baseball history has recorded many examples of prohibitive World Series favorites coming up short when it mattered most. What happened to Baltimore in 1969 also befell the 1906 Chicago Cubs, the 1914 Philadelphia Athletics, the 1926 New York Yankees, the 1954 Cleveland Indians, and the 1990 Oakland A's. In a sport where the very best professional teams routinely lose one-third of their games, occasional upsets are bound to occur. That's baseball.

In the year 98 AD, a Roman historian and philosopher named Tacitus wisely opined that success has many fathers while defeat is an orphan. He was proven correct 1,871 years later as numerous people and entire communities happily staked tenuous claims that they had been the authors of the 1969 World Series upset. For example, there was the Mets' spring training home of St. Petersburg, Florida. The editor of that city's *Evening Independent* proclaimed the day after Dave Johnson flied out to Cleon Jones: "It is our spring sunshine and our hospitality that gives a baseball team the summer momentum to be so tall in the fall. We wish spring training started today so we wouldn't have to wait until February to welcome our world champs properly."[10]

There is also Tom Seaver's heavenly explanation from 1969: "God is living in New York City and He's a Mets fan."[11]

Three decades later, Dave Johnson still had difficulty accepting that his favored Orioles had been beaten by the upstart Mets. He chalked it up to kismet. "I'm still flabbergasted we lost," Johnson said in a 1999 interview. "Destiny made all sorts of funky things happen. Gusts of wind blowing balls back to their outfielders, Swoboda's diving catch, Al Weis hitting a home run; our winning just wasn't meant to be."[12]

John G. Griffin of United Press International preferred to believe that the laws of the universe had been turned inside out and upside down. He declared, "Elephants can fly, water can flow uphill and rocks can float. Why not? The New York Mets are the amazing world champions of baseball. What next?"[13]

What the 1969 World Series represents is what makes the world of sports so compelling: The best team or individual on paper does not always win on the field of play. Sometimes the experts are proven wrong—very wrong. If the stars are aligned correctly, the underdog can sometimes triumph in a famous upset. David can defeat Goliath. A collection of college boys can beat the Soviet Union's invincible hockey team at the Olympics. Buster Douglas can knock out Mike Tyson. The New York Mets can defeat the Baltimore Orioles. Such stories are what keep fans tuned in to the unpredictable drama of sports.

In the final analysis, it is not how the 1969 Mets won it all that matters, it is that they *did* win it all, and that their surprise victory still resonates with tens of thousands of baseball fans in New York City and beyond. In a 2019 interview, Art Shamsky noted, "I've talked to a lot of people over the years, and probably 150,000 have told me they were at the last game on October 16, 1969. I think Shea Stadium at the time probably held 53,000 [spectators] at most. And either they were there in spirit, or they were there in person—it doesn't make any difference. Because I just think, you know, they were *there*."[14]

An editorial that ran in the October 17 edition of the *Toledo Blade* echoed those same sentiments. It read, in part, "No baseball team in recent memory had more Americans who never saw them play pulling for them to confound the sports world, we suspect, than the amazing New York Mets. To the delight of a nation that traditionally roots for the underdog, the Mets are the new world champions."[15]

The *Blade*'s Stan Isaacs attributed the Mets' championship to a healthy combination of very good baseball and more than a fair share of terrific luck. He wrote, "Almost nothing went wrong for the Mets in the last weeks of the [divisional] race, in the playoffs, and in the World Series. They played opportunistic baseball and got break, after break, after break."[16]

Another columnist, David Lawrence, saw something bigger and more profound in the 1969 World Series result. In the wake of the wild celebrations he wrote,

> The opportunity for the citizens of the largest city in the country to celebrate a baseball victory in which negroes and whites, with unrivaled skill, participated will long be remembered as one of the good things that happened in the United States during a period of nationwide uneasiness and unrest.[17]

With the wisdom and experience of age, in a 2019 interview 76-year-old Jerry Koosman looked back at the 1969 championship as a personal triumph that reinforces the idea of the American dream. He told a reporter,

> For me it was that you can dream big. I was born and reared on a farm in western Minnesota and dreamed of winning the World Series. To see that come true, it's almost overwhelming. I did it, though, proving that anything is possible if you set your mind to it and work hard. It doesn't matter where you come from or how you are raised. Anything is possible in this country. Anything.[18]

13

The 1969 World Series
MVP Debate

Recognition of the man named the most valuable player of each year's World Series began in 1955. Johnny Podres, who pitched and won two complete games for the Brooklyn Dodgers and compiled a sparkling 1.00 ERA, was the first.

Sport magazine, a periodical renowned for its color photography of athletics nearly a decade before *Sports Illustrated* was founded, initially sponsored the World Series MVP award. *Sport* gave the annual winner an automobile. In Clendenon's case it was a 1970 Dodge Challenger, valued at about $5,000. This custom was later taken over by a panel of officials and baseball reporters who conduct a vote to determine the winner during the final game of each year's Fall Classic. The recipient used to win a scaled-down but strikingly similar version of the Commissioner's Trophy that is presented to the winning team; it featured only one gold-plated flag instead of a ring of them.

Starting in 2017, it was renamed The Willie Mays World Series Most Valuable Player Award. Since then, a new trophy has been awarded. It features a bronze sculpture of Mays making his famous catch in Game #1 of 1954 World Series. Mays himself was never a recipient, despite appearing in four World Series, two of which came after the establishment of the award. (Mays is a curious choice to have such an honor named for him. Apart from that one memorable grab at the Polo Grounds, Mays was very ordinary in Fall Classic play. His World Series stats are markedly below his regular-season numbers. In those four Series, Mays batted just .239 with 17 hits in 71 at-bats. He knocked in six runs. Mays had just two stolen bases, no home runs, no triples and only three doubles. Any of the award's two-time winners—Bob Gibson, Reggie Jackson and Sandy Koufax—possess better credentials to have the trophy bear his name.)

Sometimes there is an obvious candidate for the most valuable player of the World Series. (For example, there probably would have been calls for a federal investigation if Brooks Robinson had not won the World Series MVP award in 1970.) Similarly, Bob Gibson in 1967 and Roberto Clemente in 1971 were the only logical candidates for the hardware.

Other times the decision is far from being clear-cut. The 1969 World Series provides an excellent example of this. One could make cases for as many as five New York Mets to have been named the top player of the Fall Classic: Donn Clendenon, Al Weis, Jerry Koosman, Gary Gentry or Tommie Agee. Of course, this plethora of candidates made for some spirited debate for baseball buffs after the 1969 season.

There was a split decision of sorts. *Sport* tabbed Clendenon as the winner, largely because of his three home runs in the World Series. Clendenon also batted .357 and drove in four runs. The Baseball Writers of America Association disagreed with the magazine's verdict, however. They gave their version of the award to Weis. The two authors of this book have differing opinions on the subject too. We both agree on one matter, though: *Sport* magazine got it wrong. Here are our respective choices and why we made them:

• WHY AL WEIS SHOULD HAVE BEEN NAMED
  THE 1969 WORLD SERIES MVP

Unheralded Al Weis, New York's 31-year-old second baseman, came out of nowhere to have a dream World Series in 1969.

In his 11 official at-bats versus the Orioles, Weis managed five hits for a terrific .455 average. No starter on either team compiled a higher batting average than Weis did. Weis' on-base average was .563. His slugging percentage was .727. That is a stratospheric number for a player who, after Game #2 was called "a banjo-hitter."[1] He got two of the most important hits of the World Series. Weis, hardly known for his power, tied Game #5 with a solo home run in the bottom of the seventh inning off Dave McNally. With the game level, Baltimore's defense now had to play to prevent a go-ahead run rather than a tying run. That indirectly made New York's two-run eighth inning possible.

In Game #2, Weis drove in the winning run in the top of the ninth inning in the Mets' 2–1 victory. That triumph evened the Series at a game apiece and turned its momentum squarely in New York's direction as the teams headed to Shea Stadium. Weis made just one error in the four World Series games he played at second base—and it turned out to be an inconsequential miscue.

More than any other Met, Al Weis represented both the New Yorkers' underdog status and also their overachieving and winning mettle during the 1969 World Series.—John G. Robertson

• WHY TOMMIE AGEE SHOULD HAVE BEEN NAMED
  THE 1969 WORLD SERIES MVP

In 1969, Tommie Agee led the New York Mets in both home runs and RBI. Yet during that year's World Series it was not his bat for which he would be remembered. It would be for two tremendous—and critical—catches in Game #3 at Shea Stadium.

For most of the five-game series, Agee, like many of the other Mets, struggled at the plate. Only three New Yorkers with at least five at-bats in the World Series produced a better batting average than Agee's .167: Al Weis batted .455, Ron Swoboda hit .400, and Donn Clendenon batted .357. Agee managed three hits. (Only four Mets could boast more—and none had more than six.) He also compiled an on-base percentage of .250 and had the Mets' only stolen base of the Series. However, it is my opinion that Agee alone won pivotal Game #3 in such a sensational fashion with his glove that his exploits in that one contest elevated him above his Met teammates.

Midseason acquisition Donn Clendenon averaged just one home run every six games during his split season with the Mets. However, he managed to crush three in just four World Series games en route to winning the coveted MVP award (National Baseball Hall of Fame and Museum, Cooperstown, NY).

His two game-saving and series-changing catches likely prevented the Orioles from scoring five runs. Those catches alone, while stellar on their own merits, stand out even more so because Agee personally stifled not one but two potential Oriole rallies. Agee himself said afterward it was his greatest one-day defensive performance.

With the Series tied at a game apiece, the stakes were probably never higher than they were when Agee shone. The pressure was on both teams to deliver in Game #3—and Agee did so with aplomb. For those still not convinced of Agee's World Series MVP credentials, he added a solo home run off Jim Palmer to lead off Game #3.—Carl T. Madden

14

Whatever Happened To…

"God gave us memory so that we might have roses in December."
—James M. Barrie

Here are brief summaries, in alphabetical order, of what became of the 21 New York Mets and the 21 Baltimore Orioles who appeared in the 1969 World Series, along with the two teams' managers, the six umpires, and the six NBC broadcasters who described the action:

Tommie Agee's exploits in Game #3—a home run and two spectacular, timely catches—will live forever in New York Mets lore. In its coverage of the Fall Classic, *Sports Illustrated* called it the greatest one-day performance by a center fielder in World Series history. Agee, who had been the AL Rookie of the Year with the Chicago White Sox in 1966, had a fine follow-up year in 1970, recording a 20-game hitting streak. He set three impressive Met club records that season for hits (182), runs scored (107), and stolen bases (31). Agee also hit for the cycle in a game versus St. Louis on July 6. But soon Agee, a native of Magnolia, Alabama, would be beset by knee injuries that severely hampered his play offensively and defensively. After batting just .227 in 1972, Agee was traded to Houston and then to St. Louis. His career ended in 1973. Upon retiring, Agee, always a Met at heart, opened an eatery near Shea Stadium called Outfielder's Lounge. He also became a very prominent figure in local charities and assisted with youth baseball clinics. On January 22, 2001, Agee suffered a fatal heart attack after leaving a Manhattan office building. He was 58 years old. During the 1969 World Series, Agee told a reporter that he had a heart murmur that disqualified him from military service. Cleon Jones, who played center field before Agee's arrival in New York, marveled at his late teammate's ability to handle the tricky, swirling winds in Shea Stadium. "I hated it; every guy before me hated it," Jones recalled. "But Tommie never complained. I watched Willie Mays, Curt Flood, Vada Pinson. Nobody played it better than Tommie Agee."[1]

One of the best defensive shortstops ever, **Mark Belanger** acquired the nickname "Blade" because of his long, thin build. He impressively won eight Gold Gloves in a span of 10 years with the Orioles. Rich Dauer, who played second base alongside Belanger for six seasons, called him "the greatest shortstop in the world. He never put you in a bad position with his double-play throws. I never had to think out there. If there was any question in my mind, I'd look at Blade, and he'd have a finger out, pointing which way I should move."[2] Belanger was not much of a threat at the plate, however. His .228 lifetime batting average is the third worst in MLB history among players who accrued at least 5,000 at-bats. After 17 seasons in Baltimore, Belanger was cut loose by the Orioles at the end of the 1981 season, a campaign in which he publicly criticized manager Earl Weaver. He spent one season with the Los Angeles Dodgers before retiring. Notorious for being a chain smoker, Belanger died in 1998 of lung cancer. He was just 54 years old.

Just six years into his MLB career when the 1969 World Series was played, **Paul Blair** of Oklahoma was already a star outfielder with the Orioles—and he still had a decade more of excellent play ahead of him. Blair loved to talk and was given the nickname Motormouth by his Oriole teammates. Blair had a three-homer game on April 29, 1970, but he also suffered a severe beaning just over a month later. On May 31 Blair suffered a broken nose and other facial injuries when a fastball thrown by Ken Tatum of the California Angels struck him. (Tatum had also hit the previous Baltimore batter, Boog Powell.) He was carted off the field on a stretcher. Nevertheless, Blair returned to the Baltimore lineup remarkably fast, played in 133 games, and led both teams in the 1970 World Series in hits, with nine, in Baltimore's five-game triumph over Cincinnati. After enduring an awful batting slump in 1972, Blair became one of the first MLB players to seek the help of a psychiatrist and a hypnotist to help him regain his confidence. It worked. He had 24 hits in 46 at-bats shortly thereafter. The book on Blair was that he was a good fastball hitter, but had trouble hitting breaking balls. (Accordingly, Blair flourished batting in front of Frank Robinson. He once said in an interview, "With 2–0 counts or 3–0 counts, I knew exactly what [pitchers] would throw me. They're not going to walk Paul Blair to get to Frank Robinson."[3]) Always a superb defensive player, Blair was a unanimous Gold Glove winner in 1973. Overall, he won eight Gold Gloves in Baltimore. Teammate Frank Robinson remembered, "[Paul] was to the outfield what Brooks [Robinson] was to the infield. He was our glue out there. I had to play such a small area in right field just to get out of his way, and so did the left fielder. It felt like we weren't even on the field."[4] In January 1977, Blair was traded to the New York Yankees. The Yankees won the World Series in both 1977 and 1978, but Blair was used mostly in a reserve role. One unproductive year with the Cincinnati Reds followed. An even more unproductive 1980 back in New York (in which he only played in 12 games) prompted the 36-year-old Blair to retire at the end of the season. On December 26, 2013, Blair collapsed and died from a heart attack while participating in a celebrity bowling event in Pikesville, Maryland. He was 69 years old.

Despite living in New York City during the baseball season, Mets second baseman **Ken Boswell** remained a Texan through and through. He was very quotable too. When the Mets became the talk of the baseball world in 1969, Boswell was just one of four bachelors on the team, and he found himself the object of quite a few smitten female fans. According to the *New York Times*, "The 25-year-old Texan says that girls from Brooklyn are always asking him home to dinner. 'They all offer to cook spaghetti,' he said. 'They'd have a better chance if they fixed spareribs and chicken.'"[5] When his strait-laced father arrived in New York City to watch the World Series, Boswell showed him the usual tourist sights of Gotham. "I also pointed out the girls with no bras and the see-throughs and things like that," Boswell recalled with a grin. "He couldn't believe those short skirts. Of course, sometimes I can't believe them either."[6] With manager Gil Hodges using a primarily right-handed-hitting lineup versus the Orioles' lefties in the World Series, the left-handed-hitting Boswell only started Game #3 when righty Jim Palmer pitched for Baltimore. Boswell got a hit and scored run in the Mets' 5–0 victory, but he was back on the bench for Games #4 and #5. Still, civic leaders from his hometown told him to expect a big celebration once he returned to Texas. He told *Sports Illustrated*, "When I get home to Austin, they are going to have a 'Welcome Home Ken Boswell Parade.' I hope they mean me and not some other Ken Boswell."[7] Boswell's greatest baseball achievement came on defense. He went from having the absolute worst fielding percentage among all MLB second basemen in 1969 to setting a Mets club fielding record at his position the next year (.996). However, injuries and declining offensive production hurt Boswell over the rest of his career. Still, Boswell had a memorable and record-tying 1973 World Series versus Oakland. He had three pinch-hit singles in three at-bats against the Athletics. All three hits came off future Hall of Famers: one off Catfish Hunter and two off Rollie Fingers. Boswell was traded to Houston at the end of 1974 and played three seasons for a struggling Astros team. He did well as a pinch-hitter, but he only started in games sporadically. Upon his retirement. Boswell returned to Austin and sold antique automobiles.

Switch-hitting Baltimore left fielder **Don Buford** was frequently described as "squat" for his compact build: 5'7" and 160 pounds. He played both collegiate baseball and football at Southern Cal. A gridiron knee injury would periodically bother him throughout his MLB career. Buford led off Game #1 of the 1969 World Series with a bang: He smacked a home run off Tom Seaver—the one that probably should have been caught by Ron Swoboda. Buford then doubled in the fourth inning. After his explosive start, however, Buford struggled mightily the rest of the way: He went a miserable 0-for-18 for the remainder of the World Series. When 1970 began, the 33-year-old Buford had to compete with promising rookie Merv Rettenmund for his position. In effect, the Orioles had four very capable outfielders vying for the three outfield jobs. That year the 5'7" Buford played all three outfield positions, batting .272 and drawing 109 walks—productive numbers for any leadoff hitter. He had a much better postseason this time, batting a combined .318 for both the 1970 ALCS and World Series. He homered once in each series as well as the dominant Orioles won everything that October. Buford put together another fine season in 1971 as manager Earl Weaver did his best to give all four of his outfielders about the same amount of playing time. Buford led the AL with 99 runs scored, batted .290 and hit 19 home runs—a career best. Buford also hit two home runs in the 1971 World Series versus Pittsburgh. That was Buford's last hurrah. His numbers dropped badly in 1972. (He batted just .206.) The Orioles did not sign Buford to a contract for 1973. Buford played four seasons in Japan before quitting baseball in 1976 at age 39. Former Oriole teammate Frank Robinson, who was managing the San Francisco Giants, persuaded him to join the team as a first base coach. Buford served in that capacity for four seasons. He also did some managing at the minor league level. In looking back at his glory days with the Orioles, Buford spoke for himself and his family, "That was the time of our lives."[8]

Don Cardwell was described in one biography as "the definition of a journeyman pitcher."[9] The 33-year-old right-hander was the oldest hurler on the Mets' staff. Even though he had started 21 games for the 1969 Mets, Cardwell saw just one inning of action in the 1969 World Series—a relief appearance where he set down the Orioles in order in the sixth inning of Game #1. It was his only career postseason appearance. However, Gil Hodges had Cardwell tentatively penciled in as the Mets' starter for decisive Game #7, if the World Series had lasted that long. Cardwell was a threat with the bat; he hit 15 career home runs. But Cardwell was also a constant threat to hit opposing batters in the early part of his career. "It took me three years before I learned how to pitch inside without hitting somebody in the head," he remembered. "You just had to hold the ball a certain way. If you hold it one way, the ball tails in. If you grip it across the seams and throw it over the top more, it's straighter."[10] Cardwell began the 1970 season in New York, but Atlanta purchased his contract in July. He finished out his 14-year career in the Braves' bullpen. For the next 36 years Cardwell operated Ford dealerships in North Carolina. The Winston-Salem resident died in his hometown on January 14, 2008, of Pick's disease. He was 72 years old.

The 1969 World Series victory truly was the last MLB hurrah for New York third baseman **Ed Charles**. The 36-year-old, nicknamed The Glider, was released by the Mets on December 1, about six weeks after the team won the championship. It was not an enormous surprise because Charles had only played in 61 regular-season games, sharing duties at the hot corner with Wayne Garrett and Bobby Pfeil. He saw no action at all in the NLCS versus Atlanta. Charles did not leave baseball entirely, however. He worked as a Met scout for nine years. When baseball fantasy camps became fashionable in the 1980s, Charles made many appearances in Florida teaching the finer points of the sport to enthusiastic middle-agers. Later he worked with juvenile offenders and disadvantaged youths in New York City. "I never tell them I played baseball," Charles told a reporter, "but most of them find out. The question they ask most is, 'Why are you here?' I tell them, 'I'm here because you're here.'"[11] Charles had an unusual hobby for a ballplayer: He was an amateur poet whose talent for crafting words was praised by Curt Gowdy during the World Series. At the conclusion of the Mets' victory parade, Charles recited a prayerful example of his work that he had written in 1962—the day he learned he had finally made it to the big leagues as a member of the Kansas City Athletics. Charles died in Queens, New York, on March 15, 2018, at the age of 84. In his *New York Times* obituary, Charles was described as "the heart and soul of the Miracle Mets."[12]

Donn Clendenon was the final person added to the roster of the 1969 Mets. The World Series MVP had a productive year in 1970—so good that the club's longtime and popular first baseman Ed Kranepool was demoted to the minors for a time. Clendenon set a Met team record in 1970 with 97 RBI, including seven in a single game. By 1971, however, it was apparent that Ed Kranepool was once again going to be the Mets' regular first baseman. Accordingly, Clendenon was released by New York at the end of the 1971 season. He was picked up by St. Louis in 1972, but he played very sparsely for the Cardinals. He was released by the Cards in August of that same year. After retiring, Clendenon worked for Scripto, a pen company, and General Electric. (At the latter business he was responsible for recruiting minority candidates for jobs.) He also earned a law degree from Duquesne University. After overcoming a cocaine addiction, Clendenon became certified as a drug counselor and worked in that field in Sioux Falls, South Dakota. In 2005, Clendenon died at age 70 of leukemia. That same disease had killed his father when Donn was an infant. Upon learning of his former teammate's passing, shortstop Bud Harrelson recalled, "When we got [Clendenon], we became a different team. We [had] never had a three-run-homer type of guy. He was always humble, never cocky. We were still young kids in that era. He was a veteran who came in and made us better. When you threw him into the mix with the rest of us, we became a dangerous force."[13]

Henry (Shag) Crawford got his unusual nickname as a child when he was teased for being "shaggy" in how he dressed. It stuck with him for his long life. Before getting into the umpiring profession, Crawford had briefly been a catcher in the Philadelphia Phillies' farm system. Crawford famously ejected Earl Weaver in Game #4 of the 1969 World Series. Later in that same game, Crawford ruled that J.C. Martin had not violated baserunning rule 6.05k on his 10th-inning bunt that dramatically ended the contest. He remained on the NL staff of umpires until 1975. On September 22, 1974, Crawford was the plate umpire when one of the craziest scenes ever witnessed on an MLB field erupted. During a Cubs-Cardinals game at Busch Stadium, Crawford became fed up with a prolonged Chicago argument. To end it he applied the rarely invoked Rule 6.02c: Crawford ordered St. Louis hurler Al Hrabosky to pitch even though no Chicago batter was in the box! Hrabosky's first pitch was automatically called a strike by Crawford. When the Cubs realized what was going on, two Chicago hitters (plus a coach!) swarmed into the two batter's boxes as the next Hrabosky pitch sailed in! A huge brawl started shortly thereafter. (A clip of the bizarre incident can be found on YouTube; it is worth watching!) Crawford worked the NLCS in 1974 and was supposed to work the 1975 World Series. However, he refused to do so on principle when MLB began assigning umpires for postseason play on a rotational basis rather than purely on the merit system. He was summarily relieved of his duties. "They said they retired me," Crawford said of his dismissal, "but, in my personal opinion, they dumped me."[14] Crawford died at age 90 in 2007. His son, Jerry, was an MLB umpire for 33 years. Another son, Joey, refereed in the National Basketball Association for a record 39 seasons.

"If there's a more superstitious man in baseball than **Mike Cuellar**, I'd like to meet him,"[15] said Orioles broadcaster Chuck Thompson during a 1970 World Series game. Indeed, Cuellar was an interesting mix of superstitions and rituals whose curveballs and screwballs made the Cuban expatriate perhaps the best left-handed pitcher in the AL in the early 1970s. His Oriole teammates lovingly called him Crazy Horse—a nickname not widely known outside the Baltimore clubhouse. It was because of the over-the-top, elaborate rituals Cuellar performed before and during pitching assignments to placate the baseball gods. In a sport where superstitions abound, Cuellar took his to quite an intense level. Paul Blair recalled just one example: "[Cuellar] would walk to the mound the same way, same steps. Step on the mound. Go to the front of the mound, and the rosin bag couldn't be there. Somebody had to come and kick the rosin to the back of the mound. Then he'd walk off the mound the same way. He would come in the dugout the same way; make the same number of steps to the water cooler. Everything had to be the same every time he went out there."[16] It all seemed to work, however, as Cuellar won a phenomenal 139 games in his first seven years in Baltimore after struggling in the NL. His best season with the Orioles was 1970 when he went 24–8, leading the AL in both victories and complete games. During the 1970 ALCS, Cuellar hit a grand slam home run versus Minnesota in Game #1. In that same postseason he was on the mound when the Orioles won Game #5 of the 1970 World Series. (When the last out was made, a photo of Cuellar, taken from the rear, shows him thrusting both arms in the air as he looks at an equally jubilant Brooks Robinson. It might be the most famous image in Oriole history.) Age caught up to Cuellar in 1976, however; he went 4–13. "I gave Mike Cuellar more chances than my first wife,"[17] quipped Earl Weaver. He was released by the Orioles and picked up by the California Angels for 1977. Cuellar pitched badly in two games to conclude his fine career on a sour note. After his retirement, Cuellar settled in Florida. He enjoyed years of fine health, but in early 2010, Cuellar was diagnosed with stomach cancer and faded quickly thereafter. He died at the Orlando Regional Medical Center on April 2 at age 72. Upon hearing of Cuellar's death, Earl Weaver praised him. "Mike was a monstrous part of the great teams we had from 1969 to 1971. He was an artist on the mound and a player [whose acquisition] put us over the top. Several times, down the stretch, he pitched with two days' rest, when we needed it."[18]

In his SABR biography of Baltimore's third-string catcher, Rory Costello penned, "Neither a star nor a 'character,' **Clay Dalrymple** still struck a chord with many fans. If you appreciate honest artisans and the game's subtle nuances, you could be one of them."[19] Dalrymple did not see much action in the 1969 World Series. That was altogether in keeping with his 1969 season in which he appeared in just 37 games. The 32-year-old catcher, who had spent nine seasons with the Philadelphia Phillies, did not play much in the final three seasons of his 12-year MLB career. However, Dalrymple spent all three of those years with an Oriole team that was in the World Series each October. With Elrod Hendricks and Andy Etchebarren seeing most of the action behind the plate, Dalrymple played sparingly and did some pinch-hitting for Baltimore. His offensive numbers had been in decline for years, but his strong arm and baseball intelligence kept him on the mighty Orioles roster. In the 1969 World Series, Dalrymple was the only man on either team to bat 1.000, having been successful twice in two pinch-hitting appearances. In 1970 and 1971 combined, Dalrymple appeared in just 36 games for the Orioles and sat on the bench during both postseasons. He retired in early 1972 but he kept in touch with his old Baltimore teammates. The good-humored Dalrymple recalled a 2008 event where he and many of the surviving Orioles from the team's glory years were brought together for an autograph session. "The line for Frank Robinson was snaking all around the place when they announced [my arrival]," he said. "About 10 minutes went by…. I had nobody [at my table]. I stood up and made an announcement: 'Can I have your attention, please. I know it's crowded over here, and you're going to have to be patient, but if you bear with me, I just might be able to squeeze you in.' The whole place broke up laughing. I got a nice group of people and we talked about baseball."[20]

Lou DiMuro, who worked the plate in Game #5 and was embroiled in two hit-by-pitch controversies in the sixth inning of that decisive game, umpired in the AL for 20 seasons. An air force veteran, DiMuro met a tragic and untimely end. He had umpired first base during a late-afternoon Chicago White Sox-Texas Rangers game at Arlington, Texas, on Sunday, June 6, 1982. Afterwards, he went out for a late dinner with Darrell Johnson, one of the Ranger coaches. While returning to his hotel on foot at about 11 p.m., DiMuro was struck by an automobile as he attempted to cross a busy street. DiMuro suffered massive head injuries and died a couple of hours later at an Arlington hospital. He was just 51 years old. (Some newspapers wrongly reported DiMuro's age as 50.) No charges were filed against the driver. DiMuro's officiating colleagues lovingly called him "Pops" because he was the oldest man in their crew. Umpire Larry Barnett, who worked with DiMuro, sadly remarked, "He was one of the most decent human beings you'd ever meet, but he always seemed to have bad luck. If someone's bag would get lost, it would be his; if someone came down with the flu bug, it would be [Lou]."[21] The luckless DiMuro was prone to on-field mishaps too. On May 30, 1979, in Milwaukee, DiMuro was knocked groggy after accidentally being flattened by Cliff Johnson—one of the biggest men in the AL—in a collision that occurred well away from home plate after Johnson had scored on a sacrifice fly! DiMuro was out for the rest of the season and had an arthritic hip for the rest of his days. Upon returning to duty in 1980, he injured his back by slipping on the damp steps of a dugout in Milwaukee during a rain delay. At the time of his death, DiMuro was just one of nine MLB umpires still using the outside chest protector when he worked home plate. DiMuro's sons, Mike and Ray, both became MLB umpires.

Mets backup catcher **Duffy Dyer** had just one brief appearance in the 1969 World Series. He saw one pitch as a pinch-hitter in Game #1. He meekly grounded out to shortstop Mark Belanger. A native of Phoenix, the 23-year-old Dyer was a rookie who earned a spot on the Mets' roster in 1969 to play occasionally in place of Jerry Grote. In effect, however, Dyer was the Mets' third-string backstop, behind J.C. Martin as well. On Opening Day at Shea Stadium Dyer hit a pinch-hit three-run homer in New York's 11–10 loss to Montreal. Dyer's weak bat—he was a lifetime .221 hitter—hurt his prospects of becoming a full-time catcher for any MLB team. Accordingly, Dyer never played more than 94 games in any season in the majors. Dyer was traded to Pittsburgh in 1974 for Gene Clines where he backed up star backstop Manny Sanguillén. Later he was acquired by Oakland. In 1978, as a free agent, he was acquired by Montreal where he backed up Gary Carter for two seasons. He finished his MLB career in Detroit. The Tigers released him in May 1981. For a time, Dyer had an unusual offseason job for a ballplayer: He did flower arrangements. "I used to watch florists and marvel at how they put together such intricate designs,"[22] he explained.

Andy Etchebarren—possessor of one of the great surnames in baseball history—continued to share the team's catching duties with Elrod Hendricks. Etchebarren, who was of Basque descent, was never much of an offensive threat, compiling a meager .235 career batting average. He was more than capable defensively, however—which kept him employed in the major leagues for more than a decade. Still, Etchebarren's weak bat sometimes caused him to sit out long stretches. Prior to the 1973 ALCS versus Oakland A's, Etchebarren was mocked by opposing manager Dick Williams. Williams sarcastically said he feared Etchebarren for the strength he must have built up from not playing much all season. Etchebarren responded by hitting a game-tying three-run homer off Vida Blue in the fourth game, although the Orioles lost the series three games to two. Boog Powell recalled Etchebarren as "a gamer"—an extremely tough competitor who was oblivious to pain. He was indeed. Powell remembered one incident from 1974 when a foul ball struck Etchebarren's throwing hand. Sitting beside him on the Oriole bench, Powell noticed that a bone was protruding from Etchebarren's skin! Powell, not Etchebarren, ended up summoning medical help. Etchebarren finished his 15-year MLB career in 1978. Twelve of them had been spent with Baltimore. He died on October 5, 2019, at age 76. "He was a terrific teammate and a good friend of mine," said Brooks Robinson, upon hearing of Etchebarren's passing. "He loved the game, and he loved being an Oriole."[23]

For a while **Wayne Garrett** was considered a godsend at third base for the Mets. Before he arrived as a rookie in 1969, New York had used 39 different players at that position since their inception in 1962. Garrett initially seemed to fit the bill. But, as biographer Les Masterson put it, "New York's National League team spent nearly every offseason during Garrett's 7½-year Mets tenure searching for some-one else to take over the third-base job."[24] Garrett hit only .218 in his rookie sea-son in 1969 while playing in 124 games and collecting 400 at-bats, but many of his hits were timely and dramatic. Garrett starred in the NLCS; he started all three games and batted .385. Over the next three years he shared duties at third base with Joe Foy, Tim Foli and Jim Fregosi. Garrett was especially productive for the Mets' pennant-winning club of 1973, but he fared poorly in the team's two postsea-son series. Struggling offensively, Garrett was traded to Montreal in July 1976. Two years later the Expos dealt Garrett to St. Louis. Unable to reach a suitable deal with the Cardinals for the 1979 season, Garrett took his services to Japan and played two years for the Chunichi Dragons. He recalled, "I just couldn't run anymore. The Cards could see that. I got an offer to go to Japan for two years and I accepted it. They paid me $125,000 for the two seasons—about twice as much as I was making in the big leagues."[25] After retiring from baseball, Garrett worked a variety of jobs, including being employed in the courier service.

Frank Robinson could be excused for not knowing who **Rod Gaspar** was when the 23-year-old rookie outfielder boldly predicted his Mets would defeat Rob-inson's Orioles in the upcoming 1969 World Series. After all, not only was Gaspar a first-year player, he was also just a part-time player in Gil Hodges' platoon system. Gaspar realized he was a small cog in the Mets' championship outfit. He recalled, "[Gil] really knew how to utilize his personnel. I always felt part of the club. I know I wasn't a star, but I knew I was a contributor. [Gil] made every player feel a part of that unit and vitally important to the team's success."[26] Nevertheless, in 1970 Gas-par found himself starting the season in the Mets' AAA affiliate in Tidewater, Vir-ginia. He was elevated to New York late in the season and only appeared in 11 games. When the Mets acquired pitcher Ron Herbel from San Diego that summer, Gas-par found himself as the "player to be named later" in the deal. He was sent to the Padres in December. Spending most of the time with San Diego's AAA farm team in Hawaii, Gaspar got into just 16 games with the Padres in 1971. He did not see big league action again until 1974 when he played in 33 games. That season was Gaspar's final one. His MLB career consisted of just 178 regular-season games; 118 of those were with the 1969 New York Mets. After baseball, Gaspar worked in the financial services business for three decades, but he still is sought out by Mets fans. "I'm sure all my teammates still get fan mail about that year. I do also," he said in a 2007 inter-view. "You can easily imagine that when people find out that I played for the 1969 world champions and they see [my World Series ring], the atmosphere changes. What a wonderful baseball year! What a great group of guys. We were the best."[27]

"His stuff was every bit as good as Seaver's. He had just as live an arm."[28] That was what Ron Swoboda said about pitcher **Gary Gentry**. Despite being a very promising rookie, Gentry only had one more winning season in his surprisingly short seven-year major league career. In 1970 he posted a mediocre 9–9 won-lost record for New York. In 1971 he was slightly better with a 12–11 mark. Gentry sometimes got himself into trouble by being too outspoken. Towards the end of the 1971 season, Gentry, an Arizona native, bluntly told a reporter, "New York is a dirty, dirty town. I can't leave soon enough when the year's out."[29] That same season he also publicly claimed that Tom Seaver was getting preferential treatment from Gil Hodges compared to other Met pitchers. Gentry also had a quick temper that occasionally alienated his fellow Mets. Once, in a game versus Cincinnati, he showed up teammate Tommie Agee after the outfielder had badly misplayed a fly ball that resulted in a bases-clearing triple. Agee was enormously popular with the New York fans; accordingly, Gentry received piles of hate mail. With his career sputtering, Gentry was traded to Atlanta in November 1972. He spent three years with the Braves battling injuries and appearing in only 26 total games. Following the 1975 season, Gentry was out of baseball at age 29.

Author John Updike once said the warm, pleasant and slightly gravelly delivery of versatile broadcaster **Curt Gowdy** made him sound like "everybody's brother-in-law."[30] The remark was intended as a compliment for the Green River, Wyoming, resident. "My flat voice sounds just the way a cowboy hat looks,"[31] Gowdy modestly wrote in his autobiography. Gowdy's fans found it quite soothing. His voice was familiar to fans of baseball, basketball and football for decades. Gowdy was even briefly loaned to ABC in 1976 so he could cover the swimming events at the 1976 Montreal Olympics. After the 1969 World Series, Gowdy continued to call baseball games for NBC's *Game of the Week* and the MLB postseason for another six years. His strong criticism of umpire Larry Barnett's controversial no-interference call in the 1975 World Series prompted accusations that Gowdy was biased towards the Boston Red Sox—the team whose games he covered locally for 15 seasons before he was employed by NBC. Gowdy's baseball work at NBC was reduced significantly from that point onward, although he continued working pro football and Rose Bowl games for the network through Super Bowl XIII in 1979. Shortly thereafter, Gowdy was part of an unusual broadcaster "trade" when CBS acquired his services in exchange for Don Criqui moving to NBC. A man who always enjoyed the outdoors, Gowdy hosted *The American Sportsman*, a weekend staple on ABC from 1965 until its cancellation in 1984. It was an unscripted program that featured Gowdy either hunting or fishing with prominent athletes. Gowdy also was the narrator for many of the official World Series films for MLB. Dick Enberg, a terrific multi-sport announcer himself, followed Gowdy as NBC's lead football broadcaster. He graciously summarized Gowdy's splendid career thusly: "He was the first superstar of sports television because he did all the big events. No one will ever be the voice of so many major events at the same time ever again."[32] Gowdy died of leukemia in Florida at age 86 on February 20, 2006. His funeral procession circled Fenway Park. One of Gowdy's pallbearers was former NBC colleague Tony Kubek.

During Game #5 of the World Series, **Jerry Grote** was described by Bill O'Donnell on NBC radio as "probably the most unheralded player on the Mets' roster."[33] That was a fair assessment. Grote's demeanor did not make him the least bit cuddly. The veteran New York backstop was a cantankerous chap, always seemingly in a testy mood—or worse. Nevertheless, Grote, who celebrated his 27th birthday on the same day his team won the 1969 NLCS over Atlanta, was also one of the leaders on the championship Mets team. Noted for his aggressive style behind the plate, Grote quickly won the respect of the entire New York pitching staff. Speedster Lou Brock rated Grote as the catcher in the NL who gave him the most problems in his base-stealing pursuits. In both 1970 and 1971, Grote led all NL catchers in putouts. Suddenly, in 1972, Grote was replaced as the Mets' first-string catcher by Duffy Dyer. It was a huge mystery in the baseball world until it was announced in September that Grote needed surgery to remove bone chips from his right elbow. (Newly installed Mets manager Yogi Berra had deliberately kept quiet about Grote's arm problem to keep the other NL teams guessing.) Grote remained the Mets' first-string catcher through 1976. In midseason of 1977 he was traded to Los Angeles for two minor leaguers. Grote retired after the 1978 World Series and was a homebody for two years until he was persuaded to make a short-lived comeback with the Kansas City Royals in 1981. The aging Grote did not play much for the Royals, but he did have one fabulous game that season: On June 3, in a 12–9 win over the Seattle Mariners, Grote drove in seven Kansas City runs; four of them came on a grand slam home run. "The older the violin, the sweeter the music,"[34] declared the 38-year-old Grote, who retired as a lifetime .252 hitter.

Dick Hall, the Orioles' veteran reliever with the quirky delivery, was put to the test three weeks after the 1969 World Series ended. It had nothing to do with baseball. The tall 39-year-old took his exam to be a certified public accountant. He passed with flying colors, recording the second-highest score in the state of Maryland. Hall knew his baseball career was winding down and he needed to find a new vocation. Hall had been the hard-luck losing pitcher of Game #4. (Jerry Grote had been gifted a two-base hit in the top of the tenth inning when Don Buford reacted too late to what should have been an easy fly ball for the left fielder to catch. Rod Gaspar, who pinch-ran for Grote, scored on J.C. Martin's infamous bunt play two batters later—after Hall had been lifted for Pete Richert. Hall ended up with the dreaded sideways eight—an ERA of infinity—for the 1969 Series.) The next year, Hall was the oldest player in the AL, but it did not matter. He was still very effective coming out of the Baltimore bullpen. Hall was credited with a win in relief versus Minnesota in the 1970 ALCS, and he picked up a 2⅓-inning save versus Cincinnati in Game #2 of the World Series. Hall's array of well-aimed, off-speed pitches—plus an occasional sneaky fastball—flummoxed the talented Reds lineup. At one point in the game, Cincinnati's Johnny Bench screamed at Hall with growing frustration, "How can you be out there with that garbage?"[35] Hall stuck around for one more season with the Orioles, getting to the World Series for a third straight season. He earned a save in Game #2. It was his final MLB appearance. Hall then embarked on a successful accounting career; he stuck with it as a full-time occupation until 2001. As of May 2021, Hall, at age 90, is the oldest living player of the 42 Orioles and Mets who appeared in the 1969 World Series.

Even as a switch-hitter, **Derrel (Bud) Harrelson** was never much of an offensive threat with a career batting average of just .236 and just seven home runs, but he earned his keep in the majors as a superb fielding shortstop. Known to his Met teammates as Mighty Mouse (and sometimes Twiggy), the diminutive Harrelson was an excellent and versatile all-around athlete. He played high school football as a safety and as a running back in California while weighing just 97 pounds. The 25-year-old Harrelson missed five weeks of the 1969 baseball season due to military obligations, but he was back at the shortstop position to turn the double play that clinched the NL East title for the Mets on September 24. Harrelson made just one error in 44 chances during the 1969 postseason. He made the NL All-Star team in 1970 and got two hits in the game. Harrelson played well for New York in 1971 too, but a variety of injuries caused him to miss about 300 games from 1972 through 1974. Harrelson is perhaps best known to baseball fans for a famous fight he had with Cincinnati's Pete Rose during Game #3 of the 1973 NLCS at Shea Stadium after a hard Rose slide into second base. (Remarkably, neither he nor Rose was ejected from the game.) Prior to the game, the Reds were irked by a flippant Harrelson comment in which he said the vaunted Reds "all look like me hitting."[36] The Mets took the NLCS in five games and then lost the 1973 World Series in seven games. New York had led the heavily favored Oakland A's three games to two. In that series, Harrelson was controversially called out on a tag play at home plate by umpire Augie Donatelli in the most hotly disputed incident of the 1973 Fall classic. Harrelson was traded to Philadelphia in 1977 and eventually became a teammate of his old adversary, Pete Rose, when the ex–Red arrived in 1979. (The two men got along just fine.) Harrelson also played with the Texas Rangers before concluding his playing career in 1980. Harrelson became a Met coach in 1981 and was the only man to be in a Met uniform for their World Series championships in both 1969 and 1986. He managed the Mets after Davey Johnson was fired in 1990. Harrelson himself was fired near the end of the 1991 season. His managerial record over parts of two seasons was 145–129. Like Tom Seaver—his longtime roommate from his playing days—in 2016 Harrelson was diagnosed with Alzheimer's disease after he had experienced noticeable memory lapses.

According to biographer Rory Costello, **Elrod Hendricks** of St. Thomas (in the Virgin Islands) "embodied Baltimore Orioles tradition; only Brooks Robinson wore the orange and black for even half as many games."[37] Hendricks' solid major-league career spanned 12 seasons from 1968 to 1979, playing the vast majority of the time with Baltimore. Often described as willowy, Hendricks ironically acquired the nickname Beef from his teammates. Beyond those dozen seasons, Hendricks also spent 28 more years as the Orioles' coach bullpen coach from 1978 through 2005. The gregarious "Ellie" easily made friends. AL umpire Ron Luciano amusingly said the Baltimore catcher "had the nicest way of arguing of anyone in baseball."[38] Even more remarkable is that Hendricks was a below-average hitter (he had a lifetime batting average of just .220) and had one of the weaker throwing arms of any MLB catcher of his era. What he did possess, however, were baseball smarts and the ability to adapt. After the 2005 season, Hendricks' position with the Orioles was somewhat up in the air. It never was clarified. On December 21 of that year, Hendricks succumbed to a sudden fatal heart attack. He was one day short of his 65th birthday. Typical of the good-hearted ex-catcher, two days before his sudden passing, Hendricks had dressed up as Santa Claus at a special event for about 100 underprivileged children in Baltimore.

Not surprisingly, **Gil Hodges** was named MLB Manager of the Year for 1969 by *The Sporting News*. In 1970, his club held a share of first place as late as September 10, but the Mets could not repeat their feat of the previous year. They finished in third place in the NL East, behind both Pittsburgh and Chicago, with a mediocre record of 83–79. Hodges' club posted the very same record in 1971 as they came home in a tie for third place as the Pirates again took top honors in the division. The Mets concluded their 1971 schedule on September 30 with a 6–1 home win over St. Louis. No one at Shea Stadium that Thursday night could have known it was Hodges' last official game as manager. To say the baseball world was deeply saddened by the sudden death of Hodges on April 2, 1972, would be a huge understatement. Hodges had just finished playing 27 holes of golf at West Palm Beach, Florida, on that Easter Sunday. He was playing with longtime friends: Met coaches Eddie Yost, Rube Walker and Joe Pignatano. (Hodges and his companions had plenty of free time on their hands as MLB's first players' strike was delaying the start of the 1972 season.) While discussing that night's dinner plans as he leisurely walked back to his motel with Pignatano, Hodges abruptly collapsed from his second heart attack in 31 months. Hodges fell backwards and hit his head on the sidewalk. He was bleeding profusely and turning blue. Pignatano recalled the awful scene: "I put my hand under Gil's head, but before you knew it, the blood stopped. I knew he was dead. He died in my arms."[39] Hodges was pronounced dead of a coronary at 5:45 p.m. at a local hospital. He was two days shy of his 48th birthday. The shocking news traveled rapidly across North America. ("Mets Miracle Worker Gil Hodges Dead," screamed a headline in the next day's *Montreal Gazette*.) On April 6, more than 10,000 people crowded inside and around Our Lady Help of Christians Church in Brooklyn for the funeral rites. Many of Hodges' current players and old Dodger teammates were inconsolable. "I'm sick," said ex–Brooklyn pitcher Johnny Podres. "I've never known a finer man."[40] Jackie Robinson tearfully told Howard Cosell that Hodges' passing rivaled the recent death of his son as the saddest day in his life. (Robinson himself would be dead, just as suddenly, less than seven months later.) Pee Wee Reese said, "If you have a son, it would be a great thing to have him grow up to be like Gil Hodges."[41] In his playing days, Hodges was a superb defensive first baseman and an offensive force. Some people steadfastly believe that Hodges, more than anyone else, was the heart and soul of the famed Brooklyn Dodger clubs of the 1940s and 1950s. The Mets retired Hodges' #14 in 1973. His exclusion from the Hall of Fame is utterly mystifying to a great many baseball fans. In June 2019, Hodges' 93-year-old widow, Joan, was present at Citi Field for the 50th anniversary celebration of the Mets' 1969 World Series championship.

Here is a fun fact about Baltimore second baseman **Dave Johnson**: Because he had a bachelor's degree in mathematics from Trinity University, his Oriole teammates comically nicknamed him Dum-Dum. Johnson recovered from a truly dismal 1969 World Series in which he managed one measly base hit in 18 at-bats. As a talented and reliable second baseman, he won Gold Gloves in 1969, 1970 and 1971. Following the 1972 season—in which Johnson only batted .221—he was traded to Atlanta in a multi-player deal. (Earl Weaver believed Johnson had lost too much fielding range by bulking up in an attempt to become a more lethal power hitter.) Rejuvenated, in 1973 Johnson hit 43 home runs with the Braves—a remarkable total considering his previous best seasonal output had been 18 in 1971. By 1975, however, Johnson was released by the Braves and ended up playing two seasons in Japan. After Johnson concluded his playing career, he managed three minor league teams before becoming the manager of the New York Mets in 1984. Now more commonly referred to as Davey Johnson, he led the Mets to the 1986 NL pennant (their first since 1973) and a World Series championship. Thus, the man whose fly ball to Cleon Jones made the final out in the 1969 World Series was the same man who managed the Mets to their next World Series title. "Davey Johnson went on to an even more decorated career as a manager," wrote one biographer. "His winning percentage of .562 is 10th all-time among managers with 1,000 victories; [a statistic] surpassed by only Earl Weaver among pilots who began their careers after 1960. But it was while playing for Weaver in Baltimore that Johnson first became a prominent name in baseball, as the valuable second baseman for four pennant winners and the 1966 and 1970 [World Series] champions."[42]

Cleon Jones played for six more seasons with the Mets, but he never again came close to hitting .340 as he did in 1969. (Moreover, it was a Mets team record until 1998.) The man who caught the fly ball to end the 1969 World Series hit .277 in 1970 and a very good .319 in 1971. Injuries began to take their toll on Jones in 1972, however. Playing in about two-thirds of New York's games that season, he batted a disappointing .245. His average improved slightly to .260 in 1973 as the Mets advanced to their second World Series. Jones batted .286 in the Fall Classic and hit a homer in Game #2. The following season, 1974, Jones rebounded with a .282 batting average in 124 games. Sadly, Jones' stay in New York came to an inglorious and acrimonious end in 1975. Batting just .240 with only two RBI in 21 games, Jones and manager Yogi Berra clashed in a July 18 game versus Atlanta at Shea Stadium. Berra sent Jones up to pinch hit for Ed Kranepool in the seventh inning. Jones lined out to shortstop, but, when the side was retired, Jones refused to take his defensive position. *The Sporting News* reported what happened next: "There was a shouting match between [Berra and Jones] on the bench and ended with Jones flinging his glove down, pulling towels off the rack, and storming up the runway to the clubhouse."[43] When the game ended, an angry Berra informed the Mets brass that if Jones did not go, he (Berra) would resign. The Mets tried to deal Jones to the California Angels, but the trade did not materialize. Jones was given his outright release by the Mets on July 27. He did not play during the rest of the 1975 season. Jones got into a handful of games with the Chicago White Sox in 1976 before being released from the AL team. After leaving baseball, Jones returned to his home in Mobile, Alabama. He worked in the restaurant and maintenance businesses. He now does community service work with the city's youth and elderly.

Ralph Kiner led the NL in home runs for a remarkable seven straight seasons (1946 through 1952) as a member of the Pittsburgh Pirates, but a back injury ended his playing career in 1955. Beginning in 1961 with the Chicago White Sox, Kiner embarked on a lengthy and distinguished baseball broadcasting career that lasted well into his eighties. The following year, 1962, Kiner joined the New York Mets for their first season and worked alongside Lindsey Nelson. As a Met broadcaster, he was selected by NBC to do radio coverage for both the 1969 and 1973 World Series. Kiner was known for making occasional—and often amusing—verbal gaffes, especially with players' names. (Once he referred to Gary Carter as "Gary Cooper.") Even being afflicted with Bell's palsy did not stop Kiner from eventually calling MLB games for 53 seasons. Upon Kiner's death at age 91 in 2014, Mets owner Fred Wilpon affectionately said of him, "Ralph Kiner was one of the most beloved people in Mets history—an original Met and extraordinary gentleman."[44]

"I feared losing."[45] That is how **Jerry Koosman** responded in a 2019 interview to why he is still widely considered the best "money pitcher" the New York Mets ever had. He also reigns as the winningest left-hander in the club's history with 140 wins. Few people realized how many injuries and ailments Jerry Koosman had to overcome in 1969 to be the man who threw the final pitch of that year's baseball season. He endured everything from a painful muscle knot in his rotator cuff to burning his hands with hot butter while making popcorn. In 1970 Koosman suffered a very public injury: On June 7 in Cincinnati he was running in the outfield during batting practice. As bad luck would have it, fellow Met hurler Gary Gentry struck him in the face with a line drive. The painful result was a broken jaw and five displaced teeth. He had his jaw wired shut for six weeks and thus could not eat solid food. Manager Gil Hodges ordered Koosman to keep his weight up by drinking milkshakes and beer—even while sitting on the Mets' bench. "In six weeks, I only lost three pounds,"[46] Koosman recalled. There was no defense of their World Series title; the Mets dropped to third place in the NL East in 1970, finishing behind both Pittsburgh and Chicago. Koosman was 12–7 in 1971. Deeply shocked by Hodges' death in April 1972, Koosman struggled that season and had to rally late in the year to raise his record to 11–12. He was 14–15 in the Mets' pennant year of 1973.

Koosman put together three consecutive quality seasons from 1974 through 1976 while the Mets faltered badly. He won 20 games in 1976—and then lost 20 in 1977 as the Mets became a terrible team. (He was the last MLB pitch to lose a score of games one season after winning 20.) Another awful season for the Mets in 1978 prompted Koosman to request a trade. He was dealt to Minnesota where he won 20 games for the 1979 Twins. Later stops in Chicago (with the White Sox) and Philadelphia rounded out Koosman's fine career. As a 41-year-old, he compiled a 14–15 record with the 1984 Phillies. That season he also surrendered Pete Rose's 4,000th hit.

Ed Kranepool was the only member of the 1969 New York Mets who spent his entire career as a Met. As a 17-year-old, he got into three games with the famously inept 1962 squad. By the time he played his last game in 1979 at age 34, Kranepool, a left-handed slugger, comfortably held eight Met club records that could be attributed to longevity. Kranepool was supposed to be the answer to the Mets' prayers at first base, but instead he evolved into a specialist. Biographer Tara Krieger wrote, "Kranepool was about as good a role player as they came. In 1974, he set the all-time season record for pinch-hit batting average [minimum 30 at bats] by compiling a mark of .486 (17 for 35) in those situations. In his career, he had 90 hits—including six home runs—off the bench."[47] As a teenager, Kranepool struggled in the major leagues. Casey Stengel once disparaged Kranepool's lack of footspeed by saying, "He's only 17 but he runs like he's 30."[48] Kranepool had a breakthrough year at age 20 in 1965; he was hitting .288 with seven homers and 36 RBI when he was selected as the Mets' lone representative at the All-Star Game. Armed with a sharp business mind, Kranepool studied during the offseason and impressively attained a stockbroker's license by his 21st birthday. After the Mets' World Series triumph, Kranepool struggled at the plate and had his playing time reduced; he spent sizable portions of those two difficult seasons at AAA Tidewater. Although he returned to the Mets' fold in 1972, his role on the club slowly but steadily moved toward specialization. Between 1974 and 1978 Kranepool was a deadly pinch-hitter compiling a remarkable .396 batting average. After 1975, Kranepool's role with the Mets began to diminish—and so did his relationship with upper management. During his team's final home stand of 1979, Kranepool felt terribly slighted when the Mets decided to honor the St. Louis Cardinals' soon-to-be-retiring Lou Brock but did not bother to acknowledge his (Kranepool's) impending departure from baseball. After playing 18 seasons and appearing in 1,853 games for the Mets—still the team's all-time team record by almost 300—Kranepool was unceremoniously released by the club in December 1979.

Tony Kubek's superb skills as a baseball analyst were utterly wasted in his being a roving reporter for NBC's 1969 World Series coverage. He mostly did brief fluff interviews with MLB dignitaries and celebrities (including Mitzi Gaynor, Louis Armstrong and Jerry Lewis whose comments added precious little to the telecasts). Kubek had done the same task in 1968 and would again in 1970 and

1971. However, the former Yankee shortstop enjoyed a fine television career working alongside Curt Gowdy, Joe Garagiola, and then Bob Costas on NBC's *Game of the Week* broadcasts. In the 1972 World Series, Kubek was promoted to the broadcast booth. Kubek also worked for two Canadian television networks (CTV and TSN) from 1977 to 1989 calling Toronto Blue Jays games nationally. The *Toronto Star* kindly said of Kubek, "[He] educated a whole generation of Canadian baseball fans without being condescending or simplistic."[49] After NBC lost the rights to MLB after 1989, Kubek worked local Yankee telecasts for a few seasons. He abruptly walked away from the sport in 1994—at least the upper echelons of it—when a labor dispute wiped out the second half of the regular season and the entire postseason. Kubek reputedly has not watched an MLB game since then. "I hate what the game's become—the greed, the nastiness," he told an interviewer. "You can be married to baseball, give your heart to it, but when it starts taking over your soul, it's time to say 'whoa.'"[50]

Dave Leonhard was among the most educated players participating in the 1969 World Series. The graduate of Johns Hopkins was often gently kidded about his scholarly achievements by his Oriole teammates. "Didn't they teach you that at Hopkins?"[51] was a typical barb Leonhard endured whenever he made a mistake. But he took the ribbing without complaint, commenting, "The only time my educational background becomes a factor with the players is when somebody needs help with a crossword puzzle."[52] In 1969, the hard-throwing, right-handed Leonhard split his duties as a starter and a reliever with the Orioles—and doing occasional military training. He compiled a 7–4 record but only saw two innings of work in the World Series, in which he gave up a home run to Ed Kranepool in Game #3. Leonhard entered the 1970 season with confidence, but he saw his playing time reduced when his ERA ballooned. In 1971 he was demoted to the AAA ranks in Rochester to start the season, but he worked his way back to Baltimore by July. In a rare start, he pitched a five-hit shutout versus Kansas City. Leonhard appeared in one game in the 1971 World Series and tossed one shutout inning versus Pittsburgh. Playing in Puerto Rico the following winter, Leonhard got himself in trouble because of an interview he did for a Spanish-language periodical. He dwelled on Puerto Rico's negatives in a piece that was titled "Leonhard Sees Island as Land of Dead Bugs, Lice, and Roaches." His comments irked the locals. Not surprisingly, Leonhard required special police protection for much of the season. Leonhard's playing time was greatly reduced by the Orioles in 1972. It proved to be his last season in the majors.

J.C. Martin only saw one pitch during the entire 1969 World Series—the pitch he bunted to end Game #4. A career .222 hitter, the controversial play is truly the only thing Martin is remembered for by baseball fans. "I don't care what some people say about the play or what I did," Martin said in an interview 20 years afterward. "The umpire said I was safe so I must have been safe. They show my old play again at first base and I see that ball bouncing off my wrist. It didn't hurt a bit then and it doesn't hurt now. I just get a kick out of seeing that ball roll away and old Rodney [Gaspar] running around those bases and getting in for the winning run. That's a satisfying scene."[53] The bunt was also the last thing Martin ever did in a Mets uniform. In March 1970 he was traded to the Cubs. Martin played three seasons in Chicago before retiring in 1972.

Dave May of Delaware came to bat twice for the Orioles as a pinch-hitter in the 1969 World Series and did not put the ball into play either time: He had a strikeout versus Tom Seaver and a base on balls versus Gary Gentry. May had a 12-season MLB career as something of a journeyman outfielder, but after 1969 he would never again appear in the postseason. In 1970, May only had 31 at-bats for Baltimore, a team heavy with talented outfielders. Partway through the season he was dealt to Milwaukee. May was both philosophical and grateful about the trade. He told a reporter, "You like to be with a winning club, but with [Baltimore], I was just sitting around. With Milwaukee, I'll get a chance to play."[54] May played with the Brewers through 1974. He was traded to Atlanta as part of the deal that brought Hank Aaron back to Milwaukee. May played two seasons with Atlanta and one with Texas. May was a good-natured ballplayer who always had time for the media and fans. A journalist for the *Dallas Morning News* called May "without question one of the friendliest players in the sport."[55] In his one year with the Rangers (1977), May had a memorable at-bat versus Nolan Ryan. Like many batters, May usually had trouble versus MLB's all-time strikeout king. In an Angels-Rangers game on September 12, May swung mightily—and missed—at a Ryan fastball, causing one of his contact lenses to fall out. The game was delayed while several people tried unsuccessfully to find it. The lull in the action irked Ryan. The pitcher chirped, "Oh, forget about it. You're going to strike out anyhow." May got his backup pair of eyeglasses from the clubhouse, put them on, and the game resumed. He proceeded to smack an RBI double. May could not resist a gibe. "Is that a strikeout?" he shouted at Ryan while standing on second base. "I'll always remember that one," May noted in an interview years later. "He didn't like it."[56] May died in Bear, Delaware, on October 20, 2012. He was 68 years old.

Between 1968 and 1971, **Dave McNally** won at least 20 games for four consecutive seasons, becoming the first AL pitcher to achieve that impressive feat since Red Ruffing did it for the New York Yankees from 1936 through 1939. McNally pitched well for Baltimore in the 1969 World Series. He recorded a 2.81 ERA over 16 innings. He just did not win a game. The next year the Montana native followed up with a 24–9 regular season record as the Orioles won the 1970 World Series. McNally made history in Game #3 of that Fall Classic by hitting a grand slam home run, the first (and only time to date) a pitcher has achieved that batting feat. While McNally and Bob Gibson are the only two pitchers to hit two career World Series homers, oddly McNally's only two World Series hits were both home runs. In the 1971 World Series, McNally—one of four 20-game winners on the Baltimore pitching staff—picked up two victories (one as a starter and one as a reliever) but lost

Game #5 as Pittsburgh upset Baltimore in seven games. By the end of the 1974 season, McNally was in a funk and asked to be traded to start afresh in new surroundings. At the time he was the Orioles all-time leader in career wins with 181. He was dealt to Montreal and spent less than half a season with the Expos before retiring at the age of 32. He had fared poorly and felt he owed the fans of Montreal an apology. "It got to the point where I was stealing money,"[57] he said of his six-figure contract. Although he never played again, he allowed his name to be used in the successful legal fight to overturn the reserve clause since he had played his last season without a contract. A chain smoker, McNally died of prostate and lung cancer on December 1, 2002, at the age of 70 in Billings, Montana. Upon hearing of McNally's passing, his old manager Earl Weaver kindly said, "Dave was an unbelievable competitor. He did it with cunning and intelligence. Plus, he was 100 percent gentleman."[58]

Curt Motton of Louisiana, used primarily as a reserve outfielder and pinch-hitter by the Orioles, saw just one pitch in the 1969 World Series. He grounded out batting for Dave McNally in the eighth inning of Game #5. He had his surname mispronounced by Shea Stadium P.A. announcer Jack Lightcap, although Lindsey Nelson got it right. (The correct pronunciation was "moe-tun.") Known for having a good eye at the plate—he walked almost as much as he struck out—Motton had some pop in his bat too, with 25 career home runs. "Earl Weaver kept him around for his power,"[59] one biographer of Motton declared. Motton appeared in about one of every three Orioles games from 1967 to 1972. He is likely best remembered for two key pinch-hits. One was the single off Ron Perranoski in Game #2 of the 1969 ALCS. The other was a double he hit off Oakland's Vida Blue in Game #1 of the 1971 ALCS. Motton was philosophical about his limited role on the powerful, pennant-winning Oriole teams. "We're winning. That's the only good thing about sitting on the bench here," he observed. "With a club like this, you can make more money because we get in the playoffs and the World Series."[60] Jim Palmer noted, however, "Guys like Curt made us more of a complete team."[61] Motton died of stomach cancer on January 21, 2010. He was 69 years old.

Whenever umpire **Larry Napp** had a plate assignment, his distinctive way of calling strikes quickly became evident: He would lift his right leg along with his right arm in what appeared to be a quirky dance. Napp (who was born Larry Albert Napodano) had a 25-year career as an AL umpire. During his tenure, Napp worked four World Series and four All-Star Games. The most famous image of Napp in action was actually one of inaction. It was captured by *Sports Illustrated* photographer Neil Leifer in Baltimore on September 3, 1960. The soles of his plate umpiring shoe are prominent, but Napp's face is obscured by people tending to him. Napp is lying flat on his back near home plate from the cumulative effect of having been struck by three consecutive pitches. Still, Napp was a thoroughly tough character. He was a judo expert who also taught and refereed boxing during the offseason. Napp had boxed professionally as a lightweight for a couple of years in the mid–1930s. He died from a heart attack at his home in Plantation, Florida, at age 77 on July 7, 1993.

Lindsey Nelson was described by one biographer as "an overworked national star in the late 1950s on NBC's college football, NBA basketball and major league baseball broadcasts."[62] He also worked Notre Dame football games between 1967 and 1979 and broadcast a record 26 Cotton Bowl games. In 1962, Nelson surprisingly stepped back from many of his national duties and agreed to call the exploits of the expansion 1962 New York Mets. Working alongside Ralph Kiner and Bob Murphy, it was a gig Nelson kept for 17 seasons. A graduate of the University of Tennessee, whatever sport Nelson worked, he always did it with a large and direct dose of folksy southern charm that greatly contrasted with the deliberately loud wardrobes he preferred when color television became the norm. Another biographer declared, "Wherever [Nelson] set up his microphone, he sounded as if there was no place he would rather be. Like many announcers trained in the heyday of AM radio, [Nelson] learned to convey excitement without screaming. His enthusiastic personality, on and off the air, was designed to offend no one, and that was one of the secrets of his survival in the often-cutthroat world of big-time sports broadcasting."[63] Nelson surprised New York's baseball fans when he voluntarily left the Mets after 17 years following the 1978 season and signed a three-year deal to call games for the San Francisco Giants. (He wanted to be close to his daughter who lived in the Bay Area.) Parkinson's disease forced Nelson into retirement in 1985. While recuperating at Emory University Hospital in Atlanta from a fall, Nelson died from pneumonia on June 10, 1995, 15 days after his 76th birthday. In his obituary, the *Los Angeles Times* said Nelson's "soothing voice and brazen sports jackets were fixtures for generations of baseball and college football fans."[64]

Originally from the Bronx, New York, Baltimore Orioles broadcaster **Bill O'Donnell** called baseball games with a pleasant voice—and a calm, professional, unflappable air presence. It stood to reason. Covering sports was an absolute picnic for O'Donnell who, as a teenager, had been a combat correspondent for the U.S. Marine Corps during the Second World War and witnessed some of the most horrific battles in the Pacific Theater. After years of calling minor league games, in 1966 he was hired by the Baltimore Orioles as their full-time radio and TV broadcaster. "I felt like my prayers had been answered,"[65] O'Donnell remembered. By chance, he had latched onto a team that was going to be the dominant force in the AL for a decade. He also partnered with the superb Chuck Thompson for 16 seasons. As well as working for the Orioles, O'Donnell was the play-by-play man for the backup game of NBC's *Game of the Week* telecasts from 1969 to 1976. It was Thompson, though, and not O'Donnell, who was chosen by NBC to be the Orioles' World Series announcer in 1970 and 1971. Sadly, in 1981, O'Donnell was diagnosed with cancer. Thompson recalled, "Bill underwent cancer surgery in 1981, and made enough progress to return to work. But a year later, he had another operation and never fully recovered."[66] An especially distressing scene from the 1982 season was forever etched into Thompson's memory: "Sometime after the second operation, [O'Donnell] wanted to come back to the booth and do his share.

The night he returned, [there was] an extended rain delay. As long as I live, I'll remember Bill stretched across three metal chairs in the back of the booth during the delay, trying to conserve as much energy as possible for the resumption of the game. I begged him to go home. But professionals don't quit—and Bill completed the game."[67] O'Donnell died on October 29, 1982. He was just 56 years old.

Baltimore manager Earl Weaver famously had a love-hate relationship with his superstar right-handed pitcher **Jim Palmer**. In praiseful times, Weaver said, "Jim Palmer knows how to rise to the occasion, plus Jim Palmer will be in the Hall of Fame—and it's hard to go wrong when you pitch a Hall-of-Famer."[68] (Palmer was indeed elected to Cooperstown in 1990, being chosen on more than 92 percent of the ballots in his first year of eligibility.) Other times Weaver lamented the seemingly endless string of injuries—both real and imagined—that afflicted Palmer. Weaver once bitterly told a scribe, "The Chinese tell time by the Year of the Horse or the Year of the Dragon. I tell time by the Year of the Back and the Year of the Elbow. This year it's the Year of the Ulnar Nerve."[69] According to one Palmer biographer, the acrimony between Weaver and the pitcher "seemed largely theater. Neither man could hide his admiration for the other."[70] The high-kicking Palmer won three AL Cy Young Awards, had eight 20-win seasons, and is universally regarded as the greatest pitcher in Orioles history. It is all quite remarkable considering he was demoted to the minors in 1968 with arm trouble and subsequently left unprotected in the draft. No other MLB team took a chance with him. Consistently reliable, Palmer spent his entire career in Baltimore, winning World Series games in three different decades. When Palmer was released by the Orioles in 1984, he was the team's all-time leader in games pitched, games started, innings pitched, batters faced, complete games, wins, strikeouts, and shutouts. As of 2020, he still leads the club in all those categories. Upon retiring, Palmer quickly went into baseball broadcasting at both the local and national levels.

Where John (**Boog**) **Powell** grew up in Lakeland, Florida, mischief-making children were known as "buggers." John's father shortened the disparaging term to Boog. The moniker stuck through adulthood, giving his muscular son one of baseball's most memorable nicknames. Following the disappointing 1969 World Series in which Powell had five hits in 19 at-bats—and none for extra bases—the slugging Baltimore first baseman had a terrific 1970 season, winning the AL MVP with a .297 batting average and clubbing 35 home runs. He also hit three postseason homers, including two in the World Series, as Baltimore upended the Cincinnati Reds in five games. (Always a good defensive player, Powell made a memorable putout on Johnny Bench during that World Series, catching a foul pop-up with his bare hand after it had fallen from his mitt.) Powell's offensive output dropped noticeably from 1971 to 1974. In 1975, he was acquired by the Cleveland Indians where an old Oriole teammate, Frank Robinson, was now the manager. Powell put up numbers almost the same as his MVP year and garnered some MVP votes. (He finished 20th.) Powell's batting stats again declined in 1976 and he spent 1977 as a part-time player with the Los Angeles Dodgers. He was forever an Oriole, though, in the minds of baseball fans. He and Brooks Robinson jointly performed ceremonial pitch duties on Opening Day 2010 when Baltimore celebrated the 40th anniversary of the 1970 World Series champions. Since 1992, Powell has been the proprietor of Boog's BBQ, located just outside of Camden Yards.

"**Merv Rettenmund** provides Earl Weaver with a pleasant problem,"[71] said Curt Gowdy during a 1970 World Series telecast. The dilemma was that Rettenmund gave the Orioles too many quality outfielders. Rettenmund played halfback at Ball State University and was drafted by the Dallas Cowboys, but he never pursued professional football as a livelihood. It was a good decision. Rettenmund had a 13-year MLB playing career distinguished by his roles as both a "super sub" and as a highly dependable pinch-hitter. Rettenmund was a player of terrific promise. In 1968 he was named Minor League Player of the Year by *The Sporting News* for his excellent season with the AAA Rochester Red Wings. As the fourth outfielder on the 1969 Baltimore Orioles, however, Rettenmund did not get many opportunities to start on such a talented squad. That season, his first full-time campaign in the big leagues, Rettenmund became hugely valuable to the Orioles as someone who could come off the Baltimore bench in numerous roles. In an interview years later, Rettenmund recalled getting into trouble with his short-fused manager during the 1970 World Series. Rettenmund did not appear in the first three games versus Cincinnati. During Game #4, when he was again not playing, Rettenmund decided he could see what was happening better on television than from his spot on the bench. Accordingly, he quietly moved to the Orioles' clubhouse and watched the action from a TV set in the manager's office! Between innings Earl Weaver caught Rettenmund—relaxing with his feet up on the desk!—and chewed him out. Nevertheless, Weaver also told him he would be starting Game #5 the next day. (He responded with a solo home run, an RBI single, a walk, and two runs scored, as Baltimore won, 9–3, to clinch the World Series.) In 1971, Rettenmund had his best MLB season. Playing in a career-high 141 games for Baltimore and batting .318, Rettenmund finished 19th in AL MVP voting. (In a heady moment before one game that year, Rettenmund told his teammates that there were only two certainties in the world: there would be snow in the wintertime and that he would get his typical two hits that day.) However, his numbers dropped off noticeably in 1972 and 1973. Rettenmund was deemed expendable after he hit just .091 in the 1973 ALCS versus Oakland. Dealt to Cincinnati—another MLB powerhouse team—he had two poor seasons with the high-flying Reds. In 1976, Cincinnati dealt Rettenmund to San Diego, where the pleasing warm climate—and the complete absence of any pressure—seemed to rejuvenate his batting eye. Pinch-hitting became Rettenmund's famed forte with the Padres. In 1977, he recorded a .313 batting average (a phenomenal 21-for-67) coming off the San Diego bench. At the time, those 21 hits were the eighth greatest pinch-hit total ever recorded in single MLB season. After retiring as a player in 1980, Rettenmund served for more than two decades as a batting coach with several MLB teams, most notably the San Diego Padres. There he helped shape Tony Gwynn into baseball's finest hitter.

Pete Richert only threw one pitch during the 1969 World Series—but it was a memorable toss. It was the one that J.C. Martin bunted to end Game #4. It, of course, sparked a belated debate about an interference call that probably should have been made but was not. Richert became a valuable reliever in Baltimore's championship teams through 1971. Richert's best season was 1970. Throwing mostly fastballs, Richert won seven games, lost two, and notched 13 saves. He compiled a 1.98 ERA and recorded a save in Game #1 of that year's World Series. Richert later pitched in the NL for the Dodgers, Cardinals and Phillies. He retired in 1974. After his active days as a player had ended, Richert served as a pitching coach for several teams in the Pacific Coast League.

One biographer summed it up well: "Setting the standard by which all who followed him are judged, **Brooks Robinson** played third base with style, class and an uncanny ability to turn in spectacular plays with startling regularity for 23 seasons."[72] A lifetime Oriole, Robinson won 16—16!—Gold Gloves in his fabulous career. For 15 years running he was the AL's starting third baseman in the All-Star Game. There is hardly an MLB career record for third sackers that Robinson does not own—and hold by a substantial margin. The 1964 AL MVP, Robinson had a poor 1969 World Series, at least offensively. He made up for it—and then some— the following October versus Cincinnati with one of the truly great performances that any player ever had in a Fall Classic. At age 33, not only did Robinson bat .429 in the Series (going 4-for-4 in Game #4), he made one highlight-reel defensive play after another as the Orioles crushed the Reds in five games. (The most remembered of Robinson's gems came off the bat of Lee May in the sixth inning of Game #1. It was so spectacular that it caused the fans in Cincinnati to audibly gasp. "Great day in the morning! What a play!"[73] exclaimed Reds broadcaster Jim McIntyre. Robinson was playing well behind third base. He fielded a fair ground ball that was already moving into foul territory. Robinson made a hurried, off-balance throw from well to the left of third base that bounced perfectly on a straight line to Boog Powell at first base. May was out by half a step. It needs to be viewed over and over again to be fully appreciated.) Cincinnati manager Sparky Anderson could only watch admiringly with awe. "I'm beginning to see Brooks in my sleep," he joked after the Series. "If I dropped this paper plate, he'd pick it up on one hop and throw me out at first."[74] The impressed Reds players abbreviated Robinson's nickname—"the human vacuum cleaner"—to one word: "Hoover." Robinson won a Dodge Charger as the 1970 World Series MVP, prompting Cincinnati catcher Johnny Bench to comment, "If he wanted a car that badly, we would have given him one."[75] Robinson also made offensive contributions to the Orioles too. He fell only 152 hits short of 3,000. Upon his retirement, Robinson became a broadcaster. Enormously popular with fans because of his willingness to interact with them, Robinson's Hall of Fame induction ceremony in 1983 drew one of the largest attendances ever at

Cooperstown. He was elected in his first year of eligibility with his name appearing on nearly 92 percent of the ballots cast. Robinson has been honored with two statues in Baltimore. One features him playing with a gold glove.

Frank Robinson was the man whom Mets fans loved to hate in October 1969, but by that point in his career, the 34-year-old Robinson was undeniably one of the best ballplayers in the majors. After seeing Robinson bat for the first time in a 1966 spring training game, teammate Jim Palmer presciently told fellow Oriole pitcher Dick Hall, "I think we've just won the pennant."[76] Years later Palmer also would insist Robinson "was the best player I ever saw."[77] Robinson already held a unique spot in baseball history as the only player to be named MVP of both major leagues (1961 with Cincinnati and 1966 with Baltimore). He also attained a rare Triple Crown with the Orioles in 1966. After the disappointment of losing the 1969 World Series to New York, Robinson enjoyed a solid year in 1970. He batted .306 and hit 25 home runs. The individual highlight of the 1970 season for Robinson occurred over two consecutive days. On June 25 at Boston's Fenway Park, he saved a game with a terrific catch in the 13th inning in which he hurt himself. Robinson could barely swing a bat, yet he drove in the winning run in the 14th inning with a well-placed bunt. The next night in Washington, Robinson recovered his batting stroke and hit *two* grand slam home runs. The Orioles, again dominant, won 108 games in 1970 and captured the World Series. In 1971, Robinson was the MVP of the All-Star Game and led his Orioles to their third consecutive AL pennant. They lost the World Series in seven games. Surprisingly, the 36-year-old Robinson was traded in December to the Los Angeles Dodgers. He struggled in his one season there and was dealt to the California Angels. Robinson spent nearly two full and productive seasons there, but often clashed with manager Bobby Winkles. He ended up with the Cleveland Indians in September 1974. Robinson was named the player-manager of the Indians for 1975—becoming the first black field pilot in MLB history. (During the 1969 ALCS, Robinson expressed interest to a Pittsburgh scribe about managing the NL Pirates.) Rachel Robinson, Jackie Robinson's widow, made a point of attending the historically significant Opening Day in Cleveland on April 8. Frank Robinson made it doubly memorable by homering in the game, won by Cleveland 5–3 over the New York Yankees. Robinson would eventually hold managing jobs in Baltimore, Montreal and Washington. Despite his serious approach to the game, Robinson had a sense of humor and a sharp wit that served him well. Wearing a mop on his head, Robinson acted as judge for the Orioles' kangaroo court, assessing good-natured fines of one dollar to teammates for missing signs, uniform violations, and any other transgressions—real or imagined—that he deemed to be an infraction. He and teammate Brooks Robinson were paired together in a famously comical 1980 beer commercial in which they explained that, although they had a lot in common, they were not identical twins. Frank could barely suppress his laughter long enough to deliver the punchline: "I'm at least two inches taller than he is!"[78] A recipient of the Presidential Medal of Freedom, Frank Robinson died of bone cancer at age 83 on February 7, 2019. That day Commissioner Rob Manfred accurately said, "[Robinson] was one of the greatest players in the history of our game, but that was just the beginning of a multifaceted baseball career."[79] Robinson was honored with three statues: one in Cincinnati, one in Baltimore, and one in Cleveland.

"You don't want to face **Nolan Ryan** without your rest," Reggie Jackson once advised. "He's the only guy I go against who makes me go to bed before midnight."[80] Ryan, who started 10 games for the 1969 Mets, had his only career World Series appearance in a relief stint in Game #3. Already well known by that time for his fearsome fastball, Ryan went on to become baseball's most overpowering and successful strikeout artist in a Hall of Fame career that spanned four decades. During his induction day speech at Cooperstown, Ryan stated, "It took me a while to figure out and realize what a gift that I had been given. And when I finally did, I dedicated myself to be the best pitcher I possibly could be, for as long as I possibly could be."[81] He succeeded. In 1971, Ryan was traded from the Mets to the California Angels in exchange for Jim Fregosi. It is often considered one of the worst trades in baseball history—especially by New York Met fans. By the time Ryan retired, he had obliterated the old MLB career strikeout record and set a new standard; it may well prove unattainable for anyone else. His 5,714 whiffs are nearly 1,000 more than what runner-up Randy Johnson accrued. Ryan also holds the modern MLB record for strikeouts in a season (383), set in 1973 with the Angels—the first season in which AL pitchers had to contend with the designated hitter. As of 2020, only 35 pitchers in MLB history have thrown multiple no-hitters. Ryan threw seven, his last coming in 1991 at age 44. Next best is Sandy Koufax—who is far in arrears with four. Ryan modestly summarized his career this way: "My job was to give my team a chance to win."[82]

Baltimore utility player Rutherford Eduardo **(Chico) Salmon** was inserted into two games of the 1969 World Series by Earl Weaver. Both times it was as a pinch-runner. Both times it was in the ninth inning. Salmon, a Panamanian, scored neither time. (He was the Oriole runner standing on first base when Dave Johnson flied out to Cleon Jones to end the Series.) The following October, Salmon batted once in the 1970 Baltimore-Cincinnati World Series as a pinch-hitter, in Game #2. He smacked a single off Reds pitcher Jim McGlothlin, making him one of just a handful of MLB players to compile a perfect World Series batting average of 1.000. Salmon knew he was far from being a star as an MLB role player—and he enjoyed joking about it. He also had no problem with others laughing about it too. Lou Piniella once kiddingly said to him, "I've been in this league for two years and I've never seen you play, Chico. What do you do for a living?"[83] Salmon was released by the Orioles in August 1972. The 31-year-old never played in the majors again. The affable Salmon died of a heart attack on September 17, 2000. He was only 59 years old.

Reggie Jackson once said of **Tom Seaver,** "Blind men come to the park just to

Remarkably, Frank Robinson has statues in three different MLB cities: Baltimore, Cleveland and Cincinnati. This is a photo of the statue of the late baseball great situated outside Great American Ballpark in Cincinnati (Library of Congress).

hear him pitch."[84] That comment is hyperbolic, but few serious baseball fans would question Seaver's status as the most popular New York Met ever. There was good reason why he was referred to as "The Franchise." "Tom was a legend," Wayne Garrett said in a 2019 interview. "[Over his career] Tom meant a lot to all of us. He meant a lot to me. Seaver just kind of stood head and shoulders over the rest of the pitching staff."[85] Seaver brought a new, positive attitude to the Mets when he first joined the woebegone club in 1967. "I didn't follow the Mets at all," Seaver later wrote. "I didn't know who Marv Throneberry was, or Choo-Choo Coleman, or any of the other Met characters. All I knew about the Mets was that they lost most of the time."[86] Seaver was not a loser. The 12-time All-Star won three NL Cy Young Awards over his career. Hank Aaron said Seaver was the toughest pitcher he ever faced. Nearly four decades after he last pitched for New York, he remains the club's all-time leader in victories with 198; that figure is 26 percent better than second-place Dwight Gooden's 157. In 1988, Seaver was the first Met player to have his uniform number (#41) retired. In a 1970 game, he struck out the last 10 San Diego Padres he faced to set an MLB record for consecutive whiffs. Unfortunately, Seaver did not leave the Mets on the best of terms. Following the 1976 season Seaver's attempts to obtain a contract he felt was in line with his skill level and past services to the Mets proved fruitless. His dealings with M. Donald Grant, the Mets chairman of the board, went nowhere. He was also getting bad press from some New York City tabloids—especially from sports columnist Dick Young who constantly labelled Seaver as greedy. Finally, Seaver asked to be traded. The man who had won 23 percent of the Mets' victories since 1967 was moved to the Cincinnati Reds on June 15, 1977. Seaver compiled a splendid 14-3 record in half a season with the Reds in 1977. Meanwhile, the Mets plummeted to the bottom of the NL East standings where they languished for three seasons. Seaver returned to the Mets in 1982 and 1983. He also spent time in the AL with Chicago and Boston. He eventually won 311 MLB games. The milestone 300th victory came at Yankee Stadium on August 4, 1985. (In a classy gesture, beloved former Met announcer Lindsey Nelson was invited by the New York Yankees to call the ninth inning.) Knowledgeable and well-spoken, Seaver not surprisingly became involved in baseball broadcasting. As early as 1978—when he was still an active player—Seaver was part of NBC's World Series crew. After baseball, Seaver and his wife got into the wine business. Starting in the late 1990s they operated and lived at a 116-acre vineyard estate in Calistoga, California. Seaver was elected to the Hall of Fame in 1992 in his first year of eligibility, getting votes on 425 of the 430 ballots. In 2013 Seaver began experiencing serious health issues and had difficulty remembering the names of his closest longtime friends. The memory loss was attributed to Lyme disease. In March 2019 it was disclosed by Seaver's family that he had been diagnosed with Alzheimer's dementia and he would no longer make public appearances. In June 2019, during the 50th anniversary celebration of the team's 1969 championship—which 74-year-old Tom Terrific did not attend—the New York Mets officially changed the address of Citi Field to 41 Seaver Way. Seaver died at his home on August 31, 2020, but his passing was not announced until September 2. According to a statement from the National Baseball Hall of Fame, Seaver, 75, died from a combination of Lewy body dementia and COVID-19. In an odd coincidence, Seaver's death was revealed shortly after the Mets defeated the Orioles in an interleague game in Baltimore.

Umpire **Frank Secory** was nearing the end of his second MLB career when he umpired the 1969 World Series at age 57. It was his fourth Fall Classic—as an official. A resident of Port Huron, Michigan, Secory played in the majors as an outfielder sporadically from 1940 to 1946, appearing in five games of the 1945 World Series as a member of the Chicago Cubs. (He went 2-of-5 at the plate in that Fall Classic.) Secory, like several other MLB players of his era, took up umpiring once his playing says had ended. Secory began his second baseball career as a professional umpire in the Class C West Texas-New Mexico League in 1948. From there he advanced up the ranks rapidly. Within four years, Secory was on the NL's staff of umpires. He officiated for 19 seasons from 1952 to 1970 in which he seemed to have a knack for umpiring no-hitters. He worked nine of them. Secory died at age 82 on April 7, 1995.

As a member of the 1966 Cincinnati Reds, **Art Shamsky** once hit four consecutive home runs over the course of two games. Another time he hit three homers in a game in which he did not start—a feat accomplished by no other MLB player!

However, Shamsky's 1969 season with the New York Mets almost ended before it started. During spring training, the Met outfielder was practicing fielding ground balls on March 15. Suddenly, Shamsky felt a sharp pain in his back and a shooting pain go down his left leg. It was diagnosed as a slipped disc pressing against his sciatic nerve. After three weeks of uncertainty and regular discomfort, Shamsky was given permission by doctors to continue with the season, but he did get sent to the Mets' AAA affiliate in Tidewater, Virginia to start the year. After hitting very well in the minors, Shamsky was recalled to the Mets on May 13. He hit exactly .300 in the regular season, but Shamsky was a blistering .538 versus Atlanta pitching in the three-game NLCS. Because of Gil Hodges' platoon system, Shamsky saw only limited playing time in the World Series. He was hitless in six at-bats versus Baltimore. Shamsky had a fine season for New York in 1970, batting .293, but he tailed off badly in 1971. He hit just .185 and was traded to St. Louis shortly after the season ended. Shamsky was cut by the Cardinals during spring training 1972 and, later that same season, he had two short-lived stints with the Chicago Cubs and Oakland Athletics. Shamsky got the message—and called it a career. "Three teams didn't want me. That was enough,"[87] he noted. After baseball, Shamsky was a restaurateur for a time and worked in the real estate field. He did some broadcasting for the Mets in 1980 and 1981. He says the passage of time has embellished his association with the 1969 Mets, noting, "You know, those [14] home runs that I hit went 550 feet instead of barely making it over the fence. But who cares?"[88]

Jim Simpson worked all five games of the World Series for NBC radio along with hosting the network's pregame television show (alongside Sandy Koufax and Mickey Mantle). Known for his professionalism and versatility, the smooth-voiced 41-year-old was a mainstay on NBC for many years, calling whatever sport came his way in a calm, methodical but pleasing style. Along with MLB, Simpson worked college football bowl games, basketball, tennis, and just about everything else on the sports menu for NBC. He worked for ABC and CBS at various times in his career too. When ESPN began in 1979, it hired Simpson to announce its first basketball telecast to give the fledgling all-sports cable network an automatic level of credibility. In 1998, Simpson received the sportscasting industry's highest honor: the Lifetime Achievement Award. In 2000, he was inducted into the National Sportscasters and Sportswriters Association Hall of Fame. Simpson died on January 13, 2016, at age 88 after a brief illness. Upon hearing of Simpson's passing, John Wildhack, an ESPN vice-president, noted, "There has never been a finer or more unassuming man to reach such heights in his profession."[89]

Hank Soar put in six more years as an AL umpire following the 1969 World Series. His last major assignment was the 1971 ALCS. Then, following his active 26-year career as an official, Soar became supervisor of AL umpires where he occasionally worked games on a fill-in basis as necessary until 1978. "There was no hemming and hawing when Hank was umpiring," recalled former Boston Red Sox third baseman Frank Malzone. "Hank called plays the way he saw them. He was always fair, and he never held a grudge."[90] Prior to becoming a professional baseball umpire, Soar had played in the National Football League for 11 seasons. He died at the age of 87 on Christmas Eve 2001.

Ron Swoboda will be known forever among baseball fans for his remarkable diving catch in Game #4 of the World Series off Brooks Robinson. (The next day, his eighth-inning double drove in Cleon Jones with the winning run to clinch the Series in Game #5, but only hard-core Met fans can generally recall that feat.) Despite his heroics, Swoboda only played one more season for the Mets. In 1970 he batted .233 in 115 games for New York, just slightly below the .235 batting average he posted during the Mets' 1969 championship season. He was traded in March 1971 to Montreal. Swoboda played in just 39 games for the Expos that season before he was dealt to the New York Yankees. (Swoboda said a feeling of awe swept over him the first time he walked onto the outfield grass at pre-renovation Yankee Stadium.) Swoboda played with the Yankees through 1973. He was released in December of that year. After appearing in 928 MLB games, Swoboda's career came to its close when he failed to latch on with the Atlanta Braves in 1974. After leaving baseball, Swoboda did some radio and TV work in several cities. At one time he and Met teammate Ed Kranepool jointly ran a restaurant. He wrote a memoir about the 1969 Mets aptly titled *Here's the Catch*. According to one biographer, Swoboda's hobby is studying impressionist art.

Ron Taylor was a member of both the World Series-winning 1964 St. Louis Cardinals and 1969 New York Mets. He was even more noteworthy because he was a Canadian playing major league baseball in the 1960s. In his era, that achievement was rarer than an American playing in the National Hockey League. Upon joining St. Louis, Taylor, a Toronto resident, impressed Tim McCarver with his outstanding velocity. "He threw so hard that it felt like he was doing something illegal,"[91] recalled the Cardinals' catcher. Taylor earned a place in Mets lore by being the first pitcher in his franchise's history to win a game on Opening Day—achieving the feat at Pittsburgh's Forbes Field in 1970. Taylor got the win by coming out of the bullpen, of course. In his four World Series relief appearances, Taylor did not surrender a single base hit. A postseason goodwill tour he made with a group of major leaguers to army hospitals in Vietnam inspired him. When Taylor's baseball career ended in 1972 due to a dead arm, the University of Toronto graduate—who had been an excellent engineering student—turned his attention to medical school and eventually became Dr. Ron Taylor in his late thirties. Later, Taylor was hired as the team physician for the Toronto Blue Jays. Pat Gillick, the Blue Jays' general manager, joked, "We're getting a three-in-one: We're getting an engineer, a batting practice pitcher, and we're getting a physician. How could you have a better deal?"[92] Taylor earned two more World Series rings in his medical capacity with Toronto. Taylor also has a keen appreciation of 20th century American history. He once told an interviewer the following about being part of the Mets' 1969 victory celebration—the grandest in New York City since V-J Day: "We were riding down

Broadway in that ticker-tape parade, and the crowds were cheering, and the paper was floating down form high above those office buildings. I couldn't stop thinking that this was the path that MacArthur, Eisenhower, and Kennedy had ridden. I never felt so euphoric."[93] Taylor is the subject of a documentary film produced by his two sons in 2015. Its title is *Ron Taylor: Dr. Baseball.*

"A short, chunky midwesterner, usually with a pronounced wad of Red Man chewing tobacco bulging in his left cheek"[94] was how one biographer described **Eddie Watt**. The 28-year-old right-handed Baltimore reliever, who had a subpar 1969 World Series, was generally a reliable mainstay in the team's bullpen through 1972. He felt the unyielding wrath of Oriole fans, however, after he surrendered a three-run homer to Cincinnati's Lee May late in Game #4 of the 1970 World Series. Never mind it was the Reds' only win in the Series, a Fall Classic that Baltimore won rather handily. For some reason it became fashionable to boo Watt from depriving them of a World Series sweep. (He was viciously heckled at a Baltimore Bullets basketball game after the 1970 baseball season ended.) Despite being out for a month in 1971 after breaking his hand making a tag in a game versus the New York Yankees, Watt led the Orioles in saves that season with 11 and had a very respectable 1.82 ERA. Watt lost Game #4 of the 1971 World Series in Pittsburgh and became even more unpopular in Baltimore. By 1973 Watt was unmercifully booed at Memorial Stadium, with fans constantly reminding him about the 1970 World Series—which Watt found utterly perplexing. By 1974 Watt was playing in the minors. He later had success coaching in the San Diego Padres' farm system.

Earl Weaver continued his battling and boisterous managerial career with the Orioles through 1982. Even at the major league level, statistics regarding ejections are a little bit fuzzy. Depending on the source one consults, Weaver was thrown out of MLB games at least 91 times, perhaps 94, or maybe even 98. Regardless of which figure is the correct one, any of them is the equivalent of more than half of an MLB season. Loathed by AL umpires—and vice versa—Weaver was a beloved figure in Baltimore, however. Over his career, the cagy Weaver became famous for analyzing statistics to try to gain an edge over his opponents. He firmly believed preparation between October and March was essential to any MLB team's success. Weaver once said, "A manager wins games in December. He tries not to lose them in July. You win pennants in the offseason when you build your team."[95] Weaver also became an advocate of platooning and using radar guns to measure his pitchers' speeds. He also maintained an aversion to small-ball tactics, insisting that his favorite offensive play was the three-run homer. Weaver continued to almost magically draw great performances from his pitching staff, especially Jim Palmer. Baseball writers enjoyed Weaver's company as he could tirelessly talk intelligently and passionately for hours on end about the sport. Weaver guided the Orioles to AL pennants in 1970, 1971 and 1979 and AL East crowns in 1973 and 1974. His club won the 1970 World Series versus the Cincinnati Reds in five games, but the Orioles lost the 1971 and 1979 World Series—both in seven-game upsets—to the

Pittsburgh Pirates. The Orioles were enduring a mediocre year in 1982, prompting Weaver to announce he would retire at the end of the season. He was only 52
years old. Remarkably, the Orioles got back into the AL East race and were locked
in a dead heat for first place with the Milwaukee Brewers on the final day of the season. Dramatically, the Orioles and Brewers faced each other that Sunday in a game
nationally televised by ABC. The Brewers won it handily, 10–2, to clinch the division, but the disappointed Baltimore crowd insisted Weaver emerge from the clubhouse to take a farewell bow. He did—and was brought to tears by the long ovation
he received. Less than three years later Weaver was lured out of retirement to manage the Orioles in 1985, but he retired for good in 1986. For a time, he did television
commentary. After baseball, Weaver led a remarkably quiet, home-centered life. "I
know exactly what I need to live on," he told a reporter. "I grow my own vegetables.
I stuff my own sausages. I look for chuck roast on sale to use in stew or to grind up
for hamburgers. Doing that takes time and I like it."[96] Weaver was elected to the
Hall of Fame in 1996. In his induction speech he sincerely praised the integrity
of MLB's umpires! On January 19, 2013, Weaver died of an apparent heart attack.
(Another Hall-of-Famer, Stan Musial, coincidentally died that same day.) Weaver's
passing occurred while he was at sea—on an Orioles-sponsored cruise—with his
wife of 49 years, Marianna. He was 82 years old. Upon hearing of Weaver's death,
renowned *Washington Post* sports scribe Thomas Boswell said of him, "No one in
baseball in my lifetime ever talked half as well on even half as many subjects as
Earl."[97]

"Among the Miracle Mets there was none more miraculous than **Al Weis**,"[98]
wrote biographer Michael Cahill. Cahill has a strong argument. Weis topped both
teams' regulars in the World Series with a batting average of .455—better than double his regular-season figure. Called "Mr. Cool" by his fellow Mets because he seldom showed his emotions, in 11 Series at-bats, Weis knocked out five hits. One was
a key homer that tied Game #5 in the seventh inning. One of his singles won Game
#2. For good measure, Weis' slugging percentage was .727 while his on-base average
was .563. Although teammate Donn Clendenon was the official 1969 World Series
MVP, Weis was given the equivalent honor (known as the Babe Ruth Award) by
the New York chapter of the Baseball Writers' Association of America. Listed at
six feet tall—which was almost certainly an exaggeration—Weis began his career
with Chicago's AL club in 1962 as someone who could be slotted into any middle
infield position. The White Sox eventually gave up on Weis because of his weak bat,
although he did hit. 296 in 135 at-bats in 1965. He was dealt to the Mets along with
teammate Tommie Agee in December 1967. The 1969 World Series was clearly the
high-water mark in what Weis himself honestly called a "journeyman" career. Weis
was on borrowed time in the majors after his stellar show in that Fall Classic. In
1970, Bud Harrelson was a fixture in New York at shortstop, Ken Boswell was the
Mets' second baseman of the future, and a highly touted infield prospect named
Tim Foli was doing well in the club's farm system. Weis played in 75 games and

batted only. 207. The 33-year-old Weis fared even worse to start the 1971 season in the few times he did see action. Hitless in 11 at-bats, and with no role to fill, Weis was released by the Mets on July 1 after playing in exactly 800 regular-season MLB games. The surprising, slugging second baseman of the 1969 World Series finished his 10-year career with a paltry .219 batting average.

Umpire **Lee Weyer** had a controversy-free World Series in 1969. Aptly known as "Big Lee" to his umpiring colleagues, the 6'6" Weyer served 26 years as an NL arbiter and officiated in four World Series. Born in Imlay City, Michigan, Weyer was prominent enough to baseball fans to do commercials for both Coca-Cola and Miller Beer. He was beset with health problems, however. In 1980, Weyer was diagnosed with Guillan-Barre syndrome, a potentially life-threating affliction that affects muscle control. It can also cause blindness. He managed to overcome that obstacle, but not hereditary heart problems. On Monday, July 4, 1988, the 51-year-old Weyer died suddenly, succumbing to a massive heart attack in the San Francisco suburb of San Mateo. Having just finished working first base at a Cubs-Giants game at Candlestick Park, Weyer was visiting the home of fellow umpire Ed Montague to celebrate the remainder of the holiday. According to the next day's *Los Angeles Times*, Weyer was playing basketball with Montague's children when he complained of a shortness of breath. Not long afterward, Weyer went inside Montague's house to make a telephone call. Several minutes later Montague found Weyer lying on the floor unresponsive. Both Weyer's father and older brother had also died in their early fifties from heart attacks. Weyer umpired two historically significant MLB games. He was stationed at third base when Hank Aaron surpassed Babe Ruth's all-time home run mark in Atlanta on April 8, 1974. On September 11, 1985, Weyer was working the plate in Cincinnati when Pete Rose overtook Ty Cobb on MLB's all-time hit list. (Steve Garvey was on the field, playing first base, in both those games!) "One thing I remember about him was the way he dusted off the plate," said Commissioner Bart Giamatti upon learning of Weyer's tragic passing. "He'd dust it clean and then he'd make this clear outline around the perimeter of the plate with his brush. Nobody else did that."[99] Weyer had officiated in the previous year's Twins-Cardinals World Series.

The following eight players were on the 25-man rosters for the 1969 Fall Classic, but none of them saw action in any of the five World Series games:

Baltimore Orioles	*New York Mets*
Bobby Floyd (infielder)	Jack DiLauro (pitcher)
Jim Hardin (pitcher)	Cal Koonce (pitcher)
Marcolino Lopez (pitcher)	Jim McAndrew (pitcher)
Tom Phoebus (pitcher)	Tug McGraw (pitcher)

15

Reports of Our Deaths
Have Been Greatly Exaggerated

On Saturday, June 29, 2019, prior to a home game against the Atlanta Braves, the New York Mets formally honored their championship team from half a century earlier with an elaborate 34-minute tribute. Fifteen white-haired veterans from the club's first World Series champions were present for an on-field ceremony at Citi Field, the Mets' home ballpark since 2009. Relatives of many deceased players and coaches were assembled too. However, the Mets' staff made an embarrassing, two-pronged mistake during the memorable and otherwise classy public event: The ballpark's scoreboard, in listing the 1969 Mets who had passed away, included two fringe players: Jim Gosger and Jesse Hudson. The trouble was that both men were very much still in the land of the living. Oops! (Obviously neither man had been invited to participate in the festivities.)

National Public Radio declared, "The whole thing put bad juju into Mets world, and they lost the game, 5–4."[1]

According to a news story that appeared the following day, the 76-year-old Gosger, who had a 10-year MLB career as an outfielder and first baseman—including three seasons with the Mets—was apprised of the Citi Field gaffe. He quickly acted from his home in Port Huron, MI to dispel the misinformation. To convincingly prove that he was quite alive, Gosger took to the technology of social media. On Facebook he sarcastically posted, "WOW LOOK AT ME. I MADE THE BIG BOARD … THANK YOU N.Y. METS FOR BRINGING ME BACK."[2]

Gosger's Facebook followers seemed more irked by the shameful boo-boo than Gosger himself was. In this modern age of instant access to vast and accurate sports data, many of them were strongly of the opinion that the Mets' blunder was inexcusable. Indeed, a simple Internet search provides detailed lists of all the living players who played at least one game for any World Series championship team dating back to 1947. The 1969 Mets had 26 such players listed—including the overlooked Gosger and Hudson.

Jesse Hudson's alleged death came as a tremendous surprise to the 70-year-old

Hudson himself. Nick Diunte, a baseball reporter from *Forbes*, telephoned Hudson in Louisiana to give him the startling news.

"No, I haven't heard that I was deceased,"[3] Hudson deadpanned from his home.

A lot of people had heard about the mistake, though, including people across the Atlantic Ocean on the Emerald Isle. The embarrassing story was picked up as a novelty story by *The Irish News* on July 1.

Diunte used the opportunity to interview Hudson, who had played mostly at the A and AA levels in the Mets' farm system. Showing promise, Hudson was elevated to the parent club when the 1969 minor league schedule ended. Thus, the 21-year-old left-handed pitcher got to experience a taste of life in the major leagues during a pennant race—and perhaps help the team out of the bullpen once in a while.

Hudson recalled, "I was just glad I was just able to be a part of that back in 1969," he said. "It was just really exciting to be there with the [top] pro ballplayers, and also with manager Gil Hodges and the rest of the staff."[4]

He got his chance to debut on Friday, September 19, when the Mets were losing badly, 7–0, to Pittsburgh in the second game of a home doubleheader—one of the scarce poor games for New York that month. He came in as a reliever at the top of the eighth inning. "I was scared to death," Hudson recalled. Before facing his first MLB batter (Pittsburgh catcher Jerry May), Hudson said to himself, "Well this is it; it's either do or die."[5] May hit a ground ball back to the mound. Hudson made the easy throw to first base for the out.

Still there was a thrill connected to pitching in Shea Stadium before a big crowd that invigorated the young pitcher. "In the minor leagues we never played [before] 40,000 people."[6] (The exact attendance in New York that night was 51,885.)

Hudson was the third Mets hurler that game. He pitched two innings of mop-up relief, facing ten batters. He allowed two hits and one earned run. He walked two Pittsburgh hitters and struck out three. (One opponent whom Hudson whiffed that night was Pirate superstar Willie Stargell who had homered earlier in the game. Stargell slugged 29 home runs in 1969.) Hudson never got a chance to bat in the game, but he handled two defensive chances without an error. The Mets lost the game, 8–0.

For the remainder of the season, he was a spectator in the Mets' bullpen, watching New York notch win after win through the end of the month and clinch the NL East title.

"It was just quite an experience to be part of that,"[7] Hudson said. Of course, the inexperienced Hudson was not included on the Mets' postseason roster—and he never saw any action in the big leagues again. Alas, those two innings were the extent of Hudson's entire MLB career.

It was a short stint at the top for Hudson, but he mostly remembered the unexpected and surprising kindness the Mets' leading stars showed to an unknown minor league pitcher.

"When we traveled," Hudson recalled, "Cleon [Jones] and [Tommie] Agee became just like family to me."[8]

When the Mets were made aware of their careless necrology mistake, they telephoned both players to offer their apologies. At the next day's game at Citi Field, the following message was read aloud and appeared on the large scoreboard:

> There was an error made in yesterday's "We Remember" segment during our 1969 anniversary ceremony in which we included the names and images of Jim Gosger and Jessie [sic] Hudson. We are sorry and deeply regret this error. We have spoken with both former players to express our sincere apologies. We want to thank Jim and Jessie [sic], along with their families and friends, for their gracefulness and understanding.[9]

Sadly, the Mets committed two more errors: In the team's formal apology, Jesse Hudson's first name was misspelled on the Citi Field scoreboard—twice!

1969 World Series: Composite Line Scores and Composite Box Scores

1969 World Series: Composite Line Score

Team	1	2	3	4	5	6	7	8	9	10	R	H	E
New York Mets	1	3	0	1	0	3	2	3	1	1	15	35	2
Baltimore Orioles	1	0	3	3	0	0	1	0	1	0	9	23	4

New York Mets Composite Box Score

Player	AB	H	R	BA	Player	AB	H	R	BA
Agee	18	3	1	.167	Jones	19	3	2	.158
Boswell	3	1	1	.333	Koosman	7	1	0	.143
Cardwell	0	0	0	.000	Kranepool	4	1	1	.250
Charles	15	2	1	.133	Martin	0	0	0	.000
Clendenon	14	5	4	.357	Ryan	0	0	0	.000
Dyer	1	0	0	.000	Seaver	4	0	0	.000
Garrett	1	0	0	.000	Shamsky	6	0	0	.000
Gaspar	2	0	1	.000	Swoboda	15	6	1	.400
Gentry	3	1	0	.333	Taylor	0	0	0	.000
Grote	19	4	1	.211	Weis	11	5	1	.455
Harrelson	17	3	1	.176	**Total**	**159**	**35**	**15**	**.220**

RBI: Clendenon 4, Weis 3, Gentry 2, Agee, Grote, Kranepool, Swoboda
Two-base hits: Grote 2, Charles Clendenon, Gentry, Jones, Koosman, Swoboda
Home runs: Clendenon 3, Agee, Kranepool, Weis
Stolen base: Agee
Errors: Garrett, Weis

Baltimore Orioles Composite Box Score

Player	AB	H	R	BA	Player	AB	H	R	BA
Belanger	15	3	2	.200	McNally	5	1	1	.200
Blair	20	2	1	.100	Motton	1	0	0	.000
Buford	20	2	1	.100	Palmer	2	0	0	.000
Cuellar	5	2	0	.400	Powell	19	5	0	.263
Dalrymple	2	2	0	1.000	Rettenmund	0	0	0	.000
Etchebarren	6	0	0	.000	Richert	0	0	0	.000
Hall	0	0	0	.000	Robinson, B.	19	1	0	.053
Hendricks	10	1	1	.100	Robinson, F.	16	3	2	.188
Johnson	16	1	1	.063	Salmon	0	0	0	.000
Leonhard	0	0	0	.000	Watt	0	0	0	.000
May	1	0	0	.000	**Total**	157	23	9	**.146**

RBI: Buford 2, McNally 2, B Robinson 2, Belanger, Cuellar, F. Robinson
Two-base hit: Buford
Home runs: Buford, McNally, F. Robinson
Stolen base: Blair
Errors: Palmer, Powell, Richert, Watt

New York Mets Composite Pitching

Pitcher	W	L	G	GS	SV	IP	ERA
Cardwell	0	0	1	0	0	1.0	0.00
Gentry	1	0	1	1	0	6.2	0.00
Koosman	2	0	2	2	0	17.2	2.04
Ryan	0	0	1	0	1	2.1	0.00
Seaver	1	1	2	2	0	15.0	3.00
Taylor	0	0	2	0	1	2.1	0.00
Total	**4**	**1**	**9**	**5**	**2**	**45.0**	**1.80**

Baltimore Orioles Composite Pitching

Pitcher	W	L	G	GS	SV	IP	ERA
Cuellar	1	0	2	2	0	16.0	1.13
Hall	0	1	1	0	0	0.0	
Leonhard	0	0	1	0	0	2.0	4.50
McNally	0	1	2	2	0	16.0	2.81
Palmer	0	1	1	1	0	6.0	6.00

Pitcher	W	L	G	GS	SV	IP	ERA
Richert	0	0	1	0	0	0.0	
Watt	0	1	2	0	0	3.0	3.00
Total	**1**	**4**	**10**	**5**	**0**	**43.0**	**2.72**

Wild pitch: McNally
Hit by pitch: McNally

Chapter Notes

INTRODUCTION

1. Curt Gowdy (narrator), *1969 World Series* (documentary film), Major League Baseball: 1969.

2. Art Shamsky with Barry Zeman, *The Magnificent Seasons* (New York: Thomas Dunne Books, 2004), 142.

CHAPTER 1

1. Casey Stengel, Baseball-Almanac.com quotes.

2. Robert Lipsyte, "Remembering the Mets' First Spring Training in 1962," *New York Times* online archives, February 19, 2012.

3. Casey Stengel, Baseball-Almanac.com quotes.

4. "How Bad (And Lovable) Were the 1962 Mets?" Jugssports.com, August 27, 2018.

5. Ken Burns, *Baseball* (documentary series), PBS, 1994.

6. *Ibid.*

7. Bill Bishop, "Casey Stengel," SABR biography project.

8. Ken Burns, *Baseball* (documentary series), PBS, 1994.

9. Edward Prell, "Cubs Beat Mets; Make Triple Play," *Chicago Tribune*, October 1, 1962.

10. Casey Stengel, Baseball-Almanac.com quotes.

11. Ken Burns, *Baseball* (documentary series), PBS, 1994.

12. *Ibid.*

13. Marv Throneberry, Miller Lite beer television commercial, circa 1976.

14. *Ibid.*

15. "Richie Ashburn," phillysportshistory.com, May 21, 2011.

16. Breslin, Jimmy, *Can't Anybody Here Play This Game?* (The Viking Press, 1963), 54.

17. "George Carlin Stand Up Routine 1965," YouTube video, March 21, 2019.

18. "We're in for a Bad Spell," *Bewitched* ABC-TV sitcom, September 30, 1965.

19. Casey Stengel, Baseball-Almanac.com quotes.

20. Peter Golenbock, *Amazin': The Miraculous History of New York's Most Beloved Baseball Team* (New York: St. Martin's Press, 2002), 191–192.

21. Tom Clavin and Danny Peary, *Gil Hodges* (New York: New American Library, 2012), 304.

22. *Ibid.*

23. *Ibid.*, 303–304.

24. Mort Zachter, *Gil Hodges: A Hall of Fame Life* (Lincoln: University of Nebraska Press, 2015), 124.

25. GilHodges.com.

26. "Gil Hodges," Topps baseball card, 1966 series.

27. Joseph Durso, "Hodges, Manager of Mets, Dies of Heart Attack at 47," *New York Times*, April 2, 1972, 1.

28. "Sports Illustrated Interviews—Gil Hodges," YouTube, July 18, 2019.

CHAPTER 2

1. Jack Lang, "Would You Believe…Mets in the Money? Grote Does," *The Sporting News*, March 22, 1969, 19.

2. "What a Difference Seven Years Has Made for the Marvelous Mets," *Schenectady Gazette*, October 7, 1969, 21.

3. "Quiet Hodges Made Champions of Clowns," *Eugene Register-Guardian*, October 17, 1969, 3B.

4. William Leggett, "The Cards are Marked Again," *Sports Illustrated*, April 14, 1969, 84.

5. *Ibid.*

6. Gary Waleik, "Art Shamsky and the '69 Mets Reunite with Ailing Tom Seaver," Wbur.com, June 21, 2019.

7. Ted Blackman, "Expos Take the Opener," *Montreal Gazette*, April 9, 1969, 1.

8. Tom Seaver, *The Perfect Game: Tom Seaver and the Mets* (New York: Bantam Books, 1970), 57.

9. "Tommie Agee Goes Deep...Real Deep..." Metsmerizedonline.com, April 10, 2020.

10. Tom Clavin and Danny Peary, *Gil Hodges* (New York: New American Library, 2012), 325.

11. Tom Seaver, *The Perfect Game: Tom Seaver and the Mets* (New York: Bantam Books, 1970), 70.

12. Bill Christine, "Met Banjo-Hitter Weis Plunks Dirge for Baltimore," *Pittsburgh Press*, October 13, 1969, 31.

13. Fred Worth, "Cleon Jones," SABR biography project.

14. *Ibid.*

15. *Ibid.*

16. Bruce Markusen, *Tales from the Mets Dugout* (Champaign, IL: Sports Publishing Inc. 2005), 41.

17. Peter Botte, "Reliving the Mets' Mysterious Black Cat Game Five Decades Later," *New York Post*, June 26, 2019.

18. *Ibid.*

19. "Seaver's 21st Puts Mets Half Game Behind Cubs," *Schenectady Gazette*, September 10, 1969, 32.

20. "Mets Sweep to East Division Top with Double Victory Over Expos," *Schenectady Gazette*, September 11, 1969, 38.

21. Richard Cuicchi, "September 15, 1969: Cardinals' Steve Carlton sets record with 19 strikeouts, but Mets, Swoboda prove to be Achilles' heel," SABR.org, 2018.

22. Jack Lang, "Lady Luck Beaming Broadly at Met Elbows," *The Sporting News*, October 4, 1969, 7.

23. "Shea: Beautiful Pandemonium," *Schenectady Gazette*, September 25, 1969, 38.

24. *Ibid.*

25. *Ibid.*

CHAPTER 3

1. Stan Hochman, "The Survivors of '64: Part Three—Clay Dalrymple," *Philadelphia Daily News*, July 18, 1989, 68.

2. William Leggett, "Baltimore in a Real Race," *Sports Illustrated*, April 14, 1969, 81.

3. Warren Corbett, "Hank Bauer," SABR biography project.

4. Ken Burns, *Baseball* (documentary series), PBS, 1994.

5. Warren Corbett, "Earl Weaver," SABR biography project.

6. *Ibid.*

7. "Weaver Re-Signed With Raise," *Schenectady Gazette*, September 28, 1968, 16.

8. Curt Smith, *The Storytellers: From Mel Allen to Bob Costas—Sixty Years of Baseball Tales from the Broadcast Booth* (New York: Macmillan, 1995), 204.

9. John Eisenberg, *From 33rd Street to Camden Yards—An Oral History of the Baltimore Orioles* (Chicago: Contemporary Books, 2001), 204.

10. Thomas Ayers, "Dave Leonhard," SABR biography project.

11. "Brooks Sits One Out," *Schenectady Gazette*, August 21, 1969, 33.

12. *Ibid.*

13. "Orioles Reward Weaver," *Schenectady Gazette*, September 1, 1969, 24.

14. William Leggett, "An Ideal Team in Harm's Way," *Sports Illustrated*, October 6, 1969, 21.

15. *Ibid.*

16. "Orioles Out to Prove Again They are the Best," *Schenectady Gazette*, October 4, 1969, 20.

17. Doug Brown, "Average Anemic, But B. Robby Still Swings Tough Bat," *The Sporting News*, October 4, 1969, 12.

18. William Leggett, "An Ideal Team in Harm's Way," *Sports Illustrated*, October 6, 1969, 21.

19. "Orioles Starting All Over," *Daytona Beach Morning Journal*, October 4, 1969, 12.

20. *Ibid.*

CHAPTER 4

1. Tom Seaver, *The Perfect Game: Tom Seaver and the Mets* (New York: Bantam Books, 1970), 169.

2. Ed Shearer, "Mets, Braves Open Best-of-Five Playoff," *Schenectady Gazette*, October 4, 1969, 20.

3. William Leggett, "A New Deal for an Old Sport," *Sports Illustrated*, October 13, 1969, 26.

4. William Leggett, "An Ideal Team in Harm's Way," *Sports Illustrated*, October 6, 1969, 21.

5. William Leggett, "Pitching—And an Omen—Favors the Mets," October 6, 1969, 23.

6. Sam Lacy, "Mets our pick in NL playoff," *Baltimore Afro-American*, October 4, 1969, 19.

7. *Ibid.*

8. "Amazin' Mets hit like Ol' Yankees," *Ellensburg Daily Record*, October 6, 1969, 5.

9. NBC radio broadcast of Game #2 of NLCS, October 5, 1969.

10. Milton Richman, "Mets Look Strong in Playoff Tussle," *Galt Evening Reporter*, October 6, 1969, 12.

11. Roy McHugh, "Jones' Hit Follows Near Miss." *Pittsburgh Press*, October 6, 1969, 32.

12. *Ibid.*

13. *Ibid.*

14. *Ibid.*

15. "Mets' Dressing Room," *Schenectady Gazette*, October 6, 1969.

16. *Ibid.*

17. *Ibid.*

18. Mike Rathet, "What a Difference Seven Years Has Made for the Marvelous Mets," *Schenectady Gazette*, October 7, 1969, 21.

19. *Ibid.*

20. *Ibid.*

21. "Mets Complete Atlanta Sweep for NL Pennant," *Schenectady Gazette*, October 7, 1969, 21.

22. "Jack Hugerich, Sports Editor," *Schenectady Gazette*, October 7, 1969, 21.

23. *Ibid.*

24. *Ibid.*

25. "We're Gonna Win It All: Cleon Jones," *Schenectady Gazette*, October 8, 1969, 32.

26. "What a Difference Seven Years Has Made for the Marvelous Mets," *Schenectady Gazette*, October 7, 1969, 21.

27. *Ibid.*

28. "Amazin' Ones Bomb Braves Again by 11–6," *Sarasota Herald Tribune*, October 6, 1969, 2B.

29. NBC radio broadcast of Game #3 of NLCS, October 6, 1969.

30. Art Shamsky with Barry Zeman, *The Magnificent Seasons* (New York: Thomas Dunne Books, 2004), 142.

31. Roy McHugh. "Mets Steal a Pennant and Shake Up New York," *Pittsburgh Press*, October 7, 1969, 50.

32. NBC radio broadcast of Game #3 of NLCS, October 6, 1969.

33. "We're Gonna Win It All: Cleon Jones," *Schenectady Gazette*, October 8, 1969, 32.

34. John Brockmann, "Sarasota's Garrett Hits Mets' Winning Home Run," *Sarasota Herald-Tribune*, October 7, 1969, 1.

35. "Amazin' Mets are in the Series," *Calgary Herald*, October 7, 1969, 27.

36. *Ibid.*

37. "Mets vs. Orioles," *Ellensburg Daily Record*, October 7, 1969, 5.

38. Lowell Reidenbaugh, "Laughingstocks? Mets Wipe Grins Off Critics' Faces," *The Sporting News*, October 18, 1969, 10.

39. NBC radio broadcast of Game #3 of NLCS, October 6, 1969.

40. "Loyalty Pays Off for Mets' Owner, Mrs. Payson," *St. Joseph News-Press*, October 10, 1969, 3B.

41. "Mets vs. Orioles," *Ellensburg Daily Record*, October 7, 1969, 5.

CHAPTER 5

1. William Leggett, "An Ideal Team in Harm's Way," *Sports Illustrated*, October 6, 1969, 21.

2. Sam Lacy, "Orioles Picked to Erase Twins," *Baltimore Afro-American*, October 4, 1969, 18.

3. Dick Couch, "Baltimore Wins Two Games in 23 Innings to Put Minnesota Twins in a 'One Foot in Grave' Series Position," *Gettysburg Times*, October 6, 1969, 10.

4. *Ibid.*

5. *Ibid.*

6. John Swol, "Dave Boswell Interview," *Twins Trivia*. twinstrivia.com.

7. Bill Christine, "Twin-Killing Orioles Relieve Baltimore Fears of Collapse," *Pittsburgh Press*, October 6, 1969, 32.

8. *Ibid.*

9. "Orioles' Dressing Room," *Schenectady Gazette*, October 6, 1969, 24.

10. *Ibid.*

11. *Ibid.*

12. *Ibid.*

13. "Baltimore Downs Minnesota, 1–0," *Spartanburg Herald-Journal*, October 6, 1969, 12.

14. *Ibid.*

15. "Orioles Go Two Up on Twins," *Calgary Herald*, October 6, 1969, 24.

16. "Baltimore Downs Minnesota, 1–0," *Spartanburg Herald-Journal*, October 6, 1969, 12.

17. "Twins backed into corner," *Ellensburg Daily Record*, October 6, 1969, 5.

18. Bill Christine, "Twin-Killing Orioles Relieve Baltimore Fears of Collapse," *Pittsburgh Press*, October 6, 1969, 32.

19. *Ibid.*

20. *Ibid.*

21. Tom Loomis, "Nervous Motton Provides Clutch Hit," *Toledo Blade*, October 6, 1969, 8.

22. Bill Christine, "Twin-Killing Orioles Relieve Baltimore Fears of Collapse," *Pittsburgh Press*, October 6, 1969, 32.

23. "Orioles' Dressing Room," *Schenectady Gazette*, October 6, 1969, 24.

24. *Ibid.*

25. Ralph Ray, "Twins Get the Message… It's Orioles Who Rule AL," *The Sporting News*, October 11, 1969, 12.

26. "Orioles' Dressing Room," *Schenectady Gazette*, October 6, 1969, 24.

27. "Orioles Bomb Twins to Take AL Pennant," *Calgary Herald*, October 7, 1969, 27.

28. "Rod Gaspar," Ultimate Mets Database.

29. *Ibid.*

30. *Ibid.*

31. "Ducats, Not Mets, Bring Orioles Series Problem," *Schenectady Gazette*, October 8, 1969, 32.

32. *Ibid.*

33. "Despite Steep Prices, Tickets Scarce at Shea," *Galt Evening Reporter*, October 8, 1969, 12.

34. Gordon Beard, "Orioles Figure 'Crowds' Mets' Only Advantage," *Schenectady Gazette*, October 9, 1969, 44.

35. *Ibid.*

36. Dick Couch, "'Just Amazing' Claims Earl Weaver as Orioles Take American League Title; Will Host Mets Saturday in World Series," *Gettysburg Times*, October 7, 1969, 18.

37. Gordon Beard, "Blair, Buford Lead Attack as Palmer Beats Twins, 11–2," *Youngstown Vindicator*, October 7, 1969, 16.

38. *Ibid.*

Chapter 6

1. "Jim Murray," *Schenectady Gazette*, October 17, 1969, 5D.

2. "Ducats, Not Mets, Bring Orioles Series Problem," *Schenectady Gazette*, October 8, 1969, 32.

3. Will Grimsley, "Blasé Baltimore Greets Mets With Amazin' Yawn," *Schenectady Gazette*, October 11, 1969, 22.

4. *Ibid.*

5. *Ibid.*

6. "Baltimore Bored by World Series?" *Galt Evening Reporter*, October 11, 1969, 9.

7. *Ibid.*

8. Will Grimsley, "Blasé Baltimore Greets Mets With Amazin' Yawn," *Schenectady Gazette*, October 11, 1969, 22.

9. Gordon Beard, "Brooks Robinson Doesn't Believe in 'Team of Destiny Bit'

Concerning Mets," *Gettysburg Times*, October 8, 1969, 22.

10. *Ibid.*

11. *Ibid.*

12. *Ibid.*

13. Gordon Beard, "Weaver Sharpens Wit; His Birds Tune Up Bats," *Schenectady Gazette*, October 10, 1969, 28.

14. *Ibid.*

15. *Ibid.*

16. "Weaver Claims Momentum Has Little to Do with Winning Pennants," *St. Joseph News-Press*, October 10, 1969, 3B.

17. *Ibid.*

18. "In Line for Tickets, Fans Catch Series Fever!" *Baltimore Afro-American*, October 11, 1969, 1.

19. *Ibid.*

20. "Yeh-h-h-h Orioles!" *Baltimore Afro-American*, October 11, 1969, 4.

21. Gordon Beard, "Weaver Sharpens Wit; His Birds Tune Up Bats," *Schenectady Gazette*, October 10, 1969, 28.

22. "Lindsay Says It in Poetry: Mets in 4," *Schenectady Gazette*, October 10, 1969, 28.

23. "Mets Fan Jets from London to Watch TV," *Schenectady Gazette*, October 11, 1969, 22.

Chapter 7

1. NBC-TV coverage of Game #1 of the World Series, October 11, 1969.

2. Jack Lang, "Would You Believe…Seaver for President?" *The Sporting News*, October 11, 1969, 3.

3. NBC radio coverage of Game #1 of the World Series, October 11, 1969.

4. "Empty Seats for World Series Tilts," *Galt Evening Reporter*, October 13, 1969, 9.

5. NBC-TV coverage of Game #1 of the World Series, October 11, 1969.

6. Bill Jones, "Kuhn's Firm Hand," *The Sporting News*, October 18, 1969, 6.

7. NBC-TV coverage of Game #1 of the World Series, October 11, 1969.

8. "Ron Swoboda Interview," Newyork.cbs. local, October 21, 2019.

9. *Ibid.*

10. "Casey Stengel Quotes," Baseballalmanac.com.

11. "The Catch: Ron Swoboda's 50th Anniversary Miracle" YouTube, September 9, 2019.

12. *Ibid.*

13. NBC-TV coverage of Game #1 of the World Series, October 11, 1969.

14. Jack Craig, "O's O'Donnell a Real Pro," *The Sporting News*, July 25, 1980, 53.

15. NBC-TV coverage of Game #1 of the World Series, October 11, 1969.

16. *Ibid.*

17. *Ibid.*

18. Mark Mulvoy, "The Vacuum Meets New York's Team of Destiny," *Sports Illustrated*, October 20, 1969, 42.

19. *Ibid.*

20. "Little Guys Kill Mets," *Eugene Register-Guardian*, October 12, 1969, B1.

21. *Ibid.*

22. NBC-TV coverage of Game #1 of the World Series, October 11, 1969.

23. "Legs Bother Seaver," *Eugene Register-Guardian*, October 12, 1969, B1.

24. "Orioles Start Strongly in Taking Series Opener, 4–1," *Galt Evening Reporter*, October 13, 1969.

25. Jack Hand, "Cuellar Pays Back Faith of Birds, Bopping Mets," *Tuscaloosa News*, October 12, 1969, 16.

26. "Little Guys Kill Mets," *Eugene Register-Guardian*, October 12, 1969, B1.

27. Jack Hand, "Cuellar Pays Back Faith of Birds, Bopping Mets," *Tuscaloosa News*, October 12, 1969, 16.

28. "And Where Were Met Fans?" *Tuscaloosa News*, October 12, 1969, 16.

29. Tom Loomis, "Mirrors of Sports," *Toledo Blade*, October 14, 1969, 35.

30. Jack Hand, "Cuellar Pays Back Faith of Birds, Bopping Mets," *Tuscaloosa News*, October 12, 1969, 16.

31. "Players Sour on Playoff," *Tuscaloosa News*, October 12, 1969, 16.

32. "Series Players Want More," *St. Petersburg Independent*, October 11, 1969, 3-C.

33. "Players Sour on Playoff," *Tuscaloosa News*, October 12, 1969, 16.

34. NBC radio coverage of Game #1 of the World Series, October 11, 1969.

35. "Opening Pickups," *The Sporting News*, October 25, 1969, 36.

36. Roy McHugh, "Happy Ending," *Pittsburgh Press*, October 17, 1969, 36.

37. "Orioles' Bat Boy Has Hands Full," *Ludington Daily News*, October 16, 1969, 6.

38. *Ibid.*

39. *Ibid.*

CHAPTER 8

1. NBC-TV coverage of Game #2 of the World Series, October 12, 1969.

2. *Ibid.*

3. "Koosman, Weis, Clendenon Star in 2–1 Victory," *Schenectady Gazette*, October 13, 1969, 80.

4. NBC-TV coverage of Game #2 of the World Series, October 12, 1969.

5. *Ibid.*

6. *Ibid.*

7. *Ibid.*

8. *Ibid.*

9. *Ibid.*

10. "Birds Weren't Thinking About Intentional Pass," *Schenectady Gazette*, October 13, 1969, 80.

11. NBC-TV coverage of Game #2 of the World Series, October 12, 1969.

12. "Birds Weren't Thinking About Intentional Pass," *Schenectady Gazette*, October 13, 1969, 80.

13. *Ibid.*

14. "Koosman, Weis, Clendenon Star in 2–1 Victory," *Schenectady Gazette*, October 13, 1969, 80.

15. *Ibid.*

16. NBC radio coverage of Game #2 of the World Series, October 12, 1969.

17. "Koosman, Weis, Clendenon Star in 2–1 Victory," *Schenectady Gazette*, October 13, 1969, 80.

18. "Long Layoff Had Mets' Star Koosman Worried," *Schenectady Gazette*, October 13, 1969, 80.

19. *Ibid.*

20. *Ibid.*

21. "Mets' Star Rose When Koosman 'Ushered' In," *St. Petersburg Independent*, October 13, 1969, 2-C.

22. *Ibid.*

23. *Ibid.*

24. "Mrs. Payson Didn't Watch Final Out," *Schenectady Gazette*, October 13, 1969, 80.

25. *Ibid.*

26. "Met Owner Could Not Stand Pressure," *Galt Evening Reporter*, October 13, 1969, 12.

27. "Mrs. Payson Didn't Watch Final Out," *Schenectady Gazette*, October 13, 1969, 80.

28. "Quiet Guy Gil Turns into Daring Gambler," *Beaver County Times*, October 13, 1969, A20.

29. Lawrence M. Stolle, "Say Buffalo to Get Major Loop Club under Labbruzzo," *Youngstown Vindicator*, October 14, 1969, 18.

30. *Ibid.*

31. Jack Dulmage, "Amazin' Mets Return to Miracle Land," *Windsor Star*, October 14, 1969, 1.

32. "World Series Telecasts Clobber Pro Football in Sunday Ratings," *Youngstown Vindicator*, October 14, 1969, 18.

33. Will Grimsley, "Baseball is a Lively Corpse, Ratings Showing," *Tuscaloosa News*, October 14, 1969, 7.

34. *Ibid.*

CHAPTER 9

1. Dan Riker, "Palmer Plans to Throw Fastballs," *Beaver County Times*, October 13, 1969, B-3.

2. Gordon Beard, "Weaver Sharpens Wit; His Birds Tune Up Bats," *Schenectady Gazette*, October 10, 1969, 28.

3. NBC-TV coverage of Game #3 of the World Series, October 14, 1969.

4. "Jack Hugerich," *Schenectady Gazette*, October 15, 1969, 44.

5. NBC radio coverage of Game #3 of the World Series, October 14, 1969.

6. "Big Difference in Years for Game Hero Tommie," *Schenectady Gazette*, October 15, 1969, 44.

7. NBC-TV coverage of Game #3 of the World Series, October 14, 1969.

8. *Ibid.*

9. NBC radio coverage of Game #3 of the World Series, October 14, 1969.

10. "Mets' 5–0 Win Give NL Kings 2–1 Series Lead," *Schenectady Gazette*, October 15, 1969, 44.

11. "Big Difference in Years for Game Hero Tommie," *Schenectady Gazette*, October 15, 1969, 44.

12. "Jack Hugerich," *Schenectady Gazette*, October 15, 1969, 44.

13. *Ibid.*

14. "New Yorkers Outpitch, Outhit, Outdefense Favored Birds," *Schenectady Gazette*, October 15, 1969, 44.

15. Big Difference in Years for Game Hero Tommie," *Schenectady Gazette*, October 15, 1969, 44.

16. Jack Hand, "Outfielder Saves 5–0 Win with Brilliant Glove Work," *Youngstown Vindicator*, October 15, 1969, 36.

17. "Mets' 5–0 Win Give NL Kings 2–1 Series Lead," *Schenectady Gazette*, October 15, 1969, 44.

18. "Jack Hugerich," *Schenectady Gazette*, October 15, 1969, 44.

19. "Tom Seaver on mound today," *Ellensburg Daily Record*, October 15, 1969, 6.

20. "Man Upstairs a Met Fan?" *St. Petersburg Independent*, October 15, 1969, 1-C.

21. "Blair Didn't Think Catches So Great," *Schenectady Gazette*, October 15, 1969, 44.

22. Mike Rathet, "Victory is Divine Enough to Suit NY," *Tuscaloosa News*, October 15, 1969, 29.

23. *Ibid.*

24. "Jack Hugerich," *Schenectady Gazette*, October 15, 1969, 44.

25. Lawrence Stolle, "Are They Amazing or Simply Superior Mets? The Orioles May Soon Join the List of Believers," *Youngstown Vindicator*, October 15, 1969, 38.

26. "New Yorkers Outpitch, Outhit, Outdefense Favored Birds," *Schenectady Gazette*, October 15, 1969, 44.

27. Steven Travers, *1969 Miracle Mets: The Improbable Story of the World's Greatest Underdog Team* (Guilford, CT: The Lyons Press, 2009), 129.

28. Jim Murray "Babe Truth," *Schenectady Gazette*, October 15, 1969, 45.

CHAPTER 10

1. "Mets Now Possessors of Good Fortune," *Galt Evening Reporter*, October 16, 1969, 14.

2. Jim Murray, "Baltimore Doves," *Schenectady Gazette*, October 16, 1969, 39.

3. "Mets Need One More to Complete Miracle," *Schenectady Gazette*, October 16, 1969, 38.

4. NBC radio coverage of Game #4 of the World Series, October 15, 1969.

5. SI Staff, "Shag Crawford 1916–2007," *Sports Illustrated*, July 23, 2007, 22.

6. Tom Seaver, *The Perfect Game: Tom Seaver and the Mets* (New York: Bantam Books, 1970), 69.

7. NBC radio coverage of Game #4 of the World Series, October 15, 1969.

8. *Ibid.*

9. *Ibid.*

10. "Weaver Gets Heave-Ho," *Schenectady Gazette*, October 16, 1969, 38.

11. Gordon Beard, "Orioles Admit Mistakes in Clutch Caused Defeat," *Washington (PA) Observer-Reporter*, October 16, 1969, B-6.

12. NBC radio coverage of Game #4 of the World Series, October 15, 1969.

13. "Weaver Gets Heave-Ho," *Schenectady Gazette*, October 16, 1969, 38.

14. Jack Hugerich, "The Unbelievers" *Schenectady Gazette*, October 16, 1969, 39.

15. Tom Seaver, *The Perfect Game: Tom Seaver and the Mets* (New Yok: Bantam Books, 1970), 119.

16. *Ibid.*

17. NBC radio coverage of Game #4 of the World Series, October 15, 1969.

18. *Ibid.*

19. *Ibid.*

20. *Ibid.*

21. NBC-TV coverage of Game #4 of the World Series, October 15, 1969.

22. NBC radio coverage of Game #4 of the World Series, October 15, 1969.

23. *Ibid.*

24. NBC-TV coverage of Game #4 of the World Series, October 15, 1969.

25. NBC-TV pregame coverage of Game #4 of the World Series, October 16, 1969.

26. Roy McHugh, "Happy Ending," *Pittsburgh Press*, October 17, 1969, 36.

27. Ron Cassie, "Season of Suck," *BaltimoreMagazine.com*, January 2019.

28. *Ibid.*

29. Roy McHugh, "Happy Ending," *Pittsburgh Press*, October 17, 1969, 36.

30. NBC-TV coverage of Game #4 of the World Series, October 15, 1969.

31. "Orioles Finding Sounds on 'Amazings' Side, Too," *Schenectady Gazette*, October 16, 1969, 39.

32. Jack Hand, "Mets Go Up 3 Games to 1 on Bunt-Play Error," *Lewiston Daily Sun*, October 16, 1969, 20.

33. Jim Murray, "Baltimore Doves," *Schenectady Gazette*, October 16, 1969, 39.

34. Tom Seaver, *The Perfect Game: Tom Seaver and the Mets* (New York: Bantam Books, 1970), 155.

35. "This May Be the Day for Incredible Mets," *Middlesboro Daily News*, October 16, 1969, 5.

36. Roy McHugh, "Somebody Up There Loves Those Mets," *Pittsburgh Press*, October 16, 1969, 23.

37. Steven Marcus, "1969 Mets: J.C. Martin's Bunt in World Series Still Controversial," Newsday.com, June 8, 2019.

38. "Orioles Finding Sounds on 'Amazings' Side, Too," *Schenectady Gazette*, October 16, 1969, 39.

39. Steven Marcus, "1969 Mets: J.C. Martin's Bunt in World Series Still Controversial," Newsday.com, June 8, 2019.

40. "AL Champs Find Out About Foes Tough Way," *Schenectady Gazette*, October 16, 1969, 39.

41. Steven Marcus, "1969 Mets: J.C. Martin's Bunt in World Series Still Controversial," Newsday.com, June 8, 2019.

42. "Orioles Finding Sounds on 'Amazings' Side, Too," *Schenectady Gazette*, October 16, 1969, 39.

43. Dick Couch, "J.C. Martin, Gaspar Join Hero List," *Washington (PA) Observer-Reporter*, October 16, 1969, B-6.

44. "Illegal Play Difference?" *Tuscaloosa News*, October 16, 1969, 8.

45. Mike Rathet, "Victory Format is Amazing, Too," *Tuscaloosa News*, October 16, 1969, 8–9.

46. "Martin Ran to First on Wrong Side of Foul Line," *Middlesboro Daily News*, October 16, 1969, 5.

47. NBC-TV pregame coverage of Game #5 of the World Series, October 16, 1969.

48. "AL Champs Find Out About Foes Tough Way," *Schenectady Gazette*, October 16, 1969, 39.

49. Steven Marcus, "1969 Mets: J.C. Martin's Bunt in World Series Still Controversial," Newsday.com, June 8, 2019.

50. *Ibid.*

51. *Ibid.*

52. "Commissioner Rules on Disputed Call," *Schenectady Gazette*, October 17, 1969, 5D.

53. "AL Champs Find Out About Foes Tough Way," *Schenectady Gazette*, October 16, 1969, 39.

54. *Ibid.*

55. Fred Girard, "Mets' Fans Not Only Ones Paralyzed; J.C.'s Bunt Froze Gaspar on Base Paths," *St. Petersburg Times*, October 16, 1969, C3.

56. "AL Champs Find Out About Foes Tough Way," *Schenectady Gazette*, October 16, 1969, 39.

57. "Nancy Seaver—Queen of Mets," *St. Joseph News-Press*, October 16, 1969, 7C.

58. Jim Murray, "Baltimore Doves," *Schenectady Gazette*, October 16, 1969, 39.

59. "AL Champs Find Out About Foes Tough Way," *Schenectady Gazette*, October 16, 1969, 39.

60. Tom Seaver, *The Perfect Game: Tom Seaver and the Mets* (New York: Bantam Books, 1970), 162–163.

61. *Ibid.*, 163.

62. Hal Bock, "Seaver Thinks Nonbelievers in Mets No Longer Exist," *Washington (PA) Observer-Reporter*, October 16, 1969, B-6.

CHAPTER 11

1. Roy McHugh "Happy Ending," *Pittsburgh Press*, October 17, 1969, 36.

2. NBC-TV pregame coverage of Game #5 of the World Series, October 16, 1969.

3. Irv Goldfarb, "Jerry Koosman," SABR biography project.

4. Jack Hand, "NL Champs End Baltimore Hopes with 5–3 Victory," *Schenectady Gazette*, October 17, 1969, 4D.

5. Gordon Beard, "Baltimore Wants Second Crack at Mets in 1970," *Schenectady Gazette*, October 17, 1969, 4D.

6. "Earl Loses Again," *Pittsburgh Press*, October 17, 1969, 36.

7. Jim Murray, "Mets Must Have Had Help," *Eugene Register-Guardian*, October 17, 1969, 4B.

8. NBC-TV coverage of Game #5 of the World Series, October 16, 1969.

9. NBC radio coverage of Game #5 of the World Series, October 16, 1969.

10. *Ibid.*

11. Wayne Coffey, "How Gil Hodges and a Little Shoe Polish Helped the Mets to Their '69 Miracle," Newyorkdailynews.co, March 30, 2019.

12. *Ibid.*

13. NBC-TV coverage of Game #5 of the World Series, October 16, 1969.

14. "Earl Loses Again," *Pittsburgh Press*, October 17, 1969, 36.

15. *Ibid.*

16. "Jack Hugerich," *Schenectady Gazette*, October 17, 1969, 5D.

17. Jim Murray, "Mets Must Have Had Help," *Eugene Register-Guardian*, October 17, 1969, 4B.

18. Gordon Beard, "Baltimore Wants Second Crack at Mets in 1970," *Schenectady Gazette*, October 17, 1969, 4D.

19. Milton Gross, "Miracle Workers," *St. Petersburgh Independent*, October 16, 1969, 1-C.

20. NBC-TV coverage of Game #5 of the World Series, October 16, 1969.

21. William Leggett, "Never Pumpkins Again," *Sports Illustrated*, October 27, 1969, 14.

22. Joseph Durso and William Borders, "The Amazin' Mets. For Once It's True," *New York Times* archives, October 16, 1969.

23. NBC-TV coverage of Game #5 of the World Series, October 16, 1969.

24. *Ibid.*

25. *Ibid.*

26. Fred Worth, "Cleon Jones," SABR biography project.

27. NBC-TV coverage of Game #5 of the World Series, October 16, 1969.

28. *Ibid.*

29. "1969 World Champion Jerry Koosman Goes Unfiltered with Howie Rose," YouTube video, July 16, 2019.

30. *Ibid.*

31. "Usual 'Innocent Chaos' Marks Mets' Win Scene," *Schenectady Gazette*, October 17, 1969.

32. NBC-TV coverage of Game #5 of the World Series, October 16, 1969.

33. Jim Murray, "Mets Must Have Had Help," *Eugene Register-Guardian*, October 17, 1969, 4B.

34. Milton Richman, "Donn's Dangerous Despite Bat Flaws," *Pittsburgh Press*, October 17, 1969, 36.

35. Roy McHugh "Happy Ending," *Pittsburgh Press*, October 17, 1969, 36.

36. Tom Clavin and Danny Peary. *Gil Hodges* (New York: New American Library, 2012), 346.

37. *Ibid.*

38. *Ibid.*

39. NBC-TV coverage of Game #5 of the World Series, October 16, 1969.

40. *Ibid.*

41. *Ibid.*

42. "Usual 'Innocent Chaos' Marks Mets' Win Scene," *Schenectady Gazette*, October 17, 1969, 4D.

43. *Ibid.*

44. NBC-TV coverage of Game #5 of the World Series, October 16, 1969.

45. "Usual 'Innocent Chaos' Marks Mets' Win Scene," *Schenectady Gazette*, October 17, 1969, 4D.

46. "Jack Hugerich," *Schenectady Gazette*, October 17, 1969, 5D.

47. *Ibid.*

48. Gordon Beard, "Baltimore Wants Second Crack at Mets in 1970," *Schenectady Gazette*, October 17, 1969, 4D.

49. Sheila Moran, "Mets Are Gutsy Bunch, Says Owner," *Tuscaloosa News*, October 17, 1969, 10.

50. Roy McHugh, "Happy Ending," *Pittsburgh Press*, October 17, 1969, 36.

51. Arthur Everett, "Delirium Grips Metsville as Dream Comes True," *Schenectady Gazette*, October 17, 1969, 1.

52. "Joy Unrestrained in Mets' Celebration," *Galt Evening Reporter*, October 17, 1969, 8.

53. "A Sweet Day for New York," *Middlesboro Daily News*, October 17, 1969, 1.

54. "New York Delirious with Joy as Mets Capture Championship," *Toledo Blade*, October 17, 1969, 1.

55. "The Mets Really Did Win," *Ellensburg Daily Record*, October 16, 1969, 5.

56. Gordon Beard, "Baltimore Wants Second Crack at Mets in 1970," *Schenectady Gazette*, October 17, 1969, 4D.

57. Ken Burns, *Baseball* (documentary series), PBS, 1994.

58. Gordon Beard, "Baltimore Wants Second Crack at Mets in 1970," *Schenectady Gazette*, October 17, 1969, 4D.

59. *Ibid.*

60. *Ibid.*

61. *Ibid.*

62. Doug Brown, "Bench-Rider Role Can Tire You Out, Dalrymple Claims," *The Sporting News*, December 13, 1969, 39.

63. Brad Willson, "Mets Showed They Were the Better Team," *Daytona Beach Morning Journal*, October 17, 1969. 14.

64. "Joe Falls," *The Sporting News*, November 1, 1969, 2.

65. Lawrence M. Stolle, "Wild Celebration as Incredible Mets Capture Series Title," *Youngstown Vindicator*, October 17, 1969, 16.

66. "Fans Still Love Birds," *Schenectady Gazette*, October 17, 1969, 5D.

67. "Returning Orioles moved by reception," *Baltimore Afro-American*, October 18, 1969, 17.

68. *Ibid.*

69. Jim Murray, "Mets Must Have Had Help," *Eugene Register-Guardian*, October 17, 1969, 4B.

CHAPTER 12

1. William Leggett, "Never Pumpkins Again," *Sports Illustrated*, October 27, 1969, 14.

2. "Melvin Durslag," *The Sporting News*, November 1, 1969, 2.

3. William Leggett, "Never Pumpkins Again," *Sports Illustrated*, October 27, 1969, 14.

4. Wayne Coffey, "How Gil Hodges and a Little Shoe Polish Helped the Mets to Their '69 Miracle," Newyorkdailynews.co, March 30, 2019.

5. *Ibid.*

6. Clayton Collier, "Frank Robinson Still Swears Miracle Mets Scuffed Ball in Game #5 of 1969 World Series," Mmetsmerizedonline, June 14, 2013.

7. *Ibid.*

8. William Leggett, "Never Pumpkins Again," *Sports Illustrated*, October 27, 1969, 14.

9. Sam Lacy, "Castoff Clendenon cops Series MVP, sports car," *Baltimore Afro-American*, October 18, 1969, 1.

10. "It Should Be Spring So We Could Fete 'Greatest,'" *St. Petersburg Independent*, October 17, 1969, 16-A.

11. Jacqueline Cutler, "When God Was a Mets Fan: How the Miracle in '69 Happened," Newyorkdailynews.com, March 17, 2019.

12. Edward Kiersch, "Davey's Destiny," *Cigar Aficionado*, September 1999.

13. John G. Griffin, "Elephants Fly, Rocks Float, Mets Win," *Middlesboro Daily News*, October 17, 1969, 7.

14. Gary Waleik, "Art Shamsky and the '69 Mets Reunite with Ailing Tom Seaver," Wbur.com, June 21, 2019.

15. "The Amazin's" *Toledo Blade*, October 17, 1969, 16.

16. Stan Issacs, "Breaks Piled Upon Breaks—Too Much to Believe," *Toledo Blade*, October 17, 1969, 24.

17. David Lawrence, "Triumph by Mets Provides Demonstration That Pleases," *Toledo Blade*, October 17, 1969, 16.

18. Marshall Field, "Jerry Koosman: A Look Back at a Mets' Hero," Metsmerizedonline.com, October 2, 2019.

CHAPTER 13

1. "Met Banjo-Hitter Weis Plunks Dirge for Baltimore," *Pittsburgh Press*, October 13, 1969, 31.

CHAPTER 14

1. John Vorperian, "Tommie Agee," SABR biography project.

2. Harvey Rosenfeld, *Iron Man: The Cal Ripken, Jr. Story* (New York: St. Martin's Press), 1995, 69.

3. Mike Huber, "Paul Blair," SABR biography project.

4. Eduardo A. Encina, "Former Orioles Recall Favorite Memories of Paul Blair," Baltimoresun.com, December 27, 2013.

5. Mike Bender, "Ken Boswell," SABR biography project.

6. *Ibid.*

7. William Leggett, "Never Pumpkins Again," *Sports Illustrated*, October 27, 1969, 14.

8. Mark Armour, "Don Buford," SABR biography project.

9. Matthew Silverman, "Don Cardwell," SABR biography project.

10. Bill Ryczek, *The Amazin' Mets, 1962–1969* (Jefferson, NC: McFarland & Company, 2007), 207.

11. Bill Bell, "A Whole New Ballgame," *New York News,* May 6, 2000.

12. George Vecsey, "Ed Charles, Infield Sage of the Miracle Mets, Is Dead at 84," *New York Times* online archives, March 15, 2018.

13. "Clendenon, 1969 World Series MVP, dead at 70," ESPN.com, September 17, 2005.

14. SI Staff, "Shag Crawford 1916–2007," *Sports Illustrated,* July 23, 2007, 22.

15. NBC-TV coverage of Game #5 of the World Series, October 15, 1970.

16. Adam Ulrey, "Mike Cuellar," SABR biography project.

17. Thomas Boswell, "Earl Weaver: Words from a Baseball Master," *Washington Post,* January 19, 2013.

18. "Cuellar Part of Famed Orioles' Rotation," ESPN.com, April 2, 2010.

19. Rory Costello, "Clay Dalrymple," SABR biography project.

20. *Ibid.*

21. Milton Richman, "Baseball Umpires Mourn Death of Lou DiMuro," *Florence Times,* June 10, 1982, 23.

22. Adam Ulrey, "Duffey Dyer," SABR biography project.

23. "'A Terrific Teammate': Ex-Orioles Catcher Andy Etchebarren, Member of '66 and '70 Championship Teams, Dies at 76," Baltimoresun.com, October 6, 2019.

24. Les Masterson, "Wayne Garrett," SABR biography project.

25. Maury Allen, *After the Miracle: The 1969 Mets Twenty Years Later* (London: Franklin Watts, 1989).

26. *Ibid.,* 208.

27. Maxwell Kates, "Rod Gaspar," SABR Biography project.

28. "Gary Gentry Trades and Transactions," Baseball-almanc.com.

29. Andrew Schiff and Matthew Silverman, "Gary Gentry," SABR biography project.

30. Matt Bohn, "Curt Gowdy," SABR biography project.

31. *Ibid.*

32. Howard Ulman, "TV-radio legend Gowdy dies at 86," *Elyria Chronicle-Telegram,* February 21, 2006.

33. NBC radio coverage of Game #5 of the World Series, October 16, 1969.

34. "Insiders Say," *The Sporting News,* June 27, 1981, 10.

35. "Cincinnati Joins Mexico in Hall's Legend," *Newsday,* October 12, 1970.

36. Bud Harrelson (with Phil Pepe), *Turning Two: My Journey to the Top of the World and Back with the New York Mets* (New York: Thomas Dunne Books, 2012), 140.

37. Rory Costello, "Elrod Henricks," SABR biography project.

38. *Ibid.*

39. Tom Clavin and Danny Peary, *Gil Hodges* (New York: New American Library, 2012), 360.

40. *Ibid.*

41. Marino Amoruso, *Gil Hodges: The Quiet Man* (Middlebury, VT: Eriksson, 1991), 165.

42. Mark Armour, "Davey Johnson," SABR biography project.

43. Fred Worth, "Cleon Jones," SABR biography project.

44. David K. Li, "Mets broadcaster Ralph Kiner Dead at 91," Nypost.com, February 7, 2014.

45. "1969 World Champion Jerry Koosman Goes Unfiltered with Howie Rose," YouTube video, July 16, 2019.

46. Irv Goldfarb, "Jerry Koosman," SABR biography project.

47. Tara Krieger, "Ed Kranepool," SABR biography project.

48. Steven Goldleaf, "The Early Mets' Unseen and Unused Advantage Over the Rest of the NL," Billjamesonline.com March 12, 2017.

49. "Tony Kubek," Baseballfandom.com.

50. *Ibid.*

51. Phil Berger, "Hopkins Accidental Big Leaguer," *The Johns Hopkins Magazine,* Volume XIX, Number 2 (Summer 1968), 21.

52. *Ibid.*

53. Maury Allen, *After the Miracle: The 1969 Mets Twenty Years Later* (New York: Franklin Watt, 1989), 122–123.

54. Larry Whiteside, "Fast-Dealing Brewers Corral 3 Pinch-Hitters," *The Sporting News,* June 27, 1970, 6.

55. Steve Pate, "Evaluating the Trade," *Dallas Morning News,* August 11, 1977, B3.

56. Charlie Weatherby, "Dave May," SABR biography project.

57. Ian McDonald, "McNally Saw the End Coming," *Montreal Gazette,* June 10, 1975.

58. "McNally Won 20 Games Four Straight Seasons," ESPN.com, December 6, 2002.

59. Malcolm Allen, "Curt Motton," SABR biography project.

60. Doug Brown, "Motton Sees Some Things Right in Winter Troubles," *The Sporting News*, February 7, 1970, 32.

61. "Curt Motton obituary," *Baltimore Sun*, January 22, 2010.

62. Mike Shatzkin (editor), *The Ballplayers*, New York: William Morrow, 1990.

63. Warren Corbett, "Lindsey Nelson," SABR biography project.

64. "Hall of Fame Sportscaster Lindsey Nelson Dies at 76," latimes.com, June 12, 1995.

65. Phil Spartano, "Bill O'Donnell: Baseball Prophet," *Utica Observer-Dispatch*, June 28, 1970.

66. Chuck Thompson and Gordon Beard, *Ain't the Beer Cold!* (Lanham, MD: Diamond Communications, 2002).

67. *Ibid.*

68. "Jim Palmer Quotes," baseball-almanac.com.

69. *Ibid.*

70. Mark Armour, "Jim Palmer," SABR biography project.

71. NBC-TV coverage of Game #5 of the World Series, October 15, 1970.

72. "Brooks Robinson," Baseballlibrary.com.

73. NBC-TV coverage of Game #1 of the World Series, October 10, 1970.

74. "Brooks Robinson Awards," Baseball-almanac.com.

75. Ted Patterson, *The Baltimore Orioles: Four Decades of Magic from 33rd Street to Camden Yards* (Dallas, TX: Taylor Publishing Company, 2000), 116.

76. "Jim Palmer Remembers the Late Great Frank Robinson," YouTube video, February 7, 2019.

77. "Hall of Famer Frank Robinson of Oakland dies at 83," mercurynews.com, February 7, 2019.

78. Miller Lite TV commercial, circa 1980.

79. "Frank Robinson, legend and pioneer, dies," MLB.com., February 7, 2019.

80. "Reggie Jackson Quotes," baseball-almanac.com.

81. "Nolan Ryan Quotes," brainyquote.com.

82. "Nolan Ryan Quotes," baseball-almanac.com.

83. *New York Times*, July 26, 1970, 5–2.

84. "Tom Seaver Quotes," baseball-almanac.com.

85. Deesha Thosar, "Mets to Honor Seaver with Citi Field Address Change; Statue Coming in 2020," Nydailynews.com, March 21, 2019.

86. Tom Seaver, *The Perfect Game: Tom Seaver and the Mets* (New York: Bantam Books, 1970), 18.

87. Maury Allen, *After the Miracle: The 1969 Mets Twenty Years Later* (New York: Franklin Watts, 1989), 201.

88. Gary Waleik, "Art Shamsky and the '69 Mets Reunite with Ailing Tom Seaver," Wbur.com, June 21, 2019.

89. Dave Nagle, "ESPN Remembers Colleague, Friend Jim Simpson," ESPNpressroom.com, January 13, 2016.

90. "Longtime AL Umpire Hank Soar Dies at 87," thedeadballera.com.

91. Sean Fitz-Gerald, "Ron Taylor's Sons Share the Story of Dr. Baseball," *Toronto Star* (online archive), October 23, 2015.

92. *Ibid.*

93. Maury Allen, *After the Miracle: The Amazin' Mets—Two Decades Later* (New York: St. Martin's Press, 1989), 45.

94. Malcolm Allen, "Eddie Watt," SABR biograph project.

95. "Earl Weaver Quotes," baseball-almanac.com.

96. Thomas Boswell, "Earl Weaver: Words from a Baseball Master," *Washington Post*, January 19, 2013.

97. "Earl Weaver Quotes to Thomas Boswell," *Washington Post*, January 19, 2013.

98. Michael Cahill, "Al Weis," SABR biography project.

99. "Baseball Quote of the Day," quote.webcicrle.com.

Chapter 15

1. "Morning Edition," National Public Radio, July 2, 2019.

2. "Mets List Jim Gosger, Jesse Hudson, Two Living Members of 1969 Team, As Dead," USAtoday.com, June 30, 2019.

3. Nick Diunte, "Despite the Grave Error, 1969 New York Mets Pitcher Jesse Hudson Says He's Alive and Well," Forbes.com, June 30, 2019.

4. *Ibid.*

5. *Ibid.*

6. *Ibid.*

7. *Ibid.*

8. *Ibid.*

9. "Baseball team apologizes for featuring two living players in memorial montage," *Irish News*, July 1, 2019.

Bibliography

Books

Allen, Lee. *The National League Story.* New York: Hill & Wang, 1965 [revised edition].

Allen, Maury. *After the Miracle: The Amazin' Mets Twenty Years Later.* New York: Franklin Watts, 1989.

Amoruso, Marino: *Gil Hodges: The Quiet Man.* Middlebury, VT: Eriksson, 1991.

Banner, Stuart. *The Baseball Trust: A History of Baseball's Antitrust Exemption.* New York: Oxford University Press, 2013.

Breslin, Jimmy. *Can't Anybody Here Play This Game?* New York: Viking Press, 1963.

Clavin, Tom, and Danny Peary. *Gil Hodges.* New York: New American Library, 2012.

Cohen, Stanley. *A Magic Summer: The '69 Mets.* San Diego: Harcourt Brace Jovanovich, 1988.

Dabilis, Andy, and Nick Tsiotos. *The 1903 World Series.* Jefferson, NC: McFarland, 2004.

Eisenberg, John. *From 33rd Street to Camden Yards—An Oral History of the Baltimore Orioles.* Chicago: Contemporary, 2001.

Elliott, Bob. *The Northern Game.* Toronto: Sports Media, 2005.

Feldmann, Doug. *Miracle Collapse: The 1969 Chicago Cubs.* Lincoln: University of Nebraska Press, 2006.

Gallagher, Danny, and Bill Young. *Remembering the Montreal Expos.* Toronto: Scoop Press, 2005.

Golenbock, Peter. *Amazin': The Miraculous History of New York's Most Beloved Baseball Team.* New York: St. Martin's Press, 2002.

_____. *Bums: An Oral History of the Brooklyn Dodgers.* New York: Contemporary, 2000.

Harrelson, Bud (with Phil Pepe). *Turning Two: My Journey to the Top of the World and Back with the New York Mets.* New York: Thomas Dunne, 2012.

Jones, Cleon (with Ed Hershey). *The Life Story of the One and Only Cleon.* New York: Coward-McCann, 1970.

Kahn, Roger. *The Boys of Summer.* New York: Signet, 1973.

Koppett, Leonard. *The New York Mets: The Whole Story.* New York: Macmillan, 1974.

Markusen, Bruce. *Tales from the Mets Dugout.* Champaign, IL: Sports Publishing, 2005.

Reichler, Joseph L., ed. *The World Series: A 75th Anniversary.* New York: Simon & Schuster, 1978.

Ryczek, Bill. *The Amazin' Mets, 1962–1969.* Jefferson, NC: McFarland, 2007.

Seaver, Tom. *The Perfect Game: Tom Seaver and the Mets.* New York: Bantam Books, 1970.

Shamsky, Art, and Erik Sherman. *After the Miracle: The Lasting Brotherhood of the '69 Mets.* New York: Simon & Schuster, 2019.

Shamsky, Art, with Barry Zeman. *The Magnificent Seasons.* New York: Thomas Dunne, 2004.

Shatzkin, Mike, ed. *The Ballplayers.* New York: William Morrow, 1990.

Smith, Curt. *The Storytellers: From Mel Allen to Bob Costas—Sixty Years of Baseball Tales from the Broadcast Booth.* New York: Macmillan, 1995.

Swoboda, Ron. *Here's the Catch.* New York: Thomas Dunne, 2019.

Travers, Steven. *1969 Miracle Mets: The Improbable Story of the World's Greatest Underdog Team.* Guilford, CT: Lyons Press, 2009.

Ward, Geoffrey C., and Ken Burns. *Baseball: An Illustrated History.* New York: Alfred A. Knopf, 2010.

Zachter, Mort. *Gil Hodges: A Hall of Fame Life.* Lincoln: University of Nebraska Press, 2015.

Documentary Films and Series

Burns, Ken. *Baseball*, PBS Video, 1994.
Gowdy, Curt (narrator). *1969 World Series*, Major League Baseball, 1969.

Newspapers

Baltimore Afro-American
Baltimore Sun
Beaver County Times
Calgary Herald
Chicago Tribune
Dallas Morning News
Daytona Beach Morning Journal
Ellensburg Daily Record
Elyria Chronicle-Telegram
Eugene Register-Guardian
Florence Times
Forbes
Fort Scott Tribune
Frederick Daily Leader
Galt Evening Reporter
Gettysburg Times
Harlan Daily Enterprise
Lewiston Daily Sun
Los Angeles Times
Ludington Daily News
Middlesboro Daily News
Montreal Gazette
New York Daily News
New York Post
New York Times
Newsday
Philadelphia Daily News
Pittsburgh Press
St. Joseph News-Press
St. Petersburg Independent
St. Petersburg Times
Sarasota Herald-Tribune
Schenectady Gazette
Spartanburg Herald-Journal
Spokane Daily Chronicle
Toledo Blade
Toronto Star
Tuscaloosa News
Utica Observer-Dispatch
Washington (PA) Observer-Reporter
Washington Post
Windsor Star
Youngstown Vindicator

Online Resources

Baltimoresun.com
Baseball-Almanac.com
Baseball-Reference.com
Baseballfandom.com
Baseballlibrary.com
Brainyquote.com
ESPN.com
GilHodges.com
Irishnews.com
Jugssports.com
Metsmerizedonline.com
MLB.com
NPR.org
Phillysportshistory.com
Retrosheet.org
SABR.org
Thedeadballera.com
Twinstrivia.com
WBUR.com
YouTube.com

Magazines

Cigar Aficionado
The Sporting News
Sports Illustrated

Index

205